THE U.S. AND WORLD DEVELOPMENT

AGENDA FOR ACTION 1975

James W. Howe
and the Staff of the Overseas Development Council

PUBLISHED FOR THE OVERSEAS DEVELOPMENT COUNCIL
PRAEGER PUBLISHERS
NEW YORK/WASHINGTON/LONDON

Library of Congress Cataloging in Publication Data

Howe, James W
    The U. S. and world development.

    (Praeger special studies in international economics
and development)
    1. Economic history—1945-   2. Economic assistance.
I. Overseas Development Council. II. Title.
HC59. H68   330. 9'04   75-11641
ISBN 0-275-05260-5
ISBN 0-275-89310-3 pbk.

PRAEGER PUBLISHERS
111 Fourth Avenue, New York, N.Y. 10003, U.S.A.

Published in the United States of America in 1975
by Praeger Publishers, Inc.

Printed in the United States of America

THE U.S. AND WORLD DEVELOPMENT

DEVELOPMENT

AGENDA FOR ACTION 1975

Foreword

Four times in this century, including the present moment, the world has faced crises of such vast dimensions that they strained the capacity of people and nations to craft responses adequate to the task. The first time we failed: In 1914, World War I engulfed much of the world as the existing international system failed to adjust to the emergence of newly powerful industrial nations. The second time we again failed: In the late 1920s, faced with a global economic crisis of extraordinary proportions, the nations of the world chose to chase the chimera of short-run nationalistic advantage; the result was a world-wide depression throwing millions out of work and leading ultimately to the carnage and devastation of World War II. The third time, in the post-World War II period, the nations of the world did rise to the challenge. They rebuilt a devastated Europe and created an international order that could accommodate the millions of the world's people who were no longer to be ruled by colonial powers, and they launched a creative surge of institution-building that gave us the United Nations and its associate institutions, including the World Bank and the International Monetary Fund.

Today we are entering a fourth period of crisis. Because it encompasses all of the market economies of both the developed and developing countries, with nearly three quarters of the world's population, this crisis is more acute—and the potential consequences of our failure to meet it more devastating—than any in peacetime history. The vast challenge before us, sharpened by the greatly intensified efforts of the nations of the South to secure more equality, is that of living with growing interdependence. The focus of *Agenda for Action, 1975* is on this challenge and on the corresponding opportunity to construct a new relationship between the rich countries of the world's North and the poorer countries of its South.

This volume is the third in the *Agenda for Action* series prepared annually by the Overseas Development Council. The first *Agenda*, published in early 1973, had as its central theme the growing interdependence among nations—a reality that came to the fore with great intensity later that year. The second ODC annual assessment evaluated the economic shocks of 1973–74—energy, food, and inflation—and foretold their tragic toll on what the *Agenda for Action, 1974* described as the "Fourth World" of most disadvantaged nations. That same *Agenda* urged nations not to set aside long-term work on the root problem of human poverty, and outlined a series of measures necessary to repair the damage done by the economic crises of the moment.

Human equality is a subject that has increasingly preoccupied us during

v

this century, and the growing pressure from the world's poor majority promises to dominate international issues even more forcefully in the years to come. In the short period since World War II, we have seen the development of mutuality among the advanced nations and the development of political freedom and juridical equality for all nations. It is only within the past eighteen months that a new search for economic equality has opened in earnest as the developing countries of the South, led by oil exporters, have begun to press their claims. This initiative comes at a time when the world has the capacity and knowledge to make a decent life for every person.

The challenge from the developing countries to the existing international hierarchy of power is part of an even broader theme of this *Agenda*—the argument that the world appears to be on the verge of one of the great economic, social, and political discontinuities of history. A global transformation is beginning to emerge that includes, but goes beyond, the immediate consequences of increasing interdependence; indeed, it is as if the molecular structure of the world order were changing. In the rich and poor nations alike, solutions to major issues such as the food and energy crises and stagflation increasingly involve a web of relationships requiring new global approaches if reasonable rates of growth are to continue. New global as well as domestic "social compacts"—involving significant changes in life styles—are needed to meet these new circumstances. Interdependence among nations is evolving to the point where the salient factor in our relations with developing countries should no longer be premised on paternalistically helping them with "their problem" of underdevelopment. Now the dependence of each nation on jointly managed international systems is so great that *their* lack of development frequently becomes *our* problem—just as our waste, pollution, and deepening recession often become their problem. Increasingly their problems and our problems are becoming common problems that afflict the whole world and that can best be treated by joint action. Given these conditions, *Agenda for Action, 1975* addresses the problem of *world development* rather than only that of the poor countries, although U.S. involvement with the developing countries remains the central concern of the Counoil's annual assessment.

Three major tasks are highlighted in *Agenda 1975*. The first is the need to renew our former sense of urgency in the campaign against gross human deprivation. Major progress on this front is possible within this century if we persevere. For example, the industrial countries can and should add $2 billion of development assistance annually over the level provided in 1973 for the Fourth World of poorest countries, and the OPEC countries should match that effort. Beyond this immediate emergency need, there are opportunities to improve international economic systems so that they not only serve the needs of all countries better, but also allocate more resources to the poor countries. A second major task emphasized in *Agenda 1975* is the need to respond to the challenge from the South *with such ingenuity that all parties gain.* This means that the too frequent U.S. view of that challenge as a "zero-sum game"—for example, in the energy negotiations or in the United Nations General Assembly—must be laid aside in favor of a broader vision, as is argued in the overview chapter, "The U.S. and World Development," and in Chapters VII and VIII. A third task is the importance of creating or redesigning institutions to deal with the problems that have overwhelmed existing institutions; these problems are analyzed in detail in this volume's chapters on food, trade, petrodollars, and systems overloads. The tasks before us will require that the United States and other nations take a new, comprehensive view of the kind of world they want to see evolve. Chapter IX assumes such a long-range perspective in identifying some of the elements of the kind of "global compact" needed to improve the distribution of income and economic opportunity both within and among nations.

Much of the rhetoric for each of these historic tasks is already at hand in recent official U.S. statements. The agenda for 1975 and beyond will consist of matching that rhetoric with action.

James W. Howe, Senior Fellow at the Council, directed the preparation of the *Agenda for Action*, drawing upon the entire staff of the Council. Mr. Howe wrote the overview chapter entitled, "The United States and World Development," which reflects the collective opinion of ODC's officers and staff on major issues. Because of the importance we attach to the views of the developing countries, we invited a distinguished Kenyan scholar, Dr. Ali Mazrui, to contribute a Southern perspective to our analysis, which is presented in his chapter, "The New Interdependence: From Hierarchy to Symmetry."

Theodore M. Hesburgh, *Chairman of the Board*
James P. Grant, *President*
April 1975   *Overseas Development Council*

Acknowledgments

The Overseas Development Council wishes to express its appreciation for the generous counsel given to those preparing this Agenda for Action *by many distinguished authorities in the World Bank, the International Monetary Fund, the United Nations, and the U.S. government. Advice was also gratefully received from several members of the Council's Board of Directors, especially from the Chairman of its Executive Committee, Davidson Sommers, as well as from John P. Lewis and Lincoln Gordon.*

The Project Director gratefully acknowledges his obligation to the entire staff of the Council, with a special recognition to each of the authors. Credit and thanks go to Mildred Weiss for critical perseverance and dedication in providing the comprehensive statistical material presented in this volume. Special recognition and thanks also are due to James P. Grant, ODC President, John W. Sewell, Vice President, and Robert H. Johnson, Visiting Fellow, who spent many hours and contributed countless insights; and to Valeriana Kallab, ODC Executive Editor, whose talents of logic and written expression and knowledge of the subject were indispensable. Special thanks also go to Nancy Krekeler, ODC Assistant Editor, Rosemarie Philips, and Judith Johnson for their capable and generous editorial assistance; to the Council's student interns, James Bever, Stephen Taran, Sharon Hewitt and Malcolm Russell; to Stephen Hellinger, ODC Associate Fellow, for comments on parts of the manuscript; to Michael O'Hare, ODC Business Manager; and to Sue Croy, Susan Epstein, Deborah Everett, Ferne Horner, Margaret Jameson, Phyllis Jansen, Kathryn Lenney, Angela LoRe, Charlene Meier, Kandi Triner, and Marie Williamson for their unstinting assistance in the production of the manuscript.

The Council also appreciates the special efforts of Marie Gangemi, Karen Romano, John Kaljee, Edward Scott, and Richard Svec in accelerating the book's production.

Table of Contents

The U.S. and World Development

As the year 1974 opened, the world was caught in a crisis that shattered human security as few events had done in living memory. It was a crisis of energy and food to be sure, but that was only an overlay on an older, deeper crisis that had begun in the late 1960s. Many of the familiar symbols of security so cherished in the industrialized nations—perpetual growth, expanding job opportunities, inexpensive automobile transportation, even the quality of the air we breathe and the biosphere that sustains our life—could no longer be taken for granted. The pace of growth had quickened to the point where the institutions that man had fashioned could not handle it. Too often the interlinked circuits of modern life became overloaded, and, unable to quickly adapt, they broke down. Whenever this happened, some major system—food for the hungry people, or oil for modern industrial life—failed to perform its essential function. The consequences were awesome in their toll on human life and well-being and on the natural environment. The combined pressures of rising global population, increasing affluence for one quarter of the earth's inhabitants, and deepening destitution for still another quarter of humanity were principal causes of the overload.

To this global disorder was added yet another challenge: the demands of the newly rich and the poor nations—the powerless and the disenfranchised—for a greater share of power and profit, and for participation as more equal partners in a reformed international economic order. The world would never again be quite the same. To regain an adequate pace of growth and give its people the dignity of a place in its productive processes, it would need human institutions that could anticipate, adapt, and reconcile on a more truly global basis.

1

In the eventful year 1974, progress was made on a major vestigial human problem when Portugal, the last of the colonial powers, dissolved its African empire. A grave new problem—worldwide "stagflation"— was added to the agenda for global action, and an existing problem—the deterioration of the Fourth World—grew more ominous. Citizens and governments of the industrialized countries, despite their acute concern over energy and stagflation, were touched by the desperate poverty and hunger of millions of their fellow humans and made preparations to attack the problem; and the developing nations, long dissatisfied with their status in the international hierarchy of nations, renewed and redoubled their efforts to improve their position. The oil-exporting developing nations made a real gain in economic power and income; exporters of bauxite, tin, copper, and other raw materials attempted—with inconclusive results so far—to follow their example. A similar bid for power was seen in the intensified developing-country negotiations within the International Monetary Fund, and in the efforts of certain developing countries to bargain more effectively with multinational corporations. Developing nations within the U.N. General Assembly also called for a "new international economic order." Indeed such challenges to those in control of the international economic order caused concern in Northern countries that the existing international "social compact" that had evolved in the two decades after World War II might be dissolving—a topic to which we will return later in this overview.

Both the mood of the times and an insight on the historic transformation now in progress were expressed by Secretary of State Henry Kissinger in a television interview on January 16:

> . . . one of the central facts of our period is that more than a hundred nations have come into being . . . and they too [along with the five major centers] must be central participants in this [international] process. So that for the first time in history foreign policy has become truly global. . . . I feel we are at a watershed. We're at a period which in retrospect is either going to be seen as a period of extraordinary creativity or a period when really the international order came apart politically, economically, and morally. I believe that with all the dislocations we now experience, there also exists an extraordinary opportunity to form for the first time in history a truly global society carried by the principle of interdependence. And if we act wisely and with vision, I think we can look back to all this turmoil as the birth pangs of a more creative and better system. If we miss the opportunity, I think there's going to be chaos.

U.S. policies in 1974 and early 1975 illustrate two possible ways of approaching this formidable array of world problems and prospects. The U.S. response to the long-range aspects of world hunger and food insecurity was—

with the exception of (inadequate and tardy) action on food aid—one of leadership in mapping out a systematic, comprehensive, and long-range program to attack the problem, involving a broad range of participants—developed, developing, socialist (both the U.S.S.R. and China) and oil-exporting nations. It was a response that did not seek short-run national gain at the expense of other nations but instead treated a common global illness with the medicine of international cooperation.

In the case of the oil crisis, by contrast, the U.S. originally responded to OPEC policies of confrontation by proposing a scheme of counterconfrontation—by organizing the members of the OECD, seeking an unrealistic cut in oil prices,[1] and decreasing the dependence of the United States on oil imports. Even the major developing-country importers, for example Brazil and India, were excluded from the organization. In contrast to the food case, no long-term global program was offered. Instead, the U.S. reaction was to protect its own narrowly defined interests first and the interests of other industrialized nations only second. Perhaps the sharp difference between the U.S. responses in the food and oil cases originated in the different nature of the threats themselves. While the food problem did not endanger the present relative standing of the North, the joint action of the OPEC countries was viewed as an explicit challenge to the economic supremacy of the industrial countries.

One fact that was lost sight of in the heat of confrontation was that, *even without the oil crisis*, a major shortage of low-cost oil would have been due in the 1980s—given the rate of increase in demand. The 1974 oil crisis could be viewed in one sense as an expensive but timely forewarning of the need to make changes in energy use patterns before it was too late.

How challenges are pressed by nations, individually or in groups, and how they are responded to by those challenged will determine the quality of interdependence in the years ahead. The Northern industrialized countries are willing to make the minimum necessary adjustment to the new power of the oil exporters but are reluctant to make other changes in the relationships between North and South. By contrast, a common view among countries of the South is that Northerners should treat the South as they treat one another: more or less as equal partners. Failing that, the South should take advantage of any opening it finds in any forum to press for changes. This degree of North-South confrontation is hardly compatible with the need to deal cooperatively with common problems. In the words of one developing-country observer, the need is to evolve a new "symmetrical" interdependence to replace the existing "hierarchical" relationship.[2]

As 1974 closes and the final quarter of the century opens, it is a time for taking stock of the course of world development. Much despair and great

---

[1]This stance, however, appeared to be softening in early 1975.
[2]See Chapter VI.

fears have been expressed about the future—and with good reason, because not only 1974 but the past few years as well have been full of stress. Yet one cannot look back over the past quarter century without observing that the human family has, after all, made important progress toward solving some of its ancient problems. Problems such as hunger, population increase, and human deprivation are still acutely with us, but, as we argue later in this chapter and in Chapter II, the world of today is in many important respects a better world than that which emerged from World War II.

This volume discusses two kinds of problems. First, and most important for the future as for the past, are certain threats to the human condition shared, albeit unequally, by the entire family of nations. Hunger, overpopulation, malfunctioning national and international economic systems, and the deterioration of the oceans and the environment would be formidable enough in any event, but their solution is complicated by the second kind of problem: the challenge of the developing nations of the South to the Northern dominated hierarchy of international power. This hierarchical challenge—a relatively new manifestation of an old theme—will be the subject of the second part of this overview. Before considering it in detail, however, we will first briefly review the current status of the commonly shared human problems from which no nation can now isolate itself. The analysis of these two categories of challenges will provide a basis for formulating an agenda for world development with particular focus on U.S. actions in 1975 and beyond.

Challenges to Human Ingenuity: New Global Problems

The increasing frequency, intensity, and persistence of certain commonly shared human problems in the 1970s have led to speculation that they are the early signs of approaching "limits to growth."[3] The unprecedented economic growth rates of the late 1960s and early 1970s, coupled with continuing expansion of the world's population, have strained the capacity of existing human institutions and have led to systemic overloads such as global inflation, recession, food shortages, declining harvests of ocean fish, occasional raw-material shortages, environmental stress, the deterioration of cities, and threats to the international trading system. One of the most tragic results of these events has been the worsening *relative* condition and—recently probably even a deteriorating *absolute* condition—of the world's poorest people, particularly those in the Fourth World. While there is no persuasive evidence that an unyielding ceiling on growth has been reached, the

---

[3]See Donella H. and Dennis L. Meadows et al., *The Limits to Growth: A Report for the Club of Rome's Project on the Predicament of Mankind* (New York: Universe Books for Potomac Associates, 1972); and Donella H. and Dennis L. Meadows et al., *The Limits to Growth,* Second Edition, (New York: Universe Books for Potomac Associates, 1975).

pace of economic and demographic growth appears to have exceeded the current ability of economic and social systems to adapt.[4]

If adequate economic growth is to be resumed, great human ingenuity and cooperativeness will be required in redesigning and adapting human institutions to tolerate its stresses. One of the critical tests of such redesigned institutions will be their ability to distribute more equitably not only the rewards of growth but also the traumas of interruptions in growth. The recent price explosions and the current economic slowdown have imposed great strains on most nations, yet efforts of the leading industrialized nations have been devoted largely to minimizing the impact of inflation and recession on their own citizens, the richest billion people on earth. The likely consequence is that the brunt of the hardship will fall most heavily upon the world's poorest billion—those least able to absorb it. Several of the challenges to the family of nations that have been sharpened by the events of the past year are discussed below.

Food and Hunger.[5] Viewed in the long term, the World Food Conference held in Rome in November 1974 may prove to have been an historic success. The Conference established some potentially useful, new international machinery to encourage expansion of production in food-deficit developing countries. It was agreed that there should be an internationally coordinated system of national grain reserves and a system to warn of impending shortfalls in world food availability. The Conference also focused widespread attention of citizens and their governments on the problem of hunger and population and was the first occasion on which the Western developed countries, the Soviet Union, China, the newly rich OPEC countries, and other developing countries joined efforts in considering a major world problem.

The near consensus reached at the Conference on the importance of increased food production in food-deficit countries calls for more effective rural development programs in those countries. In the long run, the key solution to the food problem is to grow more food in the food-deficit poor countries and to increase the incomes of the poor so that they can buy it. This will take time, however, and meanwhile there is the immediate problem of dealing with hunger and acute malnutrition. The U.S. Department of Agriculture estimated in December 1974 that the 1985 deficit might run as high as 71.6 million tons, but that it might be held as low as 15.8 million tons if appropriate steps were taken immediately to increase food production in developing countries.

To help meet these needs, U.S. food aid over the next five years should be maintained at a level of 8 to 9 million tons a year—roughly its level in the late 1960s and early 1970s, before it plummeted to a low of just over 3 million tons

---

[4]See Chapter VIII.
[5]See Chapter III.

in 1974. The decision by President Ford in early 1975 to expand food aid for the year to 5.5 million tons was welcome, although it came too late to be of maximum benefit. In addition, Public Law 480 needs revision to make the Food for Peace Program—which was originally a surplus disposal program—reflect current conditions. For instance, food aid needs to be programmed *early* in each year, rather than only after it is known how much is left over from other uses. The grant component of the program needs to be increased to meet the growing humanitarian needs to support agricultural production more effectively and to help establish food reserves in recipient countries. A major increase in food aid from the United States might be associated with a major allocation of funds by the richer of the OPEC countries to the new Agricultural Development Fund recommended by the World Food Conference.

The United States should also significantly increase its aid to agricultural production in poor countries that have food deficits. Although its bilateral aid for agricultural improvement in developing countries has expanded from about $300 million in 1973 to $600 million programmed for fiscal 1975, this amount is still too small in relation to the vast needs and potential benefits. The FAO estimates the external capital needed for investment in agriculture in developing countries is about $5 billion per year compared with the current level of $1.5 billion. The International Development Association of the World Bank is devoting increasing funds to rural development in food-deficit countries; it is presently supporting a total of 51 comprehensive projects in 42 countries, and plans are under way for additional projects to directly benefit a total of 100 million rural poor by 1980. The United States should support a major expansion of financing for IDA's programs in the negotiations for the next replenishment of IDA in 1976.

Finally, the United States should fully support the implementation of its own proposal for an internationally coordinated system of national food reserves—so that the world's food stock can be increased (as soon as surpluses begin to appear) to provide greater world food security in times of shortage and prevent sharp declines in the earnings of farmers in times of surplus.

Population. The United Nations-sponsored Population Conference held in Bucharest in 1974 was an important step in the evolution of a consensus that controlling fertility is linked not only to ensuring a more convenient and universally available range of acceptable contraceptives; but also to providing the poorest and most fertile people of the world with more of the benefits of development—including jobs, higher incomes, and better health and education services, especially for women. The Conference also served as a forum for airing some of the objections of developing countries to widespread accusations that their rates of population are burdening the entire planet. In fact, the consumption rate in the developed countries in some cases places an ever greater burden on the planet—despite the much lower rates of population growth in these countries. For example, the U.S. Department of Agriculture

6

projects an increased demand for cereals—due to both population increases and rising affluence—amounting to as much as 304 million tons between the base period (1969-1971) and 1985 in developed countries, in contrast to an increase of only about 277 million tons in the far more populous developing (including socialist) countries.[6] While the serious impact of rising affluence on global demand for resources is undeniable, the annual addition of vast numbers of new humans to the world's population by the developing countries is equally ominous. There is sympathy with the aspiration of the world's poor people for higher consumption levels, but there is also mounting concern that continued high rates of population growth, combined with higher consumption levels, will overload the planet's productive and waste-absorptive capacity.

On the positive side of the record, recent evidence indicates that seventy-two countries have made progress in reducing fertility.[7] Seventeen countries in this group have reduced births by as much as 10 per 1000 population since 1960, including—encouragingly—sixteen developing countries.

U.S. policy with respect to global population growth should be guided by an understanding that high birth rates are in part a product of extreme poverty and can be corrected only if the human condition is improved.[8] Bills now pending in Congress to deny aid to countries that are not making headway in reducing birth rates would very likely be counterproductive if enacted. Governments of countries with high birth rates may in a very few instances be unsympathetic to family planning programs. But even in such cases, it should be U.S. policy to encourage an attack on poverty; for experience indicates that where the human condition is improving, fertility has frequently been reduced even without comprehensive government support for family planning (e.g., most of nineteenth-century Europe), but that where poverty is acute and increasing, fertility is not likely to drop significantly and permanently even if family planning programs are widely available. U.S. Agency for International Development funds for family planning, which were reduced in fiscal year 1975, should be restored and increased over the years ahead as part of a dual approach including both family planning and programs designed to reduce poverty.

Overloaded Ecosystems, Finite Resources, and the "Good Life."[9] The

---

[6]Economic Research Service, U.S. Department of Agriculture, *The World Food Situation and Prospects to 1985,* Foreign Agricultural Economic Report No. 98 (Washington, D.C.: U.S. Department of Agriculture, 1974), p. 35.

[7]R. T. Ravenholt and John Chao, "World Fertility Trends, 1974," in *Family Planning Programs,* Population Report, Series J, No. 2 (August 1974), pp. J-21—J-39. Published by the Department of Medical and Public Affairs, The George Washington University Medical Center, Washington, D.C.

[8]See Chapter II.

[9]This subject was discussed in more detail in Chapters VIII (Part I) and IX in *The United States and the Developing World: Agenda for Action, 1973,* by Robert E. Hunter and the staff of the Overseas Development Council (Washington, D.C.: Overseas Development Council, 1973).

most acute environmental problems currently occur in rich countries, where economic activity is most intense; but problems of land erosion and water pollution are also serious in low-income countries, especially where population is dense in relation to the productive capacity of the land. In the United States, pressure continues to build up (especially in affluent quarters) against unrestrained economic growth. Local zoning authorities, supported by strong public opinion, resist rapid industrial and residential expansion, while scholars and environmentalists debate the continuation of such wasteful aspects of modern life as single-family homes on individual plots, throw-away containers, and reliance on individual motor vehicles. A recent survey reports that through the summer of 1974 there was no weakening of public concern about environmental issues. The survey responses showed that 64 per cent of the public believes that "sooner or later world population and economic growth will have to be regulated to avoid serious shortages."[10]

In poor countries, by contrast, there is understandably less concern about wasteful overconsumption—since poverty remains the most critical problem. Voices are being raised, however, against the emulation by domestic elites of the materialistic life style of the rich countries. Growing numbers of commentators also are questioning the values and modes of production and consumption of the North as both impractical and intrinsically undesirable for the South. These analysts call for more labor-intensive production, for systems that give priority to satisfying the needs of the poor before the desires of the rich, and for the acceptance of values that are compatible with the resource base and environmental conditions of such countries. They do not attack development in general but appeal for a resource-conserving approach (involving, for example, use of bicycles or buses rather than automobiles, or emphasis on preventive medicine rather than costly modern hospitals).

Issues for U.S. policy makers to consider include the question of government action to conserve commodities in scarce supply, notably oil and food. In the case of food, existing U.S. government policies that encourage intensive fattening of animals with grains and soybeans should be revised. A public education program is also needed on the health hazards of eating too much animal fat. Whether economic incentives to eat grass-fed rather than grain-fed meat are needed is a matter for further study.

With respect to overburdened ecosystems, U.S. policy makers are discovering that they must make trade-offs between the goals of meeting shortages and those of meeting environmental standards. Thus, for example, the energy shortage has forced countries to consider lowering environmental standards in order to increase the production of coal, postponing programs to control automobile pollution, and risking oil spills in rushing exploration for

---

[10]See William Watts and Lloyd A. Free, *State of the Nation* (Washington, D.C.: Potomac Associates, 1974), p. 173. No data are available to indicate whether the recent recession has dimmed this concern.

offshore oil. There were other trade-offs as well: the lumber shortage of a year ago challenged the efforts of environmentalists to protect forests; the food shortage may have brought some land into crop production which, from an environmental point of view, should have been kept in pasture or timber; and the high price of animal protein led to additional pressures on the world's ocean fisheries. Given time and ingenuity, some of these dilemmas may be resolved by the development of new technologies. Others will simply require U.S. governmental structures at all levels, as well as U.S. citizen groups, to make choices between health hazards (the most common choices do not involve threats to the biosphere itself) and shortages.

The Oceans and the Resource-Poor Countries. The results of the third session of the U.N. Conference on the Law of the Sea in Caracas were, perhaps predictably, disappointing. Delegates from 138 nations deliberated for ten weeks on an agenda designed to produce a comprehensive treaty covering all major ocean issues—ranging from the boundaries of territorial waters, economic zones, and continental shelves to questions concerning a regime for the use of the deep seabed, pollution, fisheries, and scientific research. The Conference had before it an agenda of more than one hundred items and sub-items.

Most observers are in agreement that the Caracas session achieved little more than a continuation of the preparatory work that has occupied the U.N. Seabed Committee and its predecessors for the past six to seven years. If there were no urgency to arrive at a comprehensive treaty more quickly, the lack of greater progress in Caracas would be of little concern. However, there are at least three major reasons to believe that time is of the essence in the handling of these issues, and that a high price may be paid in 1975 for the limited achievements of 1974. The first reason is that the Conference may collapse toward the end of 1975 if it becomes clear that the objective of securing a comprehensive and widely acceptable law of the sea treaty cannot be attained. Under these conditions, it might well prove impossible to prevent the further proliferation of unilateral decisions and declarations by major coastal and other states, with serious adverse implications for optimum usage of the world's oceans and the resources within and beneath them.

It is quite possible that the United States will follow the lead of others in taking such unilateral actions if not enough progress is made to guarantee a comprehensive treaty before the end of 1975. Many observers presently feel that in the absence of such progress, the U.S. Congress would enact legislation creating a 200-mile exclusive fishing zone and authorizing the construction of deep-water ports beyond present territorial sea limits. It is also considered more than likely that Congress would then authorize U.S. firms to begin mining operations in the deep seabeds. If the United States were to take such unilateral actions, a host of other nations would immediately follow, and the opportunity for a more optimal usage of "the heritage of mankind" would be lost, perhaps irrevocably.

9

The second reason for concern about the issue of timing is that the lack of progress thus far may lead various groups of states to negotiate and ratify regional treaties reflecting their own particular predispositions on issues before the Conference. Such a development would heighten rather than reduce present and potential international conflict over ocean use.

The third—and in many ways the most serious—concern is that after deliberating for so long, the Conference will, during the coming year, rush to conclude a comprehensive treaty that will in fact fulfill little if any of the promise inherent in the original proposal presented to the United Nations by Malta. That proposal called for a law of the sea treaty to utilize the resources of the oceans beyond the twelve-mile limit to assist the development of the world's poor nations and thereby diminish the inequities of the global distribution of wealth. The author of the original proposal, Dr. Arvid Pardo, recently characterized his view of the most likely outcome of this negotiation as follows:

> To put matters bluntly the package deal which is being negotiated and which may be concluded [in 1975], will provide exclusively for the protection in ocean space of the interests of the major groups of states, whether developed or developing. These interests will center around three areas: (a) international recognition of the extensive coastal jurisdiction in the seas (well beyond 200 miles in many instances); (b) international recognition of the exercise by coastal states of comprehensive powers within national jurisdiction areas; (c) normally unhampered commercial navigation.[11]

Dr. Pardo noted that acceptance of such a treaty would turn his original proposal on its head. His major concern about such an outcome is that if coastal states are permitted to extend their control of marine resources well beyond the 200-mile limit, international control of seabed resources in the comparatively small remaining area unclaimed by coastal states will be of little or no significance.

Unfortunately, those members of the "Group of 77" developing countries which individually stand to gain by an ocean regime allocating most benefits to coastal states rather than to the poorest nations have not hesitated to place their national interests ahead of those of the other members of the Group. This development probably should not be a surprise; there is no reason to expect poor countries to be less selfish or attentive to short-run gains than rich nations.

If the outcome feared by Dr. Pardo were to occur, the major losers would be the land-locked and shelf-locked states of the world as well as most of the

---

[11]Arvid Pardo, *Perspectives in Ocean Relations, Conflict and Order in Ocean Relations* (Washington, D.C.: U.S. Government Printing Office, 1975).

resource-poor members of the "Fourth World"—precisely the countries which stand to gain relatively the most under the original proposal. The major gainers would be the world's coastal states. But in the longer term, *all* states might prove to be losers when their actual gains under such an outcome were measured against the more optimal solutions inherent in the original proposal. That optimal outcome still is not entirely beyond reach if the developed as well as the developing nations constituting the present Law of the Sea Conference demonstrate a greater capacity to negotiate this major issue of global resource management in a long-term perspective.

U.S. policy on this subject has in general taken a global point of view. Several years ago, the United States proposed a treaty that would distribute among all nations at least some of the revenues from exploiting the seabed and provide some international standards to protect the oceans. The United States should continue to support a law of the sea treaty that is basically internationalist. However, if the prospects for such an enlightened treaty are dashed by the nationalistic views of others, it is regrettably, but understandably, likely that the United States will seek to protect its narrow national interests.

International Trade.[12] The main item on the U.S. agenda for international trade is to achieve the constructive potential for expansion of world trade in the Trade Reform Act of late 1974, thus avoiding trade wars of the kind that so devastated the world economy in the 1930s. Three pressures are edging the nations of the world toward such restrictions on trade. The first is the relatively recent threat of worldwide inflation, which presses nations to limit certain exports because of internal shortages. In the past two years, there have been increased examples of such restrictions in many developed countries, involving, for example, fertilizers from Japan, Europe, and the United States; oil from Australia and Canada, and sugar from Europe. For many years certain developing countries have imposed limitations on exports they considered essential to their economies. Together with export restrictions for the purpose of controlling the market or for political purposes, such impediments to the flow of goods disrupt trading patterns and internal economic activity.

The second impetus toward economic conflict is the threat to nations' balances of payments implicit in the oil price crisis. Hard pressed to meet the increased costs of oil imports, nations are tempted to limit imports of other items in order to pass on part of the oil-induced deficit to other oil-importing nations. Such efforts could lead to rising import barriers, competitive devaluations, and other actions that would invite retaliation.

Third, the shift in public concern from inflation to recession carries a danger of increasing barriers to imports and to the export of capital for the sake of protecting jobs at home. Once initiated by a major industrial country,

---

[12]For a more detailed discussion, see Chapter IV.

this approach would almost certainly cause retaliation by others, and thus would accentuate rather than alleviate the problem of unemployment in all countries as access to foreign markets dwindled.

While there are dangers on the present trade scene, there are also new opportunities. The Trade Reform Act of 1974 empowers the President to conduct negotiations to reduce existing tariff and non-tariff barriers to trade. It also authorizes him to extend preferences to manufactured and semi-manufactured goods from developing countries (except for a list of specifically excluded items). This offers the possibility of responding to the changing needs of these countries—in particular to their desire to process their raw materials—by removing current barriers to their export of such goods. Other essential elements of such a response are international commodity arrangements to stabilize the markets of raw-material producing countries while ensuring open access to essential supplies.

But the Trade Reform Act also provides the means for restricting trade; its mechanisms would permit the raising of barriers if a mood of protectionism were to dominate the Congress. The dangers of precipitating movement in this direction among the other industrial countries is great, since a number of them are delicately balanced between the two trends and would react quickly to a change of direction by the United States. Without doubt, this is a realm in which U.S. leadership is essential to the continued growth and health of the world economy. To be viable domestically, however, the U.S. program must implement effectively the adjustment process provided in the Act for workers in industries affected by increased imports.

A primary objective of the international trading community is to reach agreement on commodity arrangements to meet the demands of producers for reliable prices and markets and those of consumers for reasonable prices and secure supplies. The world has arrived at the point of interdependence in the flow of goods where failure to work out adequate mechanisms will continue to create upheavals—some as potentially convulsive as that initiated by OPEC. Whatever its stage of development, each country has a vital stake—both as a producer and as a consumer—in the sound functioning of the system. Hence the essentials are present for building a durable, increasingly equitable, trading relationship between North and South.

Global Inflation and Recession. The simultaneous economic boom experienced by the OECD countries and much of the rest of the world in the early 1970s had helped fuel an unprecedented rate of global inflation by mid-1973—even before the energy price rises of late 1973. The combined effect of the energy shocks and policies already introduced to arrest inflation led to a slump throughout the industrial world by late 1973, with the sharpest slowdowns in the United States and Japan. To make matters worse, inflation continued alongside rising unemployment, producing global "stagflation."

In the short run, solving the twin problems of inflation and recession of course still depends largely on internal actions by individual governments.

But if the long-run causes of "stagflation" are international, its cure likewise must be international. The standard solutions for deflation (as yet there are no standard prescriptions for stagflation) are "reflating" through public employment, eased money supply, tax cuts, and interest-rate cuts. The traditional cures for inflation are budget cuts, tax rises, and price, profit, and wage controls. But all of these must rely on national machinery and national policies, which may well be in conflict with the policies of other nations. There is no international money, and there is no international Central Bank or Treasury, or Department of Public Works. There likewise is no international budget. Unfortunately, however, the international linkages of monetary policies, trade, and investment[13] require that the cure at least be internationally coordinated.

Inevitably, stagflation interacts with development, spoiling the hopes of developing countries in two ways. First, the explosion in the prices of the essential imports of developing countries has hurt many of them so badly that the United Nations has designated the thirty-two "most seriously affected" countries a sort of global disaster area. Second, as recession grips the developed countries, demand has collapsed for jute, cotton, copper, and other raw materials that poor countries export, thus cutting their earnings as well. Tourism and emigrant workers' remittances also have declined in many developing countries. The resulting combination of rising import costs and decreased earnings is, of course, damaging to development progress.

But the interaction of development and stagflation also has a potentially positive aspect in that properly managed development can help to correct stagflation in the long run. Clearly *inflation* has been aggravated by the rising cost of food, caused by strong demand and short supply. Food deficits in poor countries have contributed heavily to those price rises. A series of massive national programs of rural development in the poor countries would help to relieve the inflation problem in the long run by increasing production and improving storage, transport, and distribution. Underutilized land and other resources in many developing countries give these countries a potential comparative advantage in producing low-cost food. Development would, moreover, help to fight *recession* in the developed world by enabling developing countries to import machinery, equipment, and services from the industrialized countries. To the extent that an increase in poor-country purchasing power through external credits increases demand for rich-country services and industrial products such as construction, heavy equipment, spare parts, and engineering services—sectors that have been hit hardest by recession—the development of poor countries can modestly help the rich to pull out of their recession.

---

[13]To be sure, the widespread practice of floating exchange rates goes some distance toward reconciling economic policies of nations, but it is by no means a complete answer to the need for international coordination.

The U.S. and other countries should harmonize their national economic policies to avoid the recent disastrous experience of simultaneous overexpansion followed by simultaneous and mutually reinforcing nosedives. However, the mandates and administrative capacity of existing international coordinating mechanisms (e.g., OECD, IMF, GATT) are too limited for these institutions to perform that harmonizing task. The evolution of improved and more comprehensive international coordinating mechanisms to achieve and maintain international economic health are critical international agenda items for the next few years and, indeed, for the remainder of the century.

The Fourth World. In 1974, the problems of a "Fourth World" came more fully into focus. The Fourth World consists of 42 countries, with a total population of almost one billion persons so hampered by economic stagnation and rising import costs that they have little prospect of extricating themselves without outside help. Many of the people of these countries live in acute poverty. The bulk of the population is uneducated. Hunger is chronic and starvation a reality in some places. Many of the world's debilitating diseases occur in these countries. Even though the Fourth World experiences the highest rates of infant mortality, it also accounts for a significant portion of the increase in world population.

Poverty is by no means confined to the Fourth World. It afflicts as many as 40 per cent of the people in many other developing countries. It is found in smaller pockets in most industrial countries, where it is accentuated by recession. What sets the Fourth World countries apart from the rest of the developing world is the magnitude of the problems confronting them in relation to their ability to deal with the situation. These countries are hampered not only by extensive poverty but also by their vulnerability to world economic events. Of all the countries in the world, they bear most heavily the brunt of the hardship resulting from the oil-price increase and from the global crop shortfalls, which magnify their dependence on grain imports. Moreover, their exports consist overwhelmingly of raw materials, the prices of which fluctuate widely and have declined by 50 per cent in the past two years in terms of purchasing power. Unfortunately, the predicament of the Fourth World is further aggravated by the fact that certain of the other international economic systems—e.g., official export credits, private investment, and private lending—generally benefit it less than they do other developing countries. This is of course in part a cause and in part a consequence of their low level of development.

On the brighter side, there has been continued progress in recent years in evolving development strategies to fit the needs and circumstances of poor countries. Growing recognition of the importance of the small farmer and of the need for a strategy that benefits the poorest people is evident, for example, in the U.S. Foreign Assistance Act of 1973, in the September 1973 statement of the World Bank President, and in the decisions of the U.N. Population Conference and the World Food Conference of 1974. A further positive sign is that scholars and policy makers are increasingly examining the results achieved by those countries—e.g., China, South Korea, Taiwan, and, in some respects, Sri Lanka—which have adopted such models of development. While this represents conceptual rather than physical progress for the Fourth World, it may portend a turn for the better in the future of the world's poorest people.

The President of the World Bank predicts that unless extraordinary efforts are made to help the Fourth World countries, they will experience negative growth rates of their economies for the rest of the decade. He estimates, however, that no more than $3 to $4 billion of additional concessional aid annually during this period would enable them to achieve a 2 per cent growth rate of per capita income. This would make it possible for the Fourth World countries to emerge from their present stagnation and to acquire enough resilience to tackle their basic problems. What is required from the outside in the way of resources to enable this to happen is an allocation of additional concessional aid giving special consideration to these worst-off countries. Assuming that the OPEC countries are willing to put up half of the additional $4 billion needed by the Fourth World, the OECD countries should supply the remainder, of which the United States should contribute an additional $1 billion in view of its strong economic position relative to other OECD countries.

At the same time that concessional aid is being reallocated, principally to Fourth World countries and to those borderline Third World countries which are in danger of joining their ranks, the needs of the Third World must not be overlooked. It is important to ensure that the more advanced of these countries have adequate access to capital markets and that the middle-ranking Third World countries have access to funds on intermediate terms through mechanisms such as a "third window" of the World Bank. The United States also should press for reform of the major resource-allocating systems—trade, finance, investment, and others—so that the benefits of these systems do not bypass the countries of the Third and Fourth Worlds.

Military Expenditures and the Need for Capital. The continuation of vast world expenditures on arms at a time when urgent human problems go unattended is obviously lamentable. Responding to the systems overloads discussed above would require additional capital to improve the capabilities of those systems. Over $1 trillion will be needed during the next decade alone to develop alternative sources of energy as traditional sources of low-production-cost oil provide an ever declining share of requirements. Meeting the present food shortage and anticipating future ones also will require large-scale investment in food production (particularly in developing countries) and in storage facilities, as well as in funds for food relief during the interim period when food deficits are being reduced. The aim of reducing birth rates, particularly in countries which now have an acute population-resource imbalance, likewise will require substantial outlays of capital for bringing health and education services and job opportunities to the poorest (and most fertile) groups in these countries. Protecting the earth's environment also will call for vast investments, as will the development programs of the oil-exporting nations that seek to make their economies viable before their oil reserves are used up.

Given these needs, there is clearly reason to be concerned about the level of world military expenditures. In the ten-year period from 1963 to 1973, such expenditures were $2.5 trillion, of which more than one third—or $765 billion—was spent by the United States, and $674 billion by the Soviet Union. In 1963, global arms expenditures were $197 billion, and by 1973 they had risen to $241 billion in constant 1972 dollars.[14] A modest diversion of the enormous amounts now expended for military purposes to constructive investments of the kind outlined above would make significant strides toward solving some of the common problems that threaten the world's people.

There is also reason to be concerned about the proliferation of modern arms throughout the world as a result of arms sales from the military powers. In 1973, U.S. arms sales to the world were $4.75 billion, and the U.S.S.R.'s sales were $2.54 billion. In 1974 the amounts were undoubtedly much larger. World arms exports have in fact doubled during the decade, and the percentage of GNP spent on arms by many developing nations has increased to the point where it is approaching the percentage level in developed countries. Moreover, since the oil price rises, and especially in recent months, sales of arms to the oil-exporting countries have skyrocketed—not only because of the efforts of Middle East oil exporters to build up military strength, but also due to attempts by the arms sellers to close balance-of-payments deficits created largely by the 1973-74 oil price rises. Along with continuing arms shipments to Indochina, this sharp rise in Middle East purchases accounts for a large part of U.S. arms sales. There is, of course, the problem that if the United States were to cut arms sales unilaterally, others probably would increase their sales to offset U.S. cuts. Clearly the problem cannot be solved without a comprehensive accord between arms suppliers and purchasers. That of course is an enormously complex problem which will not be resolved until progress has been achieved in settling the Arab-Israeli dispute, and until the oil-rich countries have further modernized their military establishments. But U.S. planning should be under way now for a comprehensive attack on the problem when events are more propitious.

The United States—as the world's largest arms seller and military spender—has an urgent responsibility to press ahead with negotiations to limit both global defense expenditures and the vast world trade in arms.

---

[14]*World Military Expenditures and Arms Trade 1963-73,* U.S. Arms Control and Disarmament Agency Publication No. 74 (Washington, D.C.: U.S. Government Printing Office, 1975).

Challenges to the Hierarchical Position of the Rich Nations

The past year marked the emergence of a number of oil-exporting developing countries as important new international powers, thereby disproving earlier predictions of the collapse of the OPEC cartel. Influenced by the visible success of the OPEC countries, other resource-rich developing countries tried to emulate their behavior, but with mixed results. Some succeeded, as did Jamaica, for example, when it raised its income from the mining of its bauxite deposits by foreign companies. Others failed, largely because the prices of their raw materials sagged due to a deepening recession in the industrial world.

Disagreements over the possibility of creating additional commodity cartels have obscured a basic change in psychology that has taken place within the developing world. The nations of the Southern hemisphere no longer will tolerate being taken for granted and will seek to advance their interests in a variety of ways in a number of different forums as opportunities present themselves. Thus last year's acrimonious exchange in the U.N. General Assembly over the "new international economic order" is only the beginning of a much more intensive phase in the long debate over equity in international economic relations. Similar developments can be seen in such forums as the International Monetary Fund and in the ongoing interaction of multinational corporations and host governments in the developing world.

Efforts by the South to Reform the International Economic Order. Attempts by the developing countries to change the existing international economic systems are not new; nor are their efforts to set down in writing an agreed statement of such reforms. This subject was the theme of the first United Nations Conference on Trade and Development more than a decade ago. Despite its limitations, the International Strategy for the Second Development Decade adopted by the U.N. General Assembly in 1970 was the most successful joint effort of rich and poor countries to date to achieve a limited bargain outlining the obligations of each side on behalf of development. The most recent attempts to formally revise the world economic order have been the controversial Declaration and Action Programme on the Establishment of the New International Economic Order adopted by the Special Session of the U.N. General Assembly in April 1974, and the Charter of Economic Rights and Duties of States passed by the General Assembly in December 1974 over the opposition of the developed countries.

In the changed economic circumstances since 1974, the assertions of economic rights contained in the two new documents should have come as no surprise to any seasoned representative in international organizations. They were largely the predictable outcome of a decade of fruitless efforts by the developing countries to evoke a significant developed-world response to their central problem: the fact that they still depend on their commodity exports for 75 to 80 per cent of their foreign exchange earnings, and that the international community has done little to alleviate—and much to ensure—the nearly exclusive dependence of their development on the demand for these exports in developed-country markets. Awareness of this central problem—and of the need for a new international economic order to, among other things, increase market access for their processed exports and establish adequate prices for their raw-material exports—has surfaced again and again in U.N. and other international forums and in less formal discussions within the international development establishment for years.

The revival of the term "new international economic order" at the spring 1974 General Assembly Special Session had significance not because what was being advanced was a totally new program of international economic policy goals, but because it was asserted by the developing countries at a time when they *perceived* themselves (directly or by proxy) to hold new bargaining strength to negotiate changes in at least some components of the old order.

What is striking about the present situation, given the fact that concern about economic insecurity is now worldwide, is that the developed countries, having first hailed the concept of interdependence, do not yet seem to be seriously grappling with the unavoidable and extraordinarily difficult task of giving it real meaning. Strangely enough, it is the developing countries— which less than a decade ago were merely demanding non-reciprocal aid transfers and trade concessions—that have been inspired by the recent events to try to "flesh out" the concept. In contrast, policy makers in the developed world, including the United States—which, after all, has been among the least seriously affected by the economic disasters of 1973-74—have not yet turned their imaginations to this enterprise. Ideas are not lacking on what the components of the new international economic order should be. On the developing-country side, proposals are being shaped at an impressive pace at meetings such as the Third World Forum of developing-world economists, the March 7 meeting of thirteen Francophone African nations, the OPEC summit conferences, the February 1975 raw-material conference held by the non-aligned states in Dakar; and the session of various UNCTAD bodies of member countries.

In developed countries also, consideration of the possible components of the new world order is accelerating—although still largely in non-governmental forums. In the United States alone, for example, projects on this subject are under way in the Institute of Science and Man, the Aspen Institute for Humanistic Studies, the Overseas Development Council, the Council on Foreign Relations, the Brookings Institution, the Carnegie Endowment for International Peace, and doubtless many other groups. In the face of these many efforts to propose at least some articles for a new international "social compact," the United States government, which was constructive and cooperative in some of the earlier efforts to consider reform of the old economic order, has been unresponsive since the oil price rises. It has objected strongly to many components of the new Declaration and Action

Programme of April 1974, and to the Charter of Rights and Duties voted in December 1974. But it has neither explained the reasons for its opposition nor made any serious efforts to engage in the dialogue with the South in a constructive vein. Having at best ignored recent Southern proposals on the shape of the world, the United States government has an obligation to respond to the recommendations of others and to outline its own proposals on the subject. Otherwise, it will be widely believed that its policy is merely to prevent change. An opportunity to respond will be provided by the September 1975 U.N. General Assembly's Special Session on development and international economic cooperation.

This Special Session is deliberately scheduled to take place at the time of the formal review of the implementation of the International Strategy for the Second Development Decade—after the recent major world conferences, and after some of the results are in on the progress of the multilateral trade negotiations and monetary reform discussions. Its difficult task after a year of much confrontation will be to attempt to renew commitment to eliminating some of the international political and economic constraints that continue to block development in the poor countries.

Living with OPEC—A New Power. For more than a decade after OPEC's establishment in 1960, its thirteen members unsuccessfully attempted to act in concert to prevent declines in oil prices. Only when rising demand for oil converted the buyers' market for this commodity into a sellers' market did OPEC's policies succeed in raising prices. Because of their control of oil and their growing ownership of the world's liquid financial assets, the OPEC nations are now collectively a major center of economic power. This is not to suggest that the OPEC nations will act in unison on all issues. But as long as OPEC presents a united front on oil prices and available supplies, the power of its more affluent members will extend to the monetary, development, and investment fields and the international political arena as well. Thus the views of Iran, Saudi Arabia, and Venezuela surely will be important in, for example, the long-term negotiations of an improved monetary system.

The oil exporters already have become surprisingly active in the field of development assistance; their concessional aid programs and contributions to international aid agencies amounted to about $10 billion of new commitments and $2.6 billion of disbursements in 1974.[15] This level of *commitments* parallels actual *deliveries* by OECD countries, which in 1974 totalled $11 billion. The early aid efforts of Venezuela, Iran, Saudi Arabia, the United Arab Emirates, Libya, and Kuwait seem particularly promising. A significant amount of OPEC assistance has been extended to the Fourth World.[16] More than $2 billion in concessional bilateral aid appears to have been committed by OPEC to these poorest countries in 1974. However, since the adverse

---

[15]See Chapter VII.
[16]See Chapter I.

19

impact on those countries from the oil price rises was about $2 billion in 1974 alone, OPEC aid is likely to barely offset the direct damage done to this group of countries by the oil price rises.

It is not possible to predict whether the level of OPEC commitments will be implemented with prompt deliveries, nor whether this is a level that will be sustained in subsequent years. One year after the oil price rises, however, the OPEC assistance record is impressive indeed. As a percentage of donor GNP, the 1974 commitment level of OPEC is ten times that of the much wealthier— but less liquid—OECD countries. It should be remembered that except for five Arab countries (Saudi Arabia, the United Arab Emirates, Qatar, Kuwait, and Libya, whose average per capita income approximates that of the United States and Germany), the oil exporters have an average per capita income one tenth that of the OECD countries.

The purposes of the major OPEC donors—Saudi Arabia, Iran, Kuwait, United Arab Emirates, Libya, and Venezuela—are obviously mixed. The strengthening of Egypt, Jordan, and Syria against Israel, amounting to more than one third of all OPEC aid in 1970-1974, has been important to Arab members of OPEC. Seeking to exercise regional leadership also has been a factor, especially for Iran and Venezuela. And certainly a key goal of aid to oil-importing developing nations has been to maintain their diplomatic support for OPEC in its confrontation with OECD—particularly the United States—over the price of oil. A closely related objective may be building and maintaining the solidarity of the Group of 77 and the non-aligned states. It is interesting that although the oil-price damage to oil-importing members of the Group of 77 has hurt them, they have not yet been very critical of OPEC pricing policies and indeed have praised them as a model for emulation by other raw-material suppliers. Whether or not their approval of OPEC will last may depend in large measure on how much aid they continue to receive from oil-exporting countries. For the time being, the solidarity of the Group of 77 appears to be intact.

Some developing-country analysts are looking to OPEC for active leadership in the struggle of the South to reduce its asymmetrical dependency on the North and to secure a greater share of power in managing the world's economic systems. This aim was reflected, for example, in the proposals of the first meeting of the Third World Forum,[17] held in Karachi in early January 1975. An excerpt from the communique issued by the Forum is interesting in the same connection (note the Forum's use of the term "Third World" to include all developing countries):

The present crisis marks the gradual crumbling of an old order in which a group of rich nations constituting the developed centre

---

[17]The Third World Forum is intended to be a periodic meeting of about fifty leading economists from developing countries.

continuously expanded by the use of energy and raw materials provided by the poor nations at the periphery at cheap prices. The increase in the price of oil by the OPEC could therefore be seen as a part of the struggle of the Third World to obtain a better deal from the world order. But this struggle would neither be complete nor meaningful until other poor nations at the periphery also obtained a fairer deal and unless the present polarization between the countries at the centre and those at the periphery was changed by different patterns of collective self-reliance among the Third World countries. . . . The participants . . . proposed . . . establishment of a Third World Development Bank financed by OPEC and other Third World countries. . . . In connection with these initiatives, the participants considered that close cooperation between OPEC and other parts of the Third World was vital in the next stage of this continuing struggle if the Third World was to succeed in its efforts to obtain more justice from the world order and if oil exporting countries were to expect to consolidate and maintain their gains.

Whether or not these high hopes for OPEC support will materialize, this excerpt illustrates the receptivity in at least some parts of the South to a major leadership role by the relatively stronger OPEC countries.

Clearly international investment, long dominated by OECD-based private multinational firms, has a new giant entrant in the OPEC countries. A considerable portion of the $250 billion that these countries will accumulate in surplus funds by 1980 will be invested by them in productive enterprises in OECD and other countries. This development is already presenting problems for the United States, which is not used to being the recipient of investments from the developing countries. But the advantages of encouraging such investment would appear to outweigh any disadvantages. The possibility of foreign control of major firms or industries being used to harm U.S. interests can be prevented by a normal amount of surveillance of such investments under laws and regulations that clearly state the permissible purposes and limits of such foreign control. Such investments in the United States give the investors a stake in keeping the U.S. economy healthy. For example, if Saudi Arabia had major investments in U.S. gasoline refining and distribution facilities and in the United States automobile industry, it would have to consider its financial losses before embargoing oil to the United States again. Moreover, in a time of high unemployment, OPEC investments can be a particularly useful element in tackling recession. Such investments could lead to a genuinely symmetrical interdependence in which both potential vulnerability and potential reciprocal benefits of cooperation are more equally matched between both the investing country and the United States.

Another problem created for the North by the rising power of OPEC is the management of huge trade imbalances. The quadrupling of oil prices brought to oil exporters in 1974 a surplus of some $50 billion in earnings beyond the costs of their imports. This surplus must be matched in oil-importing (mostly developed) countries by a deficit of $50 billion. How to reduce the deficit eventually and how to finance it meanwhile are among the most urgent and important items on the global agenda for action in 1975. But while the needs of the industrial world may be met by existing and planned mechanisms, the needs of developing countries will go unmet unless further bilateral and multilateral measures are implemented.[18]

The rise of the oil exporters to prominence and power presents U.S. policy makers with many development-related problems. There is the matter of the development goals of the OPEC countries themselves. The United States has established bilateral commissions with two of these countries to cooperate in their efforts to use their new resources to develop. This is a positive relationship that should be continued. Moreover, constructive participation by the OPEC countries is needed in the international economic mechanisms, including the World Bank and the IMF—and especially in any IMF facilities for recycling surplus funds. U.S. policies should encourage such participation. As mentioned already, the new liquidity of the OPEC nations also enables them to help finance development in the oil-importing developing countries—a relationship the United States likewise should support—since it will not only help world development but also facilitate the recycling of OPEC earnings and give the OPEC financiers a stake in a healthy world economy.

Private International Investment. In the relationship between private direct investors and host-country governments, the power balance gradually has begun to shift to favor the latter in many cases. This is not to say that all host governments are improving their bargaining position vis-a-vis all multinational corporations (MNCs) on all issues that concern them. Indeed, observers report that multinational corporations continue to maintain the upper hand in many negotiations. Yet the trend is perceptible, and the reaction of the MNCs is a sign that a significant long-term change is under way.

There are two reasons for this change. First and foremost are the rapidly increasing knowledge, skill, and determination of most developing-country governments in the negotiation process. Second is the continuing competition for both raw materials and world markets among MNCs; together with the more frequent presence and generally greater flexibility of Japanese and some European investors, this trend offers host countries a viable alternative to American investment and a greater opportunity to play off foreign firms against one another.

At one time, most U.S.-based corporations—although they acted as comparatively responsible entities that paid their taxes, contributed to

---

[18]See Chapter V.

community projects, and paid above-average wages—were often too slow to recognize the warning signals of opposition and merely continued to expand their investments and pursue their immediate corporate objectives without much concern for the broader development needs of host countries. In recent years, however, these firms are beginning to encounter strong and widespread reactions to their pervasive influence in developing countries—including new national and regional laws limiting their actions, United Nations analyses of their impact on the development process, and both scholarly and popular critiques of the political and economic effects of their activities. Many companies are responding defensively to this increased criticism as well as to the greater leverage and tenacity of developing-country governments. In the short run, such MNCs can use their relative bargaining strength to pursue their perceived self-interests while making only marginal concessions to host countries—especially in such areas as the limitation of profit remittances and the use of local components, supplies, and managerial personnel. In the longer term, however, the MNCs will be under pressure to make more important adjustments in response to the demands of more knowledgeable and better coordinated developing-country governments and because of competition from other MNCs.

Both MNCs and host governments are discovering that some important trade-offs have a bearing on their negotiations. The first of these relates to development and transfer of technology. While host governments would like to reduce the cost of the imported technology and make it more appropriate to local socio-economic conditions, the corporations often see no advantage in sharing or modifying their technology. They remain highly protective of their patents and rarely agree to adapt their technology and risk downgrading their trademarks, especially if they are producing for export. The technology issue will not subside in importance; in fact, it will become increasingly central to host-country efforts to sever ties of dependency. In the immediate future, however, each host country must weigh the advantages of getting advanced technology against the risk that it will be bypassed by MNCs that find more compliant hosts elsewhere, and the advantages of using such modern technology against the risk that it may be inappropriate to local conditions and needs. Those MNCs which choose to be unyielding in their approach must consider the gains of protecting their secrets and maintaining their trademarks against the possibility that other MNCs may make the accommodation and still obtain profitable investment opportunities.

Both host governments and MNCs also must become increasingly sensitive to the repercussions of their activities in the home countries of the MNCs. If MNCs and their hosts find too much in common and move investments and jobs too fast from home- to host-country sites, communities and labor unions in the home countries are likely to press for legislation to impede the outflow of investments. By contrast, consumers have little ability to protect themselves when the host government takes actions that increase costs and the MNC passes the increased cost along to the consumer (as has happened in the cases of oil and bauxite).

U.S. policy makers now confront two issues in this area. The first is the question of what position to take with respect to the increasing flow of foreign investments into the United States. As observed earlier in this chapter with respect to OPEC investments, the general U.S. position should be to welcome them. Second, what should the U.S. position be with respect to its own citizens' investments abroad? Given the extensive range of U.S. interests in the world, the U.S. government will need to take a broader approach than simply advocating the case of its own investors. For one thing, the U.S. government should be scrupulously careful to ensure that in the future there is no substance to the familiar charge that it uses U.S.-based MNCs to carry out U.S. policies in other countries—e.g., preventing Canadian subsidiaries of U.S. firms from trading with China at a time when Canada favored such trade and the United States did not. The formulation of a long-range U.S. policy toward its own MNCs is long overdue. As part of that policy, the United States should encourage consideration of the idea of an objective transnational authority with influence in resolving investment conflicts. Such a mechanism could help reconcile the world's interest in the continued contribution of MNCs to global development with the need of governments to protect and advance essential national interests.

Developing-Country Interests in International Monetary Reform. Developing countries have a special interest in two kinds of improvements in the International Monetary Fund, in addition to their general interest in making the Fund more useful to all participants. The first is the issue of increasing their influence in the policy-making process of the Fund, and the second is the matter of tailoring the Fund's facilities to meeting their needs for resources. Control of the Fund is exercised ultimately by the weighted votes of its members. The industrialized countries have a preponderance of votes, although the revision currently being approved will give the major oil-exporting countries 5 per cent more of the Fund's total quota, with the corresponding 5 per cent decrease in quotas being borne entirely by industrialized countries. This will leave the industrialized countries with 67 per cent of the votes in the Fund. Developing countries will probably continue to press for a greater share; they already obtained some influence in monetary decision-making through the IMF Interim Committee, which was established with nine developing-country seats out of a total of twenty.

With respect to increasing the access of the developing countries to the Fund's facilities, a number of recent proposals are in varying stages of completion from that of mere ideas to actual mechanisms in place and in operation. The special Oil Facility has been created to provide loans to countries hit hard by the oil price rises; the IMF currently is seeking funds to subsidize the interest rates paid on borrowings from the Oil Facility by the countries most seriously affected by the oil price rises. Other proposals currently under IMF consideration include: a U.S.-proposed Trust Fund made up of profits from the sale of IMF's gold stocks to be used for supporting development; improvements in the Fund's facility to compensate poor countries when their exports fall due to factors beyond their control; greater IMF support of buffer stocks used to help stabilize the price of raw-material exports from developing countries; and the reform of the formula for any future issuances of Special Drawing Rights—the Fund's so-called "paper gold"—to link them to supporting the development of the poor countries.

The massive resources of the IMF ($29 billion),[19] the increasing number of ideas and actual mechanisms for using its facilities to support development, and the ongoing process of monetary reform explain the growing interest of the developing countries in increasing their participation in IMF decisions. These countries already are spending a great deal of time and highly competent talent negotiating within the Fund for the improvements they desire.

The United States has long opposed the "link" of the Special Drawing Rights (SDR) system to development. As an alternative to such an approach, it recently proposed the establishment of the Trust Fund. Since there may not be any further issuances of SDRs until global inflationary pressures have eased, the Trust Fund appears to have more immediate potential for supporting development than the "link." However, at its January 1975 meeting, the IMF's "Group of 24"—a committee that represents the developing countries in monetary matters—reaffirmed its support for the "link" and at the same time voiced doubts about the desirability of the Trust Fund, particularly if it were offered as a substitute for the "link." The U.S. government should be mindful of the preferences of developing countries and be prepared to support some form of "link" when further issuances of SDRs become appropriate.

The Challenges in Perspective

The Common Human Problems. There have been important gains and important losses on the balance sheet of global human problems over the past year. Spreading recession is an unmitigated loss with no new policies in sight to solve it. After the 1972 and 1974 shortfalls in food production, deaths from malnutrition are up, and the world is more vulnerable to another crop failure than at any time since World War II. India's acute famine has been limited by its government's decision to spend over $1 billion of scarce foreign exchange to buy food—a decision that cuts India's outlays for investment goods imports and increases its vulnerability should there be a drought this year. The most important improvement registered in 1974 in the food area is the fact that worldwide attention was focused on the full dimensions of the problem,

---

[19]The quota is presently being enlarged by one third to SDR 39.0 billion ($47.75 billion as measured by the value of the dollar on December 31, 1974).

and comprehensive and long-term international measures have received at least preliminary approval.

With respect to population, two developments have brightened the outlook: first, the growing consensus that the problem calls for both family planning and improvement of the living conditions of the very poor, and second, the mounting statistical and case evidence that fertility is being reduced in many developing countries. At the same time, there is some back-sliding in rich-country determination to protect the environment as a result of the energy crisis; this may, however, be offset by renewed efforts to conserve at least oil and potentially other dwindling raw materials as well. The goal of protecting and assuring more equitable use of the oceans also appears to have been dealt a blow by the trends in international negotiations toward greater national and less international control of the resources of the continental margins. In the area of trade, the Tokyo Round of multilateral trade negotiations, jeopardized from the start by protectionist forces, has been given new impetus by the belated enactment of U.S. trade reform legislation.

Finally, in 1974-75, the appalling dimensions of human suffering in the Fourth World came more clearly into focus, casting a dark shadow over the entire landscape of world development. But even this grim fact has a brighter side, for it was the increasing contrast between the stagnation of the poorest countries and the relatively more rapid progress of the Third World of middle-income developing countries that alerted the world to the special needs of the Fourth World. The good news of the Third World's progress is unfortunately diluted with the potential harm that may befall some of its countries as a result of the increased prices of their imports and the falling prices of their exports.

Challenges to the Old Hierarchy. The brief enumeration earlier of attempts on the part of developing countries to gain more power and income suggests that something is astir; their efforts have moved beyond the stage of rhetoric to the point of negotiations in several forums. There is a new feeling of power on the part of developing countries and a consequent new burst of energy on their part to gain additional influence in world affairs. However, apart from the unique case of OPEC, any shift in economic-political power that has occurred or may take place in the near future is only at the margins of international decision-making. Control of the international economic order still remains firmly in the hands of the OECD countries and is not centrally challenged except by the oil-exporting nations acting in unison through OPEC. Nor are the financial problems of the developing countries (OPEC apart) about to be resolved by the meager transfers of power and resources discussed above. Still, there is an important symbolic change in process which, if it persists, will mean that major world economic decisions can no longer be made by a group of North Atlantic countries and Japan without taking into serious account the views of countries in Asia, Africa, and Latin America.

Prior to October 1973, some observers believed that the growing economic strength of middle-level countries, such as Brazil, Mexico, Taiwan, and South Korea, might at some future point constitute a competitive challenge to the industrialized countries in some areas of economic activity. However, that challenge was overshadowed and to some extent diminished by the success of OPEC in quadrupling the price of oil exports. Even the dramatic OPEC challenge shows every current prospect of being taken in stride—without significant long-range damage to the dominant nations but with a sharp increase in the power and prestige of the challengers. Oil-importing developing countries are avidly watching the struggle and searching—largely in vain—for leverage with which to press their own demands of the international economic order.

An analogous process goes on *within* societies. Thus in the United States, for example, workers challenged employers for decades for the right to organize; only in the 1930s, after a history of violence and repression, did they succeed in winning that right, along with social security pensions and unemployment compensation. Their victory is almost universally hailed today as good for the economy, the society, and the nation. Indeed, mass production in the prodigious American economy was made possible in large part by the gains of the working man, whose newly won job security made it possible for banks and department stores to extend mass credit. But the victories of the 1930s were by and large limited to white males. American women, Blacks, Chicanos, and Indians—all of whom are asserting their rights currently (thirty years later) were then still excluded from the system's benefits—even as the Fourth World and much of the Third World are today excluded from the direct gains being achieved by a handful of challenging nations.

Experience suggests that, in the economic arena, a bid for more power and income by one party does not necessarily threaten the well-being of those whose position in the hierarchy is being challenged. In short, it need not be a zero-sum game, but can be very positive for all participants as we have learned both from our domestic record and our experience with the Marshall Plan. The test for the dominant nations is to respond to hierarchical challenges with creative proposals that benefit all parties.

The U.S. Role

What should be the response of the United States government to the two fundamental varieties of challenge confronting the world in 1975? The closing section of this overview will evaluate the recent development performance of the United States, discuss the opportunities open to the United States for playing a constructive role, and suggest a broad context in which it can make a contribution.

U.S. Development Performance. In too many instances, U.S. performance in supporting world development appears to be out of phase with emerging world realities. There is a great need to vastly expand agricultural production in the food-deficit countries, yet the United States has been moving very slowly to increase its aid funds for this purpose. There is growing understanding that the population explosion can be contained only with the kind of far-reaching social transformation that accompanies development programs, yet the United States, while recognizing and forcefully stating this principle, continues to reduce its development assistance programs. There is a renewed need for behaving as world citizens in dealing with the oil crisis, yet the original U.S. proposal to deal with this global problem would have recycled funds only to the industrialized countries. However, the United States did propose a special arrangement for the 32 countries "most seriously affected" by the price rises of 1973-74, and it did accept the proposal for an IMF oil facility available to all countries.

Concern over a possible collision between lavish consumption rates and finite resources has become more widespread, but the U.S. government—despite much talk in official circles about conservation in the energy field—so far has not seriously acted on the subject. The poor countries are reasserting their strength in the United Nations General Assembly on the basis of the power shifts of the past year, but there has been an outcry from the U.S. government and much of the news media against this new coalition. There are even strong suggestions that the United States might altogether stop cooperating with international institutions because of this so-called "tyranny of the majority." The United States was inexcusably delinquent in the delay of its contribution to IDA and nearly reneged completely on this major development effort. Finally, in recent years the United States has frequently taken short-run nationalistic positions, especially in the World Bank and Monetary Fund, and as a consequence has found itself isolated from even its old friends on issue after issue. As a result, much of the trust and confidence in the United States that was built during the previous quarter century has been depleted.

In some areas, however, U.S. performance in 1974 was more positive. In response to world hunger, the United States was a leader in the call for a World Food Conference; with the important exception of food aid, on which its response was disappointingly tardy, U.S. participation in that Conference was constructive. In the field of international trade, the U.S. Trade Expansion Act of 1974, while its provisions ambiguously leave the way open to both restriction and liberalization, does offer an important opportunity for the United States to participate positively in improving the structure and functioning of world trade. At the sessions of the Law of the Sea Conference, the U.S. position, while short of the ideal in important respects, stands out as mature and responsible by contrast with the short-sighted policies of many other participants, including a number of developing countries. In the field of monetary affairs, the United States (after adamantly opposing reform of the

Special Drawing Rights system) has made a potentially useful proposal for use of profits from the sale of IMF gold to support development. In the operation of its diminishing aid program, the U.S. government is making encouraging efforts to apply seriously the new key doctrine of the Foreign Assistance Act of 1973: emphasis on projects that benefit the poor majority in the developing countries. In yet another area, Congress has taken the initiative to press the President to be more generous in the use of food aid and to use it for humanitarian rather than for political purposes.

The U.S. government also has supported some useful innovations in international machinery, including the establishment of the IMF's provisional Committee of 20, which gave developing countries nine out of twenty voices within this important committee charged with preparing a plan for global monetary reform. The U.S. also supported the establishment of the Group of 20, the Committee's permanent successor, and the creation of a joint IBRD-IMF Development Committee to consider how resources best can be channeled from North to South.

One promising new development within the U.S. government warrants brief discussion. In 1973, Congress included in the Foreign Assistance Act a provision for a new Development Coordination Committee (DCC) within the U.S. government to monitor and seek to improve U.S. performance in support of development. After a long delay, an Executive Order was finally signed establishing the DCC within the U.S. Agency for International Development. One of the important services that the DCC can render is to review U.S. governmental actions as well as proposed actions in a wide variety of fields and to comment on their actual or potential impact on world development. Such fields might include normally domestic concerns such as taxes, agricultural production and marketing, mining, stockpiling, and land management, as well as international concerns such as immigration, trade and monetary affairs, and investment among many others. If the U.S. interest in the protection of the environment warrants a major investment in preparing environmental impact statements prior to making important decisions, then the U.S. interest in development likewise justifies the preparation of development impact statements by the DCC (and hopefully also by other parts of the U.S. government at the request of the DCC) before important decisions are made. Obviously, the clout of the Committee on this range of policies will be limited, but it nevertheless should prove useful to have the development point of view consistently placed before policy makers.

Toward Global Approaches. Although the United States is not as economically dominant in 1975 as in the 1950s, it also is not as weak relative to its industrial partners as it was in 1971. It is less vulnerable to increased oil costs than can be said of its trading partners, and it also is insulated by its preeminence as a food exporter at a time of strong demand for food. It therefore still is the nation in the strongest position to take a global view of the problems enumerated above. Such a world view must be forcefully advocated by influential nations—and within the United States, by influential people—if that point of view is to survive.

Effective global advocacy requires that new international machinery be created that realistically reflects the views of all participating nations in the new context of increasing interdependence. Once the United States had the power to control most international organizations, but that power is now gone. The adjustment necessitated by that change has been difficult for the United States; regrettably, it has too often reacted by taking a short-run, narrowly nationalistic position. In the future, the United States can serve its own interests best not by attempting to manipulate others to do its bidding—an approach that in any case no longer works—but by advocating what is perceived by other nations as serving the common interest.

In the course of the next year, several international forums will present occasions for the United States and other nations to champion the common world interest. The most elemental human need, food, will be the subject of intensive institution-building efforts to carry out the agreements reached at the 1974 World Food Conference to increase agricultural production, create a world food security system, and increase food aid.

The resumption of the Conference on the Law of the Seas due to take place in Geneva this spring and perhaps to continue in Venezuela this summer may be the last opportunity for effectively supporting a global approach to this genuinely global problem. The International Monetary Fund is to resume its efforts to reform the international monetary system to meet the crises of imbalances caused by increased oil prices, and to design a more suitable replacement for the system created in Bretton Woods three decades ago. The multilateral trade negotiations started this spring will continue in Geneva over the months ahead, offering the world a chance to further improve this most vital component of the international economic order.

Another opportunity is presented by the U.N.-sponsored International Women's Year Conference in Mexico City in June 1975. The United States should, together with other nations, follow up in a practical way on the World Population Conference and the World Food Conference—both of which emphasized the importance of more education and more equal treatment for women as a means of reducing fertility and of increasing agricultural production. In many developing countries, farming is at least as much the responsibility of women as of men.

In the fall of 1975, the U.N. General Assembly—both at its brief September Special Session on development cooperation and at its regular session—will consider the state of development at the mid-point of the Second Development Decade in relation to the proposals for changing the international economic order adopted by the U.N. General Assembly's spring 1974 Special Session on raw materials. Great restraint, maturity, and creativity will be required of all countries if the forthcoming U.N. debate is to be one of constructive progress rather than of mutual recrimination. A special responsibility rests with those U.S. officials preparing for the debate to overlook the semantic heat likely to be generated in connection with the "new international economic order" and to focus on those items of solid substance which will shed light on the debate.

However, it is not only at international conferences but also in its internal policies that the United States can promote the adoption of cooperative global approaches to solving world problems. For example, by its internal handling of the energy crisis, shortages of fertilizer, domestic inflation and recession, and by its willingness to share food, the United States can set an example of internationally responsible behavior that will encourage cooperative action by others.

A Comprehensive Global Social Compact.[20] The international order that emerged after World War II among the non-communist, market-economy countries was a "compact" only in the sense that there was widespread consensus among nations and societies on many of its precepts. It was by no means the product of benign negotiation among reasonable men. Indeed there was much confrontation, contention, and even coercion involved in its evolution. While occasionally it took the form of broad accords, more often it consisted of concrete small agreements on specific problems.

Among the compact's important features were: full clemency for the powers defeated in World War II, a major cooperative effort to advance the progress of the industrialized market-economy countries, the evolution of national sovereignty for most colonial areas, the juridical concept of political equality for all nations through membership in the United Nations, the acceptance of an international economic order in which production and distribution are governed primarily by the market (with its attendant efficiencies as well as inequities), and a common effort to extend around the world the benefits of technological progress. This postwar economic system was a compact that extended progress primarily to its participants, including—in many developing countries—the ruling elite, a growing business sector, the bureaucracy, the professions, and workers with jobs in industry. But the majority of the populations of these countries—all of those working in agriculture (except commercialized agriculture for export) and a growing number of landless idle workers were too often excluded from a fair share in the benefits of the system. Growth ensured improvement to those who were participants, with the caveat that when it faltered, producers of raw materials were more vulnerable than manufacturers.

With the U.S. pioneering the way, the industrialized nations of the North undertook to share their technology, their resources, and their advice with the poor nations—many of which were just getting organized as independent

---

[20]See also Chapter IX.

nations. The poor nations, for their part, undertook to consider the advice and put the resources and technology to good use to benefit the participants in their domestic economies. The Bretton Woods institutions, the General Agreement on Tariffs and Trade, the Marshall Plan for reconstructing war-torn Europe, the Point Four Program, the Alliance for Progress, the International Development Association, the Development Advisory Committee, the United Nations Development Programme, the regional development banks, and many other institutions gave form to the compact. Many acts and declarations also helped to articulate its goals—including the Charter of the United Nations, the Universal Declaration of Human Rights, the Act of Bogota, the goals of the First U.N. Development Decade, and the International Strategy for the Second Development Decade.

The success of the postwar international social compact has been considerable. Europe and Japan recovered and grew to attain unprecedented economic strength; Europe achieved a degree of unity; and the standard of living of the entire North and some parts of the South increased at an impressive pace that has been sustained for more than two decades. Former colonies became independent and made great progress in nation-building, and international trade experienced a period of unprecedented growth.

In recent years, however, the social compact has been eroding. In part, this is due to the failure of nations to live up to important parts of the bargain. Rich nations accepted goals for official development assistance and fell far short of meeting commitments. They accepted goals for opening their markets to poor-country manufactures, and were late and inadequate in meeting those goals. Poor countries as well as rich interfered with the flow of trade and investment, and both intervened wholesale in the operations of the marketplace to the point where free markets could no longer be relied upon to signal information needed for traditional economic decisions. Labor unions, after having supported free trade during the bulk of the postwar era, became increasingly protectionist. The United States, whose currency and vast economy buttressed the entire economic system, devalued its currency—thus signaling its desire to give up the role of guardian of the system.

In part, the compact is breaking up because—however well the parties may live up to its terms—the terms themselves no longer meet the aspirations of many of the world's people and nations. To begin with, those who do not participate proportionately in the system's benefits are dissatisfied. In spite of the record growth rates achieved in the 1960s, the condition of the poorest people showed no corresponding improvement. The model of the Northern industrialized countries—socialist as well as capitalist—simply did not fit the needs of the South. At the risk of some exaggeration, it seems accurate to conclude that this model (which was, after all, chosen by the South, although encouraged by Northern intellectual, business, and political communities) tended to strongly encourage urbanization; increase the size of farms by mechanizing them (sending "surplus" labor from farm to city); tolerate

32

inequity for a time in order to increase savings, investment, and growth with the expectation that all classes would eventually benefit; establish costly modern medical facilities in urban areas first, to the neglect of the rural health and low-cost health facilities for all; provide subsidies to industry at the expense of agriculture; and opt for very modern and therefore capital-intensive, industry. Most observers now agree that these policies did not adequately meet the needs of most of the South. Moreover, technological progress and economic growth so increased the mutual dependence among nations that the South itself began to see opportunities to gain greater equality of economic opportunity by challenging the international economic systems.

In part, the compact also is breaking up because of new tensions between human economic activity and nature. The postwar system simply was not geared to meet the requirements of conserving energy, grain, or fish; nor is it able to distribute equitably the pain of adjusting to a slowdown in growth.

For these reasons among many others, the social compact is under widespread stress, and the world needs to repair some of its parts, replace others, and in some cases to create wholly new elements. That will hardly be an easy task. It would be difficult enough if all of the nations had the same basic beliefs and values on the issues of political freedom, economic equality, and the roles of fate and human will.

The evolution of a new or renovated compact becomes increasingly important as world problems accumulate and become insistent; generally these problems can only be resolved by nations working cooperatively toward goals on which there is an increasing consensus and according to a scenario in which each participant plays an agreed role. Broad agreement on the goals and roles will be the essence of the new global social compact. Some of the goals of such a compact are:

(1) Managing the immediate crises—hunger, stagflation, recycling oil funds, and avoidance of war—in the short run;
(2) Sharing power and income more equitably among and within nations;
(3) Restraining excessive fertility in both rich and poor countries (this in turn calls for economic and social policies that emphasize participation by all the people in the development process and benefits;
(4) Guiding production and consumption in the directions of resource conservation, environmental protection, and the improvement of human health;
(5) Continuing to support economic growth, especially in the production of more food, energy, and other essentials;
(6) Restraining arms expenditures and evolving peaceful methods of settling disputes;
(7) Enriching human lives in ways that are most meaningful to each society in the light of its own values—whether these are education,

material abundance, a sense of identity with community or with God, personal fulfillment through the achievement ethic, or greater leisure.

As to the roles of the participants, the writing of that part of the social compact is being attempted now—with varying effectiveness—in a dozen forums (including, among others, the Law of the Sea Conference, the IBRD, the IMF and its various committees, UNCTAD, the U.N. Environment Program, the U.N. General Assembly, the follow-up work of the World Food Conference, the SALT talks, the Middle East peace negotiations). Each forum is attempting to shape a fragment of the mosaic we think of as the new global social compact. In all likelihood, there will never be a sketch of the whole mosaic, except as it is reconstructed by historians. Certainly no single existing forum is capable of taking up the idea, debating it, and producing a consensus. But that is normally true of a social compact. There is nevertheless need for a thorough debate of the subject over the years ahead in intellectual, political, and diplomatic circles—a process that will, if it is successful, produce not a finished consensus, but a steadily evolving and increasingly useful guide.

Enlightened U.S. policies can make a vital—perhaps indispensable—contribution to the evolving consensus. But to do so, the United States must first articulate a comprehensive world view much as it did in the years after World War II. Then it was confronting a challenge that sought to overthrow established governments; now it faces a challenge that only seeks an equitable place for the underprivileged in the international establishment of nations. The United States can continue to deal with each challenge piecemeal, as it has for the last several years—parrying, counterattacking, or yielding case by case—or it can work within the community of nations to construct what Secretary of State Kissinger has called "a truly global society carried by the principle of interdependence."

CHAPTER I

Focus on the Fourth World

Helen C. Low and James W. Howe

The term "Third World" first came to be used in the late 1950s to distinguish the developing world from the Western industrial and the socialist "worlds." Since then, much has happened to the countries loosely grouped under this term. Many have made notable strides in the growth of their economies; some, like Brazil and South Korea, have progressed spectacularly, others less dramatically but nonetheless steadily. By the early 1970s, a sizable group of developing countries had achieved sustained economic growth at an annual rate above 6 per cent.

At the same time, however, it became apparent that other developing countries were not participating in the general trend, and that these nations in effect constituted a "Fourth World" still essentially trapped by poverty. The need for a distinction to be drawn and special action taken to help this group was first expressed by the developing countries themselves in the Algiers Charter in 1967. Because of the political difficulties inherent in formulating a list of such countries, however, the task was turned over by the United Nations to the Committee for Development Planning, the independent advisory group whose members serve the Economic and Social Council and the U.N. system in general.[1] In 1971, the Committee identified twenty-five countries as "least developed" on the basis of the rough criteria of per capita income, degree of manufacturing activity, and level of literacy. Recognizing that other

---

[1] Members of the Committee are appointed by ECOSOC on the nomination of the Secretary General and serve as independent experts rather than as official representatives of their countries.

developing countries also encounter similar problems on a regional and sectoral basis, the Committee stressed the particularly "difficult and distinct" problems which warranted singling out the group of least developed countries. While this list omitted a number of countries similarly hamstrung by circumstances—for example, the populous ones of the Indian subcontinent—it did focus attention on the need to identify and deal with the root causes of poverty. And it put the problem not in terms of low income alone, but also in the perspective of factors such as literacy and industrial activity, which facilitate change.

The perception of this group of the poorest countries as a "Fourth World" has been heightened by world economic events since 1973, which have added sharply higher costs of imported oil to the already mounting costs of imported food.[2] Those events thrust a new set of countries into a retrenchment so severe that the growth they had begun to generate was brought to a standstill. Concerned for their welfare, the U.N. General Assembly at its Special Session on raw materials in April 1974 called for the drawing up of a list of the countries "most seriously affected" by the 1973-74 developments, so that special measures could be taken on their behalf. This list of thirty-two countries overlaps extensively with the earlier U.N. list, but omits those ten least developed countries[3] which remain so isolated from the world economy that they have been spared some of its shocks.

In this analysis, the forty-two countries that appear on either or both of the U.N. lists (see Table 1, p. 48) will be viewed as comprising the Fourth World—with full awareness that this is an approximation and that the line could be drawn on either side of several borderline cases.[4] The crux of the distinction between the Third World and the Fourth for the purpose of this analysis is whether the means for generating momentum are at present available to a country from the sum of domestic and external sources, or whether the impetus for growth is dependent on still further measures that need to be taken by the outside world. In drawing this distinction, account was taken of each country's access not only to concessional aid, but also to any benefits derived from the world's major economic systems—trade, finance, private investment, and governmental and private loans.

Not all the lowest income countries (those with per capita incomes below $200) are included, since the economies of some of them, for example Zaire and Indonesia, do have the means at hand to move ahead with development.

---

[2]See Table B-7, p. 228.

[3]Sikkim, which is on the United Nations list of the least developed countries, has not been included in this analysis.

[4]While an alternative list could be proposed for the two U.N. lists on the basis of a slightly different choice of criteria (see Table A-5, p. 198), the marginal value of such a limited improvement would be more than offset by the disutility of disseminating still another list.

A few countries which are on neither U.N. list, for example Burma, might well be considered Fourth World countries.

Some countries which are included, among them Ivory Coast, El Salvador, and Guyana, have relatively high per capita incomes but, in their present circumstances, face a severe shortfall of the resources needed for growth. With help, they may have more resilience than some others to regain their pace of growth and move back into the Third World sooner. A number of Third World countries are also vulnerable to a continued delay in world adjustment to the present structural disequilibrium and could find themselves in the same predicament. Thus there is no fixed line between the Third World and the Fourth. Some countries are separated from the rest by a widening gap; others are temporarily in serious trouble because recent international economic events have taken the wind out of their sails.

Of the ninety-seven "developing" countries which are members of the United Nations, the Third World tier of fifty-six countries—with a total population of 818 million people[5]—ranges from those which, like the Philippines and Thailand, are barely beyond the Fourth World and maintaining a precarious momentum; to Argentina and Singapore, which have attained per capita incomes well over $1,000. There is considerable variation among the significant oil-exporting countries themselves, which range from Indonesia and Nigeria, which are very poor and populous and whose known oil reserves are quite limited; to the higher-income countries of Venezuela and Trinidad and Tobago; to countries such as Saudi Arabia and Kuwait, whose oil resources are vast. The Third World as a whole thus constitutes a middle band of countries which have widely varying resource bases and are developing at very different rates, but which are distinguishable from the Fourth World because they are growing perceptibly. Thus the division between the Third and the Fourth Worlds is not a sharp demarcation of present conditions of life but denotes the presence or absence of a growth dynamic operating in their economies at this time. Moreover, the distinction does not purport to reflect an unchanging condition; it is analogous to a snapshot taken of a moving scene.

Characteristics of the Fourth World

The great majority of Fourth World countries were colonial dependencies before World War II, some until considerably later. More than half of them are in Africa, largely in the tropical band which is humid on the coasts and parched in the interior; two are enclaves in South Africa. Six are in southern Asia—where India, Pakistan, and Bangladesh alone account for three

---

[5]This does not include the People's Republic of China, whose population is about 823 million.

quarters of the Fourth World population of 981 million people. Three are pressed into the mountains of the Himalayan system, while two of the poorest are found in the southwest corner of the Arabian Peninsula. The four in Latin America are tropical, Haiti being the only Western hemisphere country on the list of the least developed. Two tiny islands complete the list.

Many Fourth World countries have a low endowment of presently known resources. Many have a comparatively small population in relation to land area—although often it is not clear how dense a population the land can support. In most Fourth World countries, a large proportion of the population is engaged in subsistence farming or nomadic herding and thus lives largely outside the monetary sector. Movement within these countries is typically hindered by rudimentary road systems. For most Fourth World countries, the migration from country to city poses serious problems of unemployment in the towns. Some countries are quite isolated from the outside world, while others market their agricultural and mineral products abroad, largely in unprocessed form; these products tend to be largely agricultural, since countries with extensive minerals to export tend to "graduate" quickly from Fourth World ranks. Most Fourth World countries are highly dependent on the outside world for manufactured goods beyond handicrafts and small-scale items. Even in the case of India, less than 15 per cent of the gross domestic product is accounted for by manufacturing activity.

The Predicament of the Fourth World

The Fourth World exists in hard-core poverty. In general, less than one person in five is literate, a condition perpetuated by low public expenditures on education; infant mortality rates are well above one child in ten, often closer to two; life expectancy is below fifty years, yet there is little public expenditure on health care; and the nutritional intake is significantly less than the minimum considered necessary for health. Crude birth rates are among the highest in the world and, despite high infant mortality, population growth tends to be high.[6]

The cost of resources that goes into the added numbers of persons to be fed, housed, clothed, and trained—the "demographic investment," expressed as a percentage of fixed capital formation in a country—was estimated at 42.5 per cent for developing countries as a whole in the late 1960s, compared with 12.5 per cent for the developed countries. For the largest of the Fourth World countries, it was significantly higher: 47.3 per cent for India, 67.1 per cent for Pakistan, and 73.2 per cent for Bangladesh.[7] This indicates that one half to three quarters of the resources which these societies could otherwise utilize to

---

[6]See Table A-5, p. 198.
[7]Timothy King, ed., *Population Policies and Economic Development,* published for the World Bank (Baltimore: Johns Hopkins University Press, 1974), p. 29.

build up their productive capacity is dissipated in feeding and caring for the mounting numbers of persons. Demographers raise the serious possibility that a significant fall in fertility could be thwarted permanently by conditions of deep poverty. An improvement in the quality of life for the lowest 40 per cent of the population is needed if the vicious circle of fertility breeding poverty and of poverty thwarting a reduction in fertility is to be broken.

An examination of the rates of growth of the national product of Fourth World countries shows that they have typically remained at low to moderate levels. Because of the rapid increase of population, the per capita growth rate in many cases is reduced to a very low level. In the 1965-1972 period, there was negative per capita growth for seven of the Fourth World countries, a shrinkage of over 5 per cent for Niger and 7 per cent for Yemen (PDR). Only Botswana grew at the lively pace of 10 percent. The average growth for the group as a whole was negligible, slightly over 1 per cent.[8] For the more immediate past and the near future, it is quite likely that the rate of growth will be virtually nil or even negative for a sizable number of Fourth World countries. This means not only increased hardship at present, but also a lessened longer-range ability to come to grips with the basic problems of stagnation and improvement in the quality of life for their most impoverished people, who tend to be the hardest hit in stringent times.

Admittedly, the causes of stagnation are basically internal: isolation, both internal and external; limited physical resources; a harsh environment, which may at random besiege the countryside with floods or droughts; subsistence levels of living for a large part of the population, with few channels available for investment of chance savings; and population density, which puts pressure on limited resources. But long-term flows of resources from the outside world can help provide leverage on those problems. And actions taken in the international trade and monetary arenas can either boost or stifle the efforts of the Fourth World countries to come to grips with their own future.

The Impact of the Current Economic Crisis

Most of the developing world participated in the buoyant period of trade activity in world markets in the early 1970s, experiencing an increased volume of sales for exports at prices which stayed ahead of the costs of their principal imports. In many cases, this served to increase their external reserves and to provide an internal flexibility to facilitate both structural change and growth. A few countries whose principal exports, such as tea and jute, were not affected by increased demand did not, however, share in the general groundswell.

Among the factors that changed this encouraging trend were the disastrous events affecting food production: the Sahelian drought that spread

---

[8]See Table A-5, p. 198.

across Africa, crop shortfalls in much of the world, and the depletion of grain reserves in the countries that have traditionally served as the world's granary. These events not only depleted the external reserves of the affected countries to finance increased food imports at higher prices, but also brought about profound dislocations in the economies of several Fourth World countries— whether by the decimation of herds in the Sahel or the influx of humanity into the cities of the Indian subcontinent.

A sudden and dramatic factor in the changed circumstances since late 1973 was the abrupt rise in petroleum prices.[9] While pre-1974 oil import costs tended to be modest in the Fourth World countries, petroleum played a key role in productive activity, providing power for irrigation systems and facilitating the movement of crops and other products to market. Reliance on oil and gas for such uses was widespread, and hence oil imports could not be reduced easily.

More far-reaching in its global effects than either crop failures or oil price increases has been the decline in the rate of growth of the industrial world, on which the export prospects of the developing world depend. During 1974, the economies of most industrial countries grew very slowly, while the United States and Japan experienced an actual decrease of GNP in real terms. This weakened the prices of most primary products and turned the terms of trade against many Fourth World countries. The most optimistic forecasts for upswing in industrial activity are for late 1975, with demand for materials responding more slowly. Less optimistic assessments foresee a longer, much more difficult, period. Renewed potential for growth in the developing world depends heavily upon the revival of the developed economies. For the Fourth World, both trade and aid hang in the balance.

The vulnerability of Fourth World countries to world economic events over which they have no control was vividly described by Robert McNamara, President of the World Bank:

> The major impact is on the poorest nations. The rising prices of imported petroleum, fertilizer, and cereals; the slack demand for their exports to developed countries; and the erosion by inflation of the real value of development assistance, all have dealt severe blows to the growth aspirations of the poorest members of the Bank. These nations, with a population of one billion, and incomes averaging less than $200 per capita, on the most likely set of assumptions regarding commodity prices, capital flows, and growth rates in the OECD countries, would suffer an actual decline in their per capita incomes.

---

[9] See Table A-5, p. 198.

The effect of this on the already marginal condition of life of the poorest 40% within these countries is an appalling prospect.[10]

In considering what can be done to alleviate the situation faced by Fourth World countries, let us examine their special problems in the operation of the major international economic systems, including those governing trade, finance, direct investment, loans, and grants.

International Trade

International trade serves two functions essential to the development process: mobilizing internal resources productively and making external resources available in payment. Trade far outweighs the other sources of external capital to which most developing countries have access.[11] In the case of Fourth World countries, in the 1970-1972 period, the value of imports was three times that of loans and grants. The Fourth World thus has a strong stake in the health of world trade and in the terms on which it takes place, even though in terms of value it accounts for less than 2 per cent of the world total.

Within the Fourth World, the importance of exports, measured as a percentage of GNP, varies widely. For a majority of these countries, it amounts to 10-20 per cent, ranging widely from less than 1 per cent for the Khmer Republic and 4 per cent for India to over 50 per cent for Mauritania and Guyana. Moreover, many Fourth World countries—including Sudan, Sri Lanka, El Salvador, Ivory Coast, Guyana, Honduras, Sierra Leone, and Yemen (PDR)—depend on a single export item for at least 10 per cent of their GNP. Mauritania, for example, relies on iron ore exports for 40 per cent of its GNP. Such dependence on a single item makes not only export earnings but also all domestic economic activity vulnerable to changes in foreign demand.

The Fourth World has a vital interest in the arrangements under which primary products are traded, since most of their exports belong to this category. Historically, primary products have been subject to considerable fluctuation in both price and volume due to economic conditions abroad and to the sporadic emergence of substitute materials. The primary product boom, which brought prices to a twenty-five year high in the early 1970s, had peaked for many products by early 1974, as the industrial countries began to cut back production. While projections are difficult under present conditions, it is likely that, with a few exceptions such as oil, bauxite, tin, and timber, prices of primary products will soon drop back to the levels of the 1960s for much of the rest of the decade.[12]

---

[10]Robert S. McNamara, *Address to the Board of Governors of the World Bank Group,* Washington, D.C., September 30, 1974 (Washington, D.C.: World Bank, 1974), pp. 13-14.
[11]See Table D-1, p. 254.
[12]See Table B-7, p. 228.

The unreliability of demand and price remains the most acute problem encountered by the exports of Fourth World countries, since most of their exports are still unprocessed primary products and, as such, are not subject to serious trade restrictions.[13] Fourth World countries come up against much steeper barriers when they attempt to add phases of processing to their raw-material exports. Such processing in many cases is a logical progression for the Fourth World countries, as it permits them to move in the direction of more labor-intensive production and thus to best utilize both available materials and abundant manpower. During the 1960s, the share of processed exports in total exports increased for many Fourth World countries; in the cases of India and Pakistan, processed goods accounted for half of total exports by the end of the decade. Nonetheless, a few Fourth World countries are wholly dependent on raw materials for export earnings, and the vast majority are at least 90 per cent dependent.

At present, however, the structure of trade barriers is such that they increase with the degree of processing. This is so because the industrial countries still have industries that perform the same stages of processing, and these entrenched interests do not want to share the market with newcomers. Even as specialized an item as Afghan carpets is subject to tariffs in the world's major markets. The substantial reduction of tariffs on such goods was a notable accomplishment of the Kennedy Round of trade negotiations under the General Agreement on Tariffs and Trade (GATT) and will be continued in the upcoming round in Geneva. But as the tariff negotiations proved successful and the markets opened up, the struggle moved into the arena of non-tariff barriers, where devices such as quantitative restrictions have proved to be even more of an impediment. These, too, are now subject to negotiated reductions and will be a major concern again in Geneva.[14]

In the non-tariff-barrier arena, textiles and clothing have been a particularly difficult issue. Developing-country exports of these items to industrialized countries increased rapidly in the 1965-1972 period. The response to this success was the creation of a network of quantitative restrictions in the developed-country markets and the subsequent acceptance of "voluntary" restraints by the exporting countries under the threat of further import restrictions. This is a field in which Fourth World interests will be increasingly involved. For example, well over half of India's exports of manufactures in 1972 were textiles. The Multifiber Textile Arrangement that was recently worked out to regulate the situation demonstrates the limits within which progress is presently possible. Nonetheless, for the Fourth World countries, this type of arrangement offers a framework in which their

---

[13]One program to mitigate this problem is the export-earnings stabilization plan recently worked out between the European Community and forty-six African, Caribbean, and Pacific countries.

[14]See also Chapter IV.

42

special circumstances could be taken into account through such possibilities as higher basic quotas, provisions allowing new entrants to grow more rapidly, and the waiver of restrictions for small suppliers.

Fourth World countries also encounter difficulties on the import side of their trade. Before the recent price changes, manufactured goods accounted for over 70 per cent of their total expenditures on imports, primary products for about 20 per cent, and oil imports (on which they relied for an average 31 per cent of their domestic energy consumption) for only 6.5 per cent. The composition of import costs changed drastically, however, after the increases in prices of grain, fertilizer, and oil.

Thus it is estimated that developing countries spent $6 billion more on imports of cereals and fertilizer alone in 1974 than they had in 1973. Global shortfalls of almost 60 million tons of grain in 1972, repeated again in 1973-74, forced many developing countries—two thirds of which were deficient in cereal supplies—to increase the volume of imports and to pay higher unit prices. For the most seriously affected of the Fourth World countries, grain crops were 4 per cent less in 1974 than in 1973, and rice crops were down 1 per cent. It is estimated that this will result in a shortfall of 4.8 million tons of food grains in the first half of 1975 which will cost $1.2 billion to import.[15] For some countries the combination of price increases and crop shortfall was staggering. India, for example, whose annual grain import bill averaged $250 million in the period 1970-1972, was expected to spend above $1,000 million in 1974-75.

The price of fertilizer, on which the hope for rapid expansion of food production in these countries depends, also rose sharply in 1973 and 1974—with phosphate fertilizers tripling in price and nitrogenous fertilizers quintupling. It is estimated that outlays for imported fertilizer by all developing countries rose from $533 million in 1971 to $1,450 million in 1974.[16] Even at higher price levels, many developing countries were unable to buy all the fertilizer they needed and were prepared to pay for because of export restraints on fertilizer sales in the United States and other industrial countries. For the most seriously affected of the Fourth World countries, a shortfall of 337,000 tons of nutrients in the present crop year of 1974-75 means a resultant grain loss of 2.7 million tons. For the 1975-76 crop year, 2.5 million tons of imported fertilizer are required at the present cost of $1.76 billion—four times the cost of the same volume in 1972-73. Even if the funds could be found, the full need might not be filled.

Oil imports in 1973 cost the developing countries about $7 billion. In 1974, after a quadrupling of the price of oil, the outlay was only $10 billion higher, indicating the extent to which consumption had been curtailed. This

---

[15]This amount was reduced to 3.1 million tons (and $0.8 billion) by additional U.S. commitments in February 1975.
[16]See Tables B-8, p. 230 and C-14, p. 251.

cutback, viewed in the light of the historical trend of a 5-6 per cent increase in annual oil consumption, points out the true extent of retrenchment. While the impact differed widely from one Fourth World country to another, it was a severe blow for virtually all of them. In many Fourth World countries, oil import costs increased by more than 10 per cent of the total import bill from 1968-1972 to 1974. India's oil imports are expected to rise from $315 million in 1973 to $1,135 million in 1974—an increase equal to one third of its total 1972 import bill and about one half of its foreign exchange reserves.

Because manufactured goods represent the major component of imports and because they include many items basic to economic growth, it is worth noting that the prices of equipment are also expected to increase relative to the prices of primary products in the next few years. Together with the price increases of food, fuel, and fertilizer, this indicates a serious worsening of the terms of trade for Fourth World countries. It is estimated that those terms have worsened by 20 per cent in the last two years. This is a sobering conclusion in view of the central role of trade in providing the resources needed for development and the weakened ability of trade to finance development.

Monetary Transactions

The overall effect of the recent food, fuel, and fertilizer increases on a country is vividly apparent in its current account deficit. In 1974, the deficits of Fourth World countries, expressed as a proportion of their total imports, ranged from 3.6 per cent in the case of Ghana to 30.9 per cent in the case of Mali. The projections for 1975 show a deepened deficit for a number of countries, the greatest being 30 per cent for Bangladesh; only Guinea is expected to achieve a surplus that is due to capital inflows. For the thirty-two most seriously affected countries as a group, the current account deficit is estimated at over $5 billion for 1974 and $5.5 billion for 1975.[17]

The normal inflow of medium- and long-term capital, the details of which will be discussed later in this chapter, is expected to offset roughly half of this, leaving about $2.3 billion each year to be covered by some extraordinary means. To help meet their shortfalls, Fourth World countries drew down the reserves that many of them had built up in the early 1970s. The extent of these reserves varied widely among countries, with some holding the equivalent of several months' worth of imports at the outset and others very little.

Calls for help to the international community on behalf of the most seriously affected countries elicited a sizable response. The United Nations Emergency Operation set up to handle this assistance reported total

---

[17]See Table D-15, p. 270.

commitments of $2.73 billion from twenty-two donor countries by late 1974.[18] It is not clear how much of this sum was additional to already projected programs, on what terms it was offered, or how much will be disbursed in 1975. All but $0.2 billion was handled directly by the contributing country rather than through the Special Account set up for the program.

Fourth World countries also made substantial (and increasing) use of the International Monetary Fund (IMF), whose central function is to assist countries in meeting short-term deficits. In 1974, Fourth World countries made aggregate drawings from the IMF of $751 million under already existing IMF arrangements. In addition, twenty-three of these countries made use of the Oil Facility set up in June 1974—with funds totalling about $3.6 billion—to handle acute balance-of-payments problems resulting from the increased price of oil. Fourth World countries drew a total of $674 million, on which they pay 7 per cent interest, with repayment of the principal to be completed within seven years. It is expected that in 1975 Fourth World countries will draw up to $1.3 billion from this new facility, which has been expanded by SDR 5 billion ($6.1 billion).[19] Support is being sought from other IMF members to subsidize the interest payments on drawings by the most seriously affected countries.

The overall position of Fourth World countries in the IMF can best be seen in terms of their quotas, on the basis of which all drawings on Fund facilities except for the Oil Facility are made. At the end of 1974, the global quota was SDR 29.2 billion ($33.75 billion)—with developing-country members as a group accounting for 28 per cent, and Fourth World members only 8 per cent, of the total. Quotas are now being enlarged by almost one third, to a global level of SDR 39 billion ($47.75 billion). Proportionate shares are also being changed—notably to increase the share of OPEC countries, but without reducing the share of the other developing countries as a group.

Since 1969, when the Fund set up a new international reserve asset, the Special Drawing Right (SDR), a total of SDR 9.3 billion ($11.4 billion) has been created. It was decided to allocate these to members without charge, which amounted to an equivalent gift to each member according to its quota. In January 1975, the Interim Committee of the Board of Governors of the Fund decided to move toward establishing the SDR as the principal reserve asset of the international monetary system. Considerable debate has centered on the question of whether more of the windfall from any future allocations should be used for the benefit of developing countries, and if so, how this should be carried out. A more equitable means than allocation according to quota should be worked out for future additions of SDRs into the system.

Over time, as the needs of the international economic community have

---

[18]United Nations Document A/C.2/SR.1643, 6 December 1974, p. 2.
[19]The value of the dollar in terms of the SDR ($1.22 as of December 31, 1974) has been used in stating equivalent figures.

grown and changed, the Fund has worked out new mechanisms to help members bridge the gap to payments equilibrium on a more extended basis than was originally envisaged. Since 1952, Stand-by Arrangements, which make available drawings up to a certain amount for a specified period, have been the basis of most drawings on the Fund. Of the thirteen such arrangements in effect at the end of 1974, totalling SDR 1,361.8 million (with Italy alone accounting for SDR 1,000 million), six—amounting to SDR 163.8 million ($200.5 million)—were with Fourth World countries.

Since 1963, another IMF facility, Compensatory Drawings, has been made available to bridge medium-term shortfalls in export proceeds, with the sums repayable over a three- to five-year period. Of the sixteen such arrangements (totalling SDR 534.6 million) that were in effect at the end of 1974, six (totalling SDR 192 million, or $235 million) were with Fourth World countries. Another arrangement, the Extended Facility, has been set up recently to provide a three-year instead of the usual one-year Stand-by Arrangement in order to open up access to drawings on the basis of less stringent criteria and to lengthen the time for completion of repayment to as much as eight years. This new facility may prove of considerable use to Fourth World countries, since the criteria explicitly cover slow-growth economies whose weak balance-of-payments position prevents pursuit of an active development policy.

These mechanisms enable the Fund to handle an increasingly large level of international transactions and to provide its members with an increasing degree of flexibility in pursuing their domestic economic policies. At the end of 1974, Fourth World use of Fund credit amounted to $1,531 million, or one third of global use of such credit.[20]

Long-Term Resource Transfers

Even if they cut back on badly needed import items and draw heavily on reserves and on funds extended by the IMF, Fourth World countries face a sizable resource gap which can only be met either by further belt-tightening or by an increased flow of funds from abroad. It is necessary to examine the extent and the sources of medium- and long-term external funds—that is, private investment and governmental and private loans and grants—to evaluate their role in the present position and future prospects of Fourth World countries.

As Table 1 shows, by the end of 1972, total resources received by the developing world as a whole in the form of grants, debt outstanding, and

---

[20]"Use of Fund credit" is the difference between Fund holdings of the currency of a member and that member's quota at a certain date. It is not directly comparable to the amounts authorized to be drawn under the various facilities.

direct investment amounted to over $200 billion.[21] The Fourth World countries accounted for about one quarter of these externally financed resources, or $47 billion. Examination of the resources at the disposal of the developing world at the end of 1972 shows that roughly one quarter of the total was composed of direct private investment, half was in the form of medium- and long-term borrowings from foreign governments and private institutions, and one quarter was accounted for by grants given by DAC countries[22] in the period 1960 to 1972. For the Fourth World, the composition was significantly different from the developing-world average, with direct private investment accounting for 11 per cent, borrowing for 53 per cent, and grants for 36 per cent. The several sources of these funds and the terms on which they have been forthcoming, as well as the projected trends, will be examined below.

Direct Private Investment. The stock of direct private investments by DAC countries in the 142 countries and territories of the developing world amounted to over $35 billion at the end of 1967.[23] By the end of 1972, it had grown to over $51 billion.[24] However, only $4 billion of this total was invested in the Fourth World at the end of 1967. While the total sum invested there had increased to $5.3 billion by the end of 1972, the Fourth World share actually decreased from 11.4 per cent to just over 10 per cent. The smallness of this figure is indicated by the fact that the entire stock of direct private investment in Fourth World countries was about equal to their combined current account deficit in 1974.[25]

The composition of direct private investment in the Fourth World showed manufacturing activity accounting for 33.6 per cent; agriculture (with some processed commodities included) for 19.6 per cent; and the petroleum industry for 19 per cent (about half in marketing). Mining and smelting amounted to 14 per cent of the total. Compared with the distribution for the developing world as a whole, including the oil producers, agriculture accounted for a significantly larger share for the Fourth World, and mining and manufacturing for a slightly greater share.

Loans, Grants, and the Debt Burden. Grants from DAC countries, including technical assistance, totalled $46.7 billion for the developing world

---

[21]That sum, minus undisbursed funds and technical assistance, amounts to about $87 per person and is estimated by the OECD to comprise about 12 per cent of the total capital stock at work in the developing world. Organisation for Economic Co-operation and Development, *Total External Liabilities of Developing Countries* (Paris: OECD, 1974), p. 7.

[22]Those member countries of the Organisation for Economic Co-operation and Development who are represented on the OECD's Development Assistance Committee.

[23]Development Assistance Directorate, OECD, *Stock of Private Direct Investments by DAC Countries in Developing Countries—End 1967* (Paris: OECD, 1972), p. 13.

[24]Development Assistance Directorate, OECD, *Stock of Private Investment by Member Countries of the Development Assistance Committee in Developing Countries—End 1972* (Paris: OECD, 1974), p. 3.

[25]See Table D-15, p. 270.

Table 1. Volume and Cost of External Resources to Fourth World Countries, 1972 ($ millions and percentages)

	External Resources Received			Cost of External Resources, 1972		
	Cumulative Grants, 1960-1972	External Public Debt (including undisbursed), End 1972	Stock of PODI,[a] End 1972	Interest Payments as Percentage of Disbursed Debt	Interest and Profit Payments as Percentage of Disbursed Debt and PODI[a]	Interest and Profit Payments as Percentage of Disbursed Debt, PODI[a], and Grants[b]
	($ millions)			(percentages)		
Africa						
Cameroon[c]	447	302	210	3.3	6.6	3.7
Dahomey[cd]	221	91	25	1.3	5.1	1.5
Ghana[c]	181	625	360	1.1	4.6	4.2
Guinea[cd]	100	169	175	1.4	5.9	5.1
Ivory Coast[c]	479	700	340	4.8	7.2	4.9
Sierra Leone[c]	81	101	75	3.3	6.8	5.6
Chad[cd]	279	27	20	3.9	7.1	1.1
Central African Republic[c]	213	62	50	0.9	6.3	2.2
Mali[cd]	260	324	8	0.2	0.6	0.3
Mauritania[c]	135	82	150	1.1	8.3	5.3
Niger[cd]	293	70	35	2.7	6.4	1.8
Senegal[c]	616	191	210	4.0	7.9	5.5
Upper Volta[cd]	266	41	18	2.6	6.8	1.0
Ethiopia[cd]	290	360	70	3.6	5.1	3.7
Sudan[cd]	160	382	35	4.0	4.8	4.0
Somalia[cd]	282	232	15	0.7	2.3	0.9
Burundi[d]	152	8	18	5.7	9.6	2.3
Rwanda[d]	179	14	17	3.3	10.5	1.7
Malawi[d]	214	231	55	2.4	4.5	2.8
Uganda[d]	196	215	30	2.9	3.9	3.0
Kenya[c]	438	510	235	4.0	6.5	4.9

Tanzania[c,d]	337	646	65	2.2	3.7	2.7
Malagasy Republic[c]	586	141	95	2.4	6.6	2.0
Botswana[d]	125	78	35	2.8	6.5	2.9
Lesotho[c,d]	120	8	2	2.5	4.0	0.4
Asia						
Bangladesh[c]	225	334	55	—	5.2	1.8
India[c]	5,308	11,653	1,660	2.5	3.6	2.5
Pakistan[c]	2,316	4,647	485	1.8	2.8	1.9
Sri Lanka[c]	167	672	130	3.2	4.7	4.0
Khmer Republic[c]	291	38	85	7.4	9.6	3.6
Laos[c,d]	732	19	8	4.3	7.3	0.4
Afghanistan[d]	404	774	16	1.6	1.8	1.4
Bhutan[d]	1	e	—	n.a.	—	—
Nepal[d]	190	60	5	0.8	6.5	0.8
Yemen, Arab Rep.[c,d]	75	35	e	2.2	e	0.6
Yemen, People's Dem. Rep.[c]	156	52	1	—	e	—
Latin America						
El Salvador[c]	96	156	100	3.4	6.6	5.3
Guyana[c]	70	205	135	3.7	6.8	5.9
Haiti[c,d]	78	39	55	0.8	6.9	4.6
Honduras[c]	80	170	200	3.3	7.5	6.7
Islands						
Maldives[d]	5	e	e	n.a.	e	n.a.
Western Samoa[d]	7	—	e	—	n.a.	—
Fourth World Total	16,851	24,464	5,283			
Developing World Total[f]	46,716	102,482	51,553			

a Private Overseas Direct Investment.
b Excludes technical assistance grants.
c A "most seriously affected" country, as defined by the United Nations.
d A "least developed" country, as defined by the United Nations.
e Nil or negligible.
f Includes Malta, Israel, Spain, and Yugoslavia.

SOURCE: Organisation for Economic Co-operation and Development, *Total External Liabilities of Developing Countries* (Paris: OECD, 1974), Tables 9 and 10, pp. 45-49, 52-56.

in the period 1960-1972. For the Fourth World, they amounted to $16.9 billion, well over one third of the total.

Total medium- and long-term foreign debt owed by Fourth World countries amounted to $24.5 billion at the end of 1972—about one quarter of the $102.8 billion then outstanding for all developing countries. Only about 10 per cent of this total was owed to private sources, compared to over 30 per cent in the case of the developing world as a whole. Sixty-four per cent of Fourth World debt was owed to the DAC countries of the OECD; 23 per cent to multilateral agencies; 11 per cent to the developed socialist countries; and 2 per cent to other developing (including OPEC) countries.

In general, the terms on which the Fourth World received loans were easier than the terms for developing countries as a whole. Interest payments by Fourth World countries averaged 2.4 per cent of disbursed debt compared with 3.5 per cent for the developing countries as a group. Total debt service (interest and amortization) averaged 6.5 per cent of disbursed debt for the Fourth World compared with 12 per cent for all developing countries.

A substantial portion of the overall sums lent by DAC countries to the developing world have been made available on concessional terms, that is, with a grant element of at least 25 per cent. Debt arising from bilateral official development assistance (ODA) loans from DAC countries to the developing world amounted to $28 billion at the end of 1972, of which $12.5 billion, or almost half, was owed by Fourth World countries. In addition, of the $4.8 billion owed by the developing countries on concessional aid from multilateral agencies, $3.7 billion, or more than three fourths, was owed by these countries.[26]

Clearly loans on concessional terms were dominant in the overall picture of external borrowing by Fourth World countries. Even so, when measured by the ratio of debt service to their export earnings, the debt burden on the Fourth World of this borrowing was substantial; in 1972, debt service ranged from 3 per cent of total export earnings for Ghana to 24 per cent for India and 25 per cent for Pakistan. With the pressures to acquire funds on any terms in the present period, there is concern that some countries may have taken on more debt obligations than they can handle. Lenders need to consider the overall burden faced by a borrowing country before advancing funds; in some cases, help may well be needed to reduce some already excessive debt levels. In the future, it is important to make funds for constructive uses available to such countries on terms they can afford to pay.

Concessional Aid in the Total Picture

In the past three years, an increasing volume of funds of various types has

---

[26]It is worth noting that ODA loans accounted for virtually all of the governmental lending from DAC countries and for two thirds of the total lending from multilateral agencies to the Fourth World.

flowed into the developing world from DAC countries and the multilateral agencies. While the amount going to the Fourth World has increased slightly, its *share* of the total has dwindled. In 1973, the total net inflow of funds to the developing world amounted to $22.5 billion, of which only $3.3 billion, or 15 per cent, went to the Fourth World.[27] Three billion dollars of the funds received by the Fourth World were on concessional terms.[28] While $25.3 billion in private funds was invested in developing countries as a whole in 1973-74 through Eurocurrency loans and the bond markets, less than $0.6 billion of this went to Fourth World countries, mostly in the form of Eurocurrency loans.[29] In global terms, the developing world as a whole accounted for 40 per cent of the Eurocurrency credits and 10 per cent of bond placements. The Fourth World accounted for 10 per cent of the export credits extended by DAC countries to the developing world at the end of 1972, that is, $3.3 billion out of $33.2 billion.[30]

In spite of their high degree of dependence on concessional loans, Fourth World countries received only 35 per cent of the ODA and multilateral concessional lending to the developing world in 1973. The increase in volume of ODA funds made available to the developing world, from $8.7 billion in 1972 to an estimated $11.9 billion in 1975, conceals the impact of inflation; measured in constant dollars, total ODA funds could amount to half a billion dollars less in 1975 than in 1972.[31]

Moreover, aid funds are not as readily forthcoming from the DAC countries as a whole as they once were. While some countries have increased the fraction of GNP that they devote to aid, others, including the United States, have let theirs decline. Consequently, the average share of GNP allotted to official development assistance has dropped from 0.52 per cent in 1960 to 0.34 per cent in 1970 and to 0.30 per cent in 1973—with a probable further shrinkage to 0.29 per cent by 1975. When this is compared with the 2.79 per cent of GNP which the United States made available to start the Marshall Plan in 1949, it is clear that a persuasive edge of urgency and commitment to development is lacking.

If this is an indication of the present trend, Fourth World countries face the possibility of decreasing funds in real terms. To offset such an effect, it is important for the DAC countries to reconsider the overall resource-acquiring capability of all developing countries and to allocate concessional lending

---

[27]Report by Chairman of the Development Assistance Committee, *Development Co-operation: 1974 Review* (Paris: OECD, 1974), pp. 270-71.
[28]This figure cannot be compared with the $3.3 billion figure which shows net inflow. In 1972, the latest year for which detailed data are available, ODA lending to Fourth World countries amounted to $2.9 billion and non-ODA lending to $0.7 billion, about one quarter of the total.
[29]See Table D-13, p. 267.
[30]The total had grown to $37.2 billion by the end of 1973, but data were not available to identify the share of the Fourth World.
[31]See Table D-4, p. 258.

specifically to those countries which cannot at present acquire external resources on any other terms.[32]

Bilateral loan commitments from OPEC countries to the Fourth World have been increasing. For the period 1970-1974, $2.34 billion was committed to twenty Fourth World countries. Most of this, $1.85 billion, was committed in 1974, with over $1.4 billion going to India and Pakistan and the remainder to fourteen other countries. The terms on which this assistance was extended are not known in detail, but some of it was extended on concessional terms. OPEC countries were also moving to set up several regional development funds and had made loans to multilateral agencies for their operations. The impact of OPEC loans had not been widely felt by late 1974, as few of the funds had been disbursed by that time.

It is not clear to what extent this level of loan activity by OPEC countries will be a continuing trend as far as the Fourth World is concerned. Recent assessments of OPEC accumulations of reserve funds see them tapering off much more rapidly than had been expected. Even more immediately, it is likely that these transfers represent the marginal uses of funds and may be the first to be cut back if revenues from oil slacken. For example, Iranian sources, noting a 10 per cent decrease in petroleum sales in January 1975, indicated that Iran's foreign aid program would necessarily be reduced as a consequence.[33]

Conclusion

The present study points up the degree of stagnation with which the Fourth World countries are contending and their dependence on outside help to overcome inertia. Otherwise there will be not only more grinding poverty for the bulk of the population but also little chance to achieve self-reliant growth.

Unfavorable trade projections for the rest of the 1970s further darken the picture, since trade is the chief self-help tool available to Fourth World countries. What would be most helpful to them on the trade side would be a liberalization of trade in primary and processed goods and in simple manufactures. This would permit them to utilize to best advantage the resources they do have—the available materials and abundant manpower.

---

[32]Part of the problem of redistribution of concessional assistance arises from the fact that aid is not worked out by a mathematical formula, nor obtained from a single, coordinated source, but reflects historical relationships between donor and recipient countries. To some extent, these special ties have evened out as the numbers of bilateral connections have increased. But they continue into the present period with treaties such as that signed at Lome on February 28, 1975, between the European Community and the group of forty-six African, Caribbean, and Pacific countries. The DAC has itself called attention to discrepancies, pointing out countries whose per capita receipts of aid diverge widely from the norm and urging a more equitable distribution, as well as increased concentration of receipts to the Fourth World.

[33]The New York Times, January 26, 1975.

But they cannot make these changes; rather, it is up to the community of nations to do so for their mutual good.

On the score of international payments, the impact of increased costs of oil and grain are just now beginning to be fully felt as Fourth World financial reserves have been depleted and payment is due on previous deliveries. In spite of the fact that the industrial world has dramatized their plight, the help which has been pledged is not sufficient to avert crises; and no donors have as yet come forward to subsidize payments for use of the Oil Facility. Moreover, since the bulk of the imports of most Fourth World countries consists of investment goods and such basic consumer goods as food, curtailment means a cutback on the very items needed to break the grip of stagnation. While IMF facilities provide increasingly greater flexibility, these should be expanded further to help both Third and Fourth World countries handle fluctuations in export proceeds which could otherwise truncate domestic growth programs.

The study has also shown the limitations of the other major component of the picture, the flow of medium- and long-term resources from abroad. As far as private funds are concerned, not only have a very small proportion been put to work in the Fourth World, but also in some countries, the cumulative price tag is beyond what those countries can afford. The prospects of being able to acquire funds on market terms are extremely limited and the ability to pay for them dubious under present no-growth conditions. Concessional terms are virtually the only appropriate ones for Fourth World countries, and concessional funds on a substantially expanded basis are a key element in a program to overcome the inertia of their economies. Donors should revise their aid programs to allocate the bulk of concessional aid to the Fourth World.[34]

The World Bank has concluded that a 2 per cent rate of growth in countries with per capita incomes below $200 could be achieved in the years 1974-1980—and a 4 per cent increase in countries with per capita incomes above $200—if DAC countries would maintain the level of ODA funds at the present share of projected GNP (with other concessionary aid maintained at the same proportionate level as in the past) and if a comparable volume of funds were made available on market terms to the rest of the developing world.[35] Given the continuing difficulties of the middle ranks of the developing world in acquiring finance, the availability of funds on intermediate rather than fully market terms, such as a "third window" at the World Bank, would significantly improve their access to needed capital. The picture would be further improved if the United States would reverse the downward trend in the share of GNP it commits to ODA and restore its

[34]See Henry Kissinger's speech of March 1, 1975, Houston, Texas. In this connection, see also Robert S. McNamara, *Address to the Board of Governors,* op. cit., p. 24. McNamara estimates that the poorest countries need $3-$4 billion more per year of concessional aid for the remainder of the decade.

[35]Robert S. McNamara, *Address to the Board of Governors,* op. cit., p. 18.

contribution to a level commensurate with that of other DAC countries—that is, increase its share from 0.2 per cent to 0.3 per cent of GNP.

Such a two-pronged program on the concessional assistance side is needed both to provide the necessary impetus for growth to Fourth World countries and to provide a firm footing for the weaker of the Third World economies. Only with a comprehensive program of this sort—one which takes account of the special needs of the Fourth World countries as well as of the economically vulnerable Third World countries—can the problem of stagnation be overcome, growth sustained, and the human condition improved.

CHAPTER II

Triage and Other Challenges to Helping the Poor Countries Develop

James W. Howe and John W. Sewell

In recent months, the long-accepted moral arguments in favor of supporting economic and social development[1] have been subjected to three serious challenges. The arguments advanced by the recent critics of development support are very different from past opposition to U.S. foreign assistance programs, which has been aimed at halting the dubious practice of combining appropriations for development assistance with those for military assistance.

The first of the new challenges attributes the miserable physical conditions of the life of people in the Fourth World to "unjust" ruling structures and argues that even economic support for those structures only perpetuates human misery. The second alleges that the poorest "Fourth World" countries are beyond being saved—that nothing the rich countries do, no matter how generous or wise, can rescue them; and that helping such hopeless countries merely wastes resources needed by other countries that do have a chance to develop. A third challenge goes a step further to say that any assistance to the poorest countries not only wastes resources that the successful countries need but is also cruel to the countries that are being assisted; helping them reduce death rates when there is no chance of reducing fertility merely ensures that death rates will eventually go up to match fertility

---

[1] The challengers' conceptions of "support for development" vary widely. Some focus their criticism on food aid alone, others explicitly oppose any governmental economic aid programs, and a few argue against any action whatsoever to help the poorest countries—whether trade preferences, liberal immigration policies, or anything else. In this Chapter, except where otherwise noted, the term means official development assistance as defined by the Development Assistance Committe (DAC) of the OECD.

rates after the population has multiplied. Therefore, this neo-Malthusian challenge holds that the sum of human suffering will increase.

The Question of Buttressing "Unjust" Structures

The first challenge to the morality of extending development assistance is raised by critics who argue that "unjust" domestic structures inflict great suffering on certain developing societies, and that outside assistance, by helping to keep such structures from collapsing, only perpetuates the suffering. The concept of justice as used by many of these critics has to do with the distribution of economic benefits rather than with personal freedom or justice in the courts. There is an implication in this criticism that poor countries are frequently governed by structures that are less "just" (as they define the term) than those of developed countries. Although this is at best an unproven hypothesis, it is not central to the logic of these critics. For the sake of debate, we accept the proposition that at least some aid recipients are "unjust" (i.e., their systems of income distribution are generally less equitable than those characterizing most donor countries). Debate aside, however, in real life there is of course an infinite variety of gradations of "just" and "unjust" elements in ruling structures.

Four assumptions seem to underlie this point of view. The first is that the condition of the poorest people is primarily due to unjust domestic structures and not to other factors, both domestic and external, such as low total productivity or inadequate institutional, nutritional, or educational development—or, importantly, to flaws in the operation of international trade and other economic systems. In at least some cases, unjust structures probably are at fault. Yet there are other cases, such as Tanzania, for example, where the fact that poverty and human suffering continue unabated does not seem attributable to unjust or corrupt ruling structures. It is probably undeniable, however, that this first assumption is true at least with respect to some countries (though of course not developing ones only).

The second assumption, that external assistance keeps unjust structures from collapsing, suffers from an exaggerated perception of the importance of external economic aid. It is in general rare for external aid to be a major factor in determining whether a ruling structure stands or falls. It may have a modest effect in cases where massive financial assistance provides support for a regime based on repressive force. Such aid has played an important role in the foreign policy of some donors, including, for example, the United States, France, and Portugal. It may also be true that large-scale capital assistance projects such as dams or roads may be of marginal value to repressive governments in consolidating their political support and quelling opposition by giving an appearance of governmental effectiveness. But the most common kind of development assistance project, involving, for example, agricultural research or vocational training, probably has little or no effect on the ability of a repressive or corrupt elite to remain in power. Certainly such projects do not increase the repressive power of governments.

It is conceivable, however, that aid in any form may give a government an aura of international acceptance. How important that may be in keeping a populace from rebelling against an unjust regime is difficult to measure objectively. Certainly donors should do what they can to make it clear that support for development projects carries with it no implication of support for the ideology of the ruling government. Indeed, willingness to provide assistance through governments with a variety of ideologies, and to sustain it uninterrupted through changes in governments, would do much to avoid such an implication. Channeling a greater share of concessional aid through multilateral agencies and private voluntary organizations would also help, as would the transfer of more resources through automatic devices in the international trade, finance, and other systems.

There is an offsetting possibility to the argument that development aid gives modest support to regimes: certain types of externally financed projects may in the long run and indirectly, have the effect of countering the inequitable ruling groups. To cite one example, it has been suggested that the thousands of South Korean students educated in the United States in the late 1940s and early 1950s had much to do with the downfall of Syngman Rhee. The typical emphasis in foreign aid programs on education for the lower economic classes, and policy ideas such as progressive income taxes, competitive bidding for public contracts, and the auditing of public expenditures probably erodes the ability of regimes and elites to retain special privileges for themselves. Admittedly, these latter influences are indirect and—at least in the observable short run—not very significant, but they probably are not without some effect.

The third assumption is that the withdrawal of assistance will help to bring down the "unjust" structures. This proposition is very doubtful, even if one hypothesizes that the ruling regime's capacity to repress opposition or revolt is indirectly supported by such assistance. The withdrawal of outside support might merely lead the repressive regime to cut out development activities altogether—and to continue to purchase the instruments of repression and to impose even harsher forms of repression because it feels threatened by the withdrawal of external assistance.

The fourth and most doubtful assumption is that if a regime is overthrown as a result of the withdrawal of assistance, it will be replaced by one that is more just. Unfortunately, it is just as likely to be replaced by a stronger and more ruthless one drawn from the same ruling class. Certainly the ruling class will not fall unless power is wrested from it by a challenging class. And nothing in the withdrawal of economic aid is likely to nurture such a challenge. It is possibly more likely (though still not very likely) that a continuation of outside assistance will offer contacts and exposure to ideas that indirectly encourage reform or revolt.

What then is the proper course for outsiders when they are convinced that basic changes must be made but are opposed to outside intervention to support armed revolt? Is it to withdraw all support entirely, to decrease it, or to continue it despite the existence of unjust structures? Continuing aid would seem warranted only in those cases where it clearly brings some benefit to the oppressed. In those cases, the obligation of the donor is to provide assistance in such a manner that those managing the unjust structures cannot divert it to their sole benefit. It should again be noted that these considerations pertain only to the extreme and hypothetical cases and not to the normal donor-recipient relationship, in which opportunities to use aid to help the underprivileged are not lacking.

For any action-trained, results-oriented American, it is particularly unsettling, however, to be told—even in the rare, extreme case—that he should help poor people through inequitable systems where that is the only way to reach them—obviously with no assurance that he can stop the injustice within his own lifetime and with only incomplete evidence that he can persuade the existing ruling classes to permit gradual reforms. But it is better for outsiders to accept this practical limitation than to continue to delude themselves that they can control events in other countries—a lesson the United States learned in Vietnam. The hard decision for the outsider in such cases is whether or not his help is of sufficient benefit to the oppressed to make the effort worthwhile, for there may be some cases in which little of the outside aid will get past elitist or corrupt governments to the intended recipients.

The above discussion has deliberately overemphasized the dark side of the picture—since partisans of development so seldom expose themselves to that side. In truer perspective, many people both within and outside the ruling classes of course *are* concerned about the consequences of deep poverty and know full well that in the long run their countries will be better off if poverty is reduced. Clearly governments and elites (anywhere in the world) are not monolithic, but sprinkled with occasional reformers—many of whom are willing to make some sacrifice of their own material benefits in the interest of justice. For that reason, persuasion and education play an important role. The campaign by the President of the World Bank in behalf of policies that favor the poorest 40 per cent of the population of developing countries has at least helped make it permissible—even popular—for reformers in certain countries ruled by repressive regimes to urge government-sponsored actions designed to benefit the poorest part of the population. Moreover, the rhetoric of justice is becoming more widespread, and although proclaimed norms can endure at wide variance from the facts for a time, they cannot endure together forever.

Finally, it is well to recall that development is reinforced not only by official development assistance (ODA), but also by a variety of other means of channeling more of the world's resources to the poor countries. Included under this broad definition are any efforts to improve the price of developing-country exports or widen the market for them, or to improve the access of developing countries to international monetary assets that are available to the members of the IMF completely outside the context of ODA, or to increase the developing countries' share of the oceans' bounty. In fact, in the array of resource-transfer mechanisms, trade, investment, and monetary affairs are quantitatively more important than ODA. And the more important steps to transfer resources may with some justice be regarded not as a subsidy to the developing countries but merely as a fair share of the benefits of these international systems. Consequently, those outsiders desiring change must decide not only whether or not to channel ODA through unjust regimes, but also the far larger issue of whether or not to support the reform of international systems (trade, investment, or monetary) to make them more beneficial to developing countries as a group—on the ground that some of the benefits of the reform may be used to support inequitable structures. Quite apart from the implicit moral issue, however, it simply is not feasible to design these systems to punish countries with "unjust" structures and reward those with "just" ones.

The search for equity is frustrating. The decision to reform or revolt must rest with the people of each country. The role of the outsider who is genuinely concerned about the condition of mankind clearly is circumscribed—for the alternative of fomenting revolution is so uncertain and the alternative of abandoning development entirely so defeatist, that as long as his support can be kept biased somewhat toward greater equity, he must rest content to continue supporting development. Fortunately, in most cases, these are not the choices confronting the outsider, since developing countries can make progress toward greater equity.

The "Triage" and "Lifeboat Ethic" Challenges

The second group of challengers to the morality of supporting Fourth World countries holds that certain of these countries are incapable of becoming viable and that "subsidizing" them merely diverts resources from other potentially viable ones, thus threatening the entire human enterprise. Since such lost countries cannot gain from outside help, these critics argue, assisting them only jeopardizes the chance for the rest of the world to preserve a humane existence. Some of those who argue in this vein invoke the battlefield principle of "triage,"[2] whereby the wounded are divided into three groups: those who will survive with minimal or no treatment; those who will die no

---

[2]The term "triage," from the French "trier" (to select), came into use on the battlefields of World War I, where surgeons were forced to select from among the overwhelming numbers of wounded soldiers.

matter what is done; and those who are likely to live only if they receive intensive care. In this situation, it makes sense to concentrate limited medical resources on the last group, because doing so will ensure that the maximum number will survive.[3]

Other critics make use of the analogy of the "lifeboat"; they claim that the rich countries can be likened to survivors in a lifeboat of limited capacity surrounded by others in the water waiting to be saved. If too many of those who are drowning are rescued, the boat will be swamped and all will perish.[4] Proponents of both of these analogies say that, given the lack of any viable alternative, the only moral course of action is for the rich to take some hard decisions as to which nations are to be "saved" and which left to "die."

Three premises underlie the lifeboat ethic: first, that certain nations are beyond being saved; second, that the resources of the entire world are not adequate and cannot be made adequate to meet the needs of all; and, third, that the sacrificed nations will disappear and cease to be world problems. There is much evidence that contradicts the first assumption. Indeed, the experience of the past three decades shows precisely the reverse. At the close of World War II, Europe, Japan, China, and virtually all of the vast underdeveloped areas of Asia, Africa, and Latin America were devastated by war or economically stagnant, or both, and thus highly dependent on assistance from North America. Today, of the 135 nations listed as U.N. member states (of which 97 are considered "developing"), only 42 are in a comparably serious condition. Another score or so countries are making progress but are still in a precarious condition. All other countries—including 16 oil exporters, 12 socialist countries, about a score of middle-level developing countries, and 24 industrialized countries—are either making reliable, self-sustaining progress toward solving their problems, or have the financial resources to do so. This is not a bad record to have achieved in a period of time as short as three decades. Indeed, it would be hard to find a comparable period of human progress in history. Whereas 25 years ago the population in countries that received aid or were stagnating without it constituted perhaps 90 per cent of the globe, such countries today make up less than half of the population; and the Fourth World—comprising those countries most in need of outside financial support—constitutes only 25 per cent of the world's population. In short, spectacular progress has been recorded by many countries which pessimists once considered to be hopeless cases.

Even the experience of India, often considered a very poor prospect, is encouraging. In the mid-1960s, India, suffering a large food deficit, changed

---

[3]This argument was first made by William and Paul Paddock in *Famine, 1975!* (Boston: Little, Brown and Company, 1967). See also Wade Green, "Triage," *The New York Times Magazine,* January 5, 1975, pp. 9 ff.

[4]See Garrett Hardin, "Lifeboat Ethics: The Case Against Helping the Poor," *Psychology Today* (September 1974), pp. 38 ff.

its policies to place more emphasis on agriculture. New high-yielding varieties of seeds and other essential agricultural inputs were made available, and their use spread with great speed throughout the subcontinent. By 1971, India had essentially closed its food deficit; its food output was sufficiently high to enable it to respond to the food crisis in Bangladesh in 1971. The reversal of this trend at present is a product of three factors: first, adverse weather in 1972 and 1974; second, a shortage of fertilizer during 1974; and third, a shortage of fuel to operate irrigation pumps during 1974. The result of these three conditions has been an import deficit of more than 8 million tons of grain. However, there is good reason to believe that, barring these three unusual factors, India could today be producing essentially all the cereals required for its people.

Thus there is no reason to conclude from the record of recent decades that any nation is beyond being helped—although enormous problems of course remain to be solved.

As for the second premise of the "lifeboat ethic"—that the earth's supply of resources is not large enough to go around—the world in fact does ordinarily produce enough food to keep well ahead of population growth, but disparities in its distribution remain striking. Between 1954 and 1973, per capita food production in developing countries as a whole increased by 8 per cent.[5] The United Nations estimated in 1970 that providing each of the 460 million people suffering from malnutrition with an additional allotment of 250 calories per day would call for about 12 million additional tons of cereals. This is only about 1 per cent of world consumption, about 30 per cent of what the United States feeds its livestock, and less than half of the grain directly and indirectly lost each year through food waste by American families.

In developing countries, far too often individual families, lacking enough food, must give the bulk of it to the breadwinner; mothers must make the tragic decision—actually a form of triage—to let one child starve so the rest of the family can survive. But in a world which spends more on arms than the poorest countries spend for all purposes and where both waste and material abundance in some countries proliferate to a point where they lower the quality of life, it is a travesty to suggest it is necessary to make such a decision with respect to whole nations.

Even if the ceiling on world food production actually had been reached, there still would be much that could be done to alleviate hunger by some modicum of redistribution. Presently North Americans consume nearly one ton of grain per person, mainly indirectly, in the form of milk, meat, and eggs. In contrast, individuals in a developing country on average consume only 400 pounds of grain, mostly in direct form. Thus it takes five times as many

---

[5]Economic Research Service, U.S. Department of Agriculture, *The World Food Situation and Prospects to 1985,* Foreign Agricultural Economic Report No. 98, (Washington, D.C.: U.S. Department of Agriculture, 1974) p. 12.

agricultural resources to feed an average American as it does to feed the average Indian, Nigerian, or Colombian. And the disproportionate consumption of energy and raw materials by developed countries follows an even more exaggerated pattern.

Thus neither of the first two assumptions underlying the lifeboat and triage analogies is valid. But both analogies have a still more serious weakness. Their third assumption is that nations, like those persons drowning or bleeding to death, simply die, and thereupon cease to be "problems" for those who are saved. But in the real world, nations do not drown or die; nor do they cease to be problems to themselves or the rest of the world. Abandoning them does not solve the problem, but merely postpones it and ensures that it will be all the more painful when finally faced. National boundaries may be inadequate to quarantine permanently the tensions that build up when whole nations begin to disintegrate. Such problems and tensions may spread beyond borders to threaten the rest of the world, forcing it eventually to deal with them at much greater cost than if they had been handled earlier.

Indeed, the kind of "lifeboat" analogy we are hearing so much about today does not accurately describe the current global crisis. The rich *are not* in possession of a secure lifeboat that they *alone* command. Instead, the rich and the poor *share* the same lifeboat, which is surrounded by "waters" teeming with "sharks" such as war, violence, economic breakdown, and over-population among others. Although there is a hole in the lifeboat, and it is slowly sinking, the rich are quite sanguine, and continue to insist that the hole is not on their side, and hence not their responsibility. Indeed, all of the evidence of recent history supports this different version of the lifeboat analogy, which is virtually identical with the "spaceship earth" analogy in that it recognizes and emphasizes the interdependence of all nations and people. Every passing season brings new problems of great variety but with one consistent theme: the problem can only be solved by international cooperation, not by nations acting independently.

The Neo-Malthusian Challenge

The third challenge to the morality of supporting development—especially the direct provision of food or medicine—is that it prevents people from dying, causing populations to continue to grow until they are finally held in check by starvation and disease. According to this viewpoint, there would be less human suffering if these neo-Malthusian restraints on population growth were permitted to come into play earlier, when population levels were lower. Thus, for example, if a country received no outside help, its population might stabilize at a level of 100 million, with 40 births and 40 deaths per thousand, or a total of 4 million deaths per year. But if food aid, medicines, and other outside help were provided, the population would double to 200 million in twenty-five to thirty-five years. If that population then came into balance at 40 births and 40 deaths per thousand, there would be 8 million deaths per year. According to this neo-Malthusian calculus, aid would in the long run actually raise the annual number of deaths and hence the quantum of human suffering—an achievement of questionable morality.[6]

Like the triage and lifeboat arguments, the neo-Malthusian critique assumes that the countries being assisted will never be able to lower their *birth* rates and consequently must "inevitably" experience a Malthusian balance of awesome proportions at some point in the future. But this central premise—shared by all of these challenges to the morality of helping the poor countries—ignores a crucial point of fact: there is no clear evidence that birth rates *cannot* be brought down in these countries. There are already indications, moreover, that when combined with certain innovative and effective domestic policies, outside support can help bring down birth rates just as surely as it now helps to lower death rates.[7]

What is the connection between governmental policies and birth rates? This was the central question considered by the U.N. World Population Conference held in Bucharest, Romania, in the summer of 1974. One consensus reached at this Conference was that even a far more effective and universally available contraceptive technique could not, by itself, solve the population problem—although it would be a major factor in reducing births. The root problem is that far too many parents want more children despite the fact that the planet cannot long tolerate such increases. But the reasons for wanting many children, which the mere *availability* of a good contraceptive will not alter, must be changed if world fertility is to be significantly reduced.

At least three factors may have some influence in supporting the relatively greater desire for large families in developing countries. The first is a value system that measures the worth of individuals and their acceptability in the dominant religion or society by the number of children they produce. This value system is the product of the legacy of having a child as often as nature decrees in order to ensure continuation of the family line. This, after all, has been the "formula" for family survival throughout the four million years of human history. The second factor is that children are economically *useful* to parents—not only as farm laborers but also as providers of some security in old age. For parents living close to the brink of economic disaster, this may be the only practical way to achieve such security. Third, having children may be the only personally fulfilling event in the lives of people with little or no education, few material possessions, and little to relieve the tedium of the bleak struggle to keep alive.

In the developed countries, the desire for large families has diminished as education and access to a variety of material goods have become more

---

[6]This argument ignores the possibility that it may be feasible to provide an improving level of life for the 200 million people.

[7]See Lester R. Brown, *In the Human Interest* (New York: W. W. Norton and Company, Inc., 1974), Chapter 9.

widespread. But does this mean the poor countries—where 85 per cent of the world's population expansion occurs—must achieve the same educational and economic level before their families' preferences for numerous children will change? If so, the whole prospect for solving the problem by reducing births becomes very distant, and those who argue that the short-run cruelty of letting death rates rise is in the long run an act of mercy may have a point.

But there is encouraging evidence that parental desires for many children have been sharply moderated in developing countries at income levels *even below $200*. For example, reports from China suggest a recent significant drop in the birth rate, and the same appears to be true in such culturally and ideologically diverse countries as Taiwan, Sri Lanka, Singapore, Hong Kong, Egypt, and Barbados. Relatively low and still declining fertility levels were also noted in Argentina, Uruguay, Costa Rica, and Cuba. One element common to all these countries is the presence of effective national policies favorable to low-income groups—including policies to raise their income levels as well as policies to provide the same groups with improved health and education services.

How might such policies change the three basic reasons for wanting large families? First, although there is no hard evidence, one can speculate that one effect of fundamental education and modernization is to challenge the values born of the ancient pro-natalism by substituting modern measures of the worth of the individual, such as productivity or erudition, for fertility. This may be especially important in the case of women. Education and modernization also challenge and force changes of interpretation in religious prescriptions favoring large families. Second, with respect to the need people feel for economic security in old age, development, if it provides a margin of income above the survival level, permits even poor families to set aside some savings to provide them with security in old age. Some governments are also considering old-age security programs as a means of discouraging fertility. Third, with respect to the pleasure of having children, development, by permitting some material amenities, intellectual enrichment, and a variety of entertaining distractions, offers alternative pleasures and makes it clear that there is a trade-off for each family between a higher economic level of living and a large number of children.

Preliminary evidence of this cause and effect relationship is provided in a recent study which reports that, of the 82 developing countries with reliable statistics, 72 experienced a decrease in birth rates between 1960 and 1970. Seventeen of these decreases amounted to as many as ten births per 1,000 of population, which is a significant decline. However, most of the countries examined in this study have small populations and, unfortunately, the heavily populated countries for the most part have not yet made similar progress.[8] It is

---

[8]R. T. Ravenholt and John Chao, "World Fertility Trends, 1974," in *Family Planning Programs,* Population Report, Series J, No. 2 (August 1974), pp. J-21—J-39. Published by

instructive to note that none of the countries identified by the United Nations as "least developed" experienced a decrease in birth rates.[9]

The most fertile groups within the developing countries are the poorest ones, especially the rural poor. Fortunately, a carefully designed policy of rural development—if successful in raising health, education, employment, production, and incomes—could help to solve both of the world's most pressing problems, hunger and high birth rates. Experience suggests that birth rates do not decline until certain basic social needs have been satisfied, including an assured food supply, reduced infant mortality rates, literacy, and at least rudimentary health services.[10]

This finding changes the moral equation raised earlier. If the country in our example doubles its population from 100 million to 200 million in a generation, but in the process cuts its birth and death rates and comes into balance at 15 births and deaths per thousand, then only 3 million might die. That would be a very substantial reduction in human suffering compared with the original condition of the country, in spite of the doubling in population. Where there is a prospect of reducing fertility, food aid and other outside help to prevent deaths cannot be challenged as immoral. Indeed, failing to provide such help would be immoral.

Outside assistance would be of doubtful morality only if it were absolutely certain that fertility could not be reduced over the decades ahead. Those who are tempted to conclude that the prospects of countries such as India and Bangladesh are hopeless, and that they therefore should be "abandoned," should ponder carefully the position that they are taking. For to assume a permanent inability to reduce births is to say there is no hope that these countries ever will escape the Malthusian dilemma. Faced with such an attitude on the part of the world, how would the abandoned countries react? Are we certain that uncontrolled elements within such countries have no means of bringing their case to the world's attention through acts of violence as groups with a grievance have done so often?[11] This raises the question of whether the rest of the world, confronted with that threat, would not be compelled to quarantine—and indeed patrol—such vast areas of concentrated human misery to ensure that they are denied the power to take revenge on the rest of the world for abandoning them. This would be a high price to pay in terms of the implicit self-brutalization. Moreover, it is in fact an *unnecessary* price, since the record in a growing list of countries shows that it

the Department of Medical and Public Affairs, The George Washington University Medical Center, Washington, D.C.

[9]See also Chapter I, p. 35, and Table A-5, p. 198.

[10]See Timothy King, ed., *Population Policies and Economic Development,* published for the World Bank (Baltimore: Johns Hopkins University Press, 1974); and William Rich, *Smaller Families Through Social and Economic Progress,* Monograph No. 7 (Washington, D.C.: Overseas Development Council, 1973).

[11]For instance, Robert L. Heilbroner, in *An Inquiry Into the Human Prospect* (New York: W. W. Norton and Company, Inc., 1974), raises the prospect of "wars of redistribution" between rich and poor countries.

is possible to reduce fertility, and that there consequently is reason to help save people's lives and to struggle to improve their living conditions.

A Question of Political Will

The most sophisticated variant on the neo-Malthusian theory holds that disaster is inevitable not because of a series of natural constraints inherent in a finite globe, but because the rich countries may lack the political will necessary to mount and support programs that would provide the developing countries with the resources needed for the sustained progress that is a precondition for reducing births.[12]

This formulation of the problem poses the question of whether Americans are prepared to do their share in a sustained effort to help the poorest countries develop. For if the ability of poor countries to develop, and thus ultimately to limit births, turns in part on the response of the industrial countries, then, to that degree, responsibility falls directly upon policy makers and the public in these countries. Are Americans willing to undertake this effort, or has this country turned inward, bruised by Vietnam, recession, and other pressing domestic problems? If Americans are indeed willing to ignore the plight of the poorest in the poor countries, then, as former U.S. Ambassador to India, Daniel P. Moynihan, has said, "We are going to have to face up to the fact that we are a different people from what we thought we were."

What is the state of the American "political will"? Political will in any society is a result of governmental leadership working within the bounds set, however unclearly, by the broad limits of public opinion. Until recently it had become fashionable to downplay the impact of public opinion on American foreign policy. But that opinion is important in determining the general direction of national policies, although scholars have argued for a number of years about just what its precise impact is and how it takes place. Public opinion is important because policy makers pay attention to it. For the policy maker, public opinion may be a matter of concern even though it may not tell him clearly what to do. It has political force as long as the policy maker either receives encouragement for positions he wants to take, or, in contrast, sees some limitations on effective action. The key to the importance of public opinion in the policy process therefore is whether or not it will accept or strongly oppose the policies proposed by Congress and the Executive Branch.

Within these bounds, government policy depends largely on its leaders' views of U.S. national interest. In the case of policy toward developing

---

[12]This view is set forth by Philip Handler, President of the National Academy of Sciences, in his address "The State of Man" (Paper delivered at the Annual Convocation of Markle Scholars, Hot Springs, West Virginia, September 1974). For an adapted, published version of the speech, see Office of Public Affairs, U.S. Agency for International Development, *War on Hunger* (February 1975), p. 1.

countries, U.S. national interest in a livable world and our moral precepts coincide. But governments often are slow to take a mature and long-range view of the national interest which recognizes that coincidence. Indeed, one can make the case that in some ways the U.S. government in 1974 was practicing a form of disengagement from the problems of the developing countries despite Secretary of State Kissinger's rhetoric concerning global interdependence. This disengagement was seen in the slow U.S. response to the appeal by the Secretary-General of the United Nations for emergency assistance to help the countries most severely affected by price increases in food, fuel, and fertilizer, as well as in the gradually diminishing amount of U.S. development assistance.

Occasionally in the past, the U.S. government's appreciation of problems has fallen too far behind the perceptions of the general public, and the latter has expressed its vigorous disapproval. Certainly the antiwar movement of the late 1960s was such a manifestation. For more than a year now, moreover, there have been at least three indications that the American public is not in step with the government's current low level of interest in the problems of poor countries. The first of these signs is the current high level of public concern about the world hunger situation; the second is the participation of citizens' groups in the legislative fight for the replenishment of the World Bank's International Development Association (IDA), whose programs are targeted mainly at the poorest developing countries; and the third is the steadily rising trend in voluntary contributions to private aid programs.

The response of Americans to the current world food crisis has been widespread and intense. Some months prior to the World Food Conference of November 1974, a number of organizations traditionally associated with overseas programs—including CARE, Church World Service, Lutheran World Relief, and the American Freedom from Hunger Foundation—established a temporary coalition, the World Hunger Action Coalition (WHAC), to coordinate their contribution to the Conference. The Coalition, which attracted participation by some 70 member organizations, used a variety of measures to mobilize American opinion on these issues, including special publications and newsletters, programming suggestions for radio and television, and the organization of a campaign involving a petition signed by nearly 300,000 Americans and addressed to the Secretary of State. The petition called for U.S. support of an international grain reserve, U.S. provision of additional food aid to meet the immediate needs of the most severely affected countries, and U.S. policies to support long-range agricultural development in the poor countries.

The Coalition's efforts were paralleled by a number of other spontaneous private endeavors to help Americans better understand the nature of the long-term world food crisis. OXFAM-America organized a program of fasts on some 600 college campuses and contributed the money saved by fasting to relief organizations. American religious organizations—Protestant, Catholic, and Jewish—all became deeply involved in educating and mobilizing their constituencies on the facts of world hunger. In June 1974, leaders of all three denominations met in Aspen, Colorado, to plan a long-range strategy to mobilize Americans on issues of hunger and global development. In November, U.S. church leaders made a nation-wide public appeal to President Ford to increase food aid immediately to the countries most severely affected by hunger and malnutrition.

The response of newspapers, radio, and television was equally striking and reinforced the already strong American interest and activity on this set of problems. Each of the major news weeklies devoted special features to the hunger situation—despite competition for space from the severe domestic political crisis that the United States was going through at the same time. *The New York Times*, *The Washington Post*, *The Christian Science Monitor*, *The St. Louis Post-Dispatch*, and other daily newspapers not only devoted numerous articles to the immediate aspects of starvation and malnutrition on the Indian subcontinent and in the African Sahel, but also delved into some of the possible causes of and short- and long-term solutions to the food dilemma. Similarly, radio and television gave extensive coverage to food issues. The result of all these efforts has been rising pressure on the U.S. government and on private organizations themselves to increase their assistance to the countries severely affected by hunger and malnutrition.

A second illustration of the influence of the public was provided in 1974 by the public debate on the question of the U.S. contribution to the International Development Association, the soft loan "window" of the World Bank. When the legislation authorizing American funds for IDA was introduced in the House of Representatives in January of 1974, it was defeated by a vote of 248 to 155, in part due to congressional resentment of the oil embargo and the arbitrary price increases of the oil-producing countries, but also due to inept handling on the part of the Administration. Following the defeat of this effort in the House of Representatives, there was a determined effort on the part of public and private groups to reverse the decision. An extensive educational campaign was launched, and citizens' groups pressed individual legislators about the merits of the issue. Such public support was reinforced by editorials in over one hundred major American newspapers. This campaign grew in intensity and reached a peak in early July 1974, when the Congress reversed itself and voted 225 to 140 to provide the U.S. share to IDA. This reaction illustrates the concern of U.S. public opinion over the American responses to the pressing problem of the world's poor. It also illustrates that when the public is sufficiently aroused by governmental policies, it can act to change those policies.

The third indicator of public concern has been the upward trend in private contributions to such voluntary organizations as CARE and Church World Service. It is indeed ironic that at a time when the U.S. government is doing much less on development issues than in earlier decades, voluntary contributions to development programs from American people have risen to an all-time high of $229 million (excluding aid to Israel), an increase of nearly 82 per cent since 1964. This trend has been continuous over the past ten years, but moved steeply upward in 1974 despite the worsening economic situation in this country. CARE's contributions, for instance, were 42 per cent higher in 1974 than in 1973. With diminishing government assistance and rising private contributions from individuals, about 32 cents in every dollar provided as aid to the developing countries now comes from private contributions.

The rise in American concern for the developing countries also was reflected in the 1974 edition of *State of the Nation*, Potomac Associates' biennial survey of the state of American public opinion,[13] which showed an increase in support for foreign economic aid since their survey of two years ago. The new survey results indicated that more than half of all Americans favored increasing foreign aid or keeping it at its present level—a finding similar to that of a survey conducted two years earlier under the auspices of the Overseas Development Council.[14]

But many people maintain that, despite this evidence of public concern about human suffering and poverty, current public opinion polls provide evidence of a swing toward isolationism that seems to parallel the disengagement policies of the U.S. government. Two trends are clear from the existing opinion surveys: first, there is a marked decline in concern about "cold war" issues and a corresponding drop in support for military outlays; second, there is a strong increase in concern about domestic issues, particularly inflation and social problems. A Gallup poll conducted last year indicated that the public's preoccupation with domestic problems overshadows worry about "international" problems by the widest margin ever recorded since such survey work began in the 1930s.

But does this mean that Americans want to "disengage" from the rest of the world? There is reason to doubt this. Most judgments that there is now a shift toward isolationism have been made on the basis of questions keyed to issues of military security alone rather than to the broader questions of economic interdependence. When the questions are changed, the results differ dramatically. A recent survey conducted by Louis Harris for the Chicago Council on Foreign Relations shows quite clearly that Americans exhibit a high degree of understanding of the growing economic interdependence of the United States with the rest of the world, and that they are prepared to make sacrifices for U.S. cooperation with other countries.[15]

It would be hazardous indeed to predict future trends in public opinion,

---

[13]See William Watts and Lloyd A. Free, *State of the Nation* (Washington, D.C.: Potomac Associates, 1974).

[14]See Paul A. Laudicina, *World Poverty and Development: A Survey of American Opinion,* Monograph No. 8 (Washington, D.C.: Overseas Development Council, 1973).

[15]John E. Rielly, ed., *American Public Opinion and U.S. Foreign Policy 1975* (Chicago: Chicago Council on Foreign Relations, 1975).

but there is much evidence (related perhaps to increasing levels of education) that Americans are less prone to follow slogans than to make up their own minds. For example, the number of Americans who rank themselves as "independent" when questioned about party affiliation has now grown to about one third of the electorate. Thus American opinion on global issues is likely to be different in the future from what it was in the past. In an earlier study of opinion on such issues as Vietnam, women's rights, domestic poverty, and crime, pollster Louis Harris concluded that "the public is far more sophisticated, far more concerned, and far more advanced than the leadership believe. It can be said with certainty that the people by and large have been well ahead of their leaders."[16]

This period may be a moment in which public opinion is fluid and could go either way. It could turn inward on the mistaken assumption that a more "independent" policy can effectively protect the current U.S. position of relative economic strength; or it could support policies designed to meet the realities of an increasingly interdependent world—including support for programs designed to meet the needs of the world's poor majority.

The developments of the past year provide some hope that Americans will not support either a "triage" or a neo-Malthusian policy. Indeed, there is evidence that most Americans would find both concepts alien to their traditional concern for those in need. In the Chicago Council's survey, nearly three of every four Americans indicated they would be willing to go without meat one day each week and to cut out all unessential uses of fertilizer at home so that food and fertilizer could be shipped to countries abroad to combat food shortages. The crucial point, however, will come when this country is faced with difficult choices not on aid issues or on voluntary development assistance, but on such painful adjustments as would, for example, be involved in accepting labor-intensive imports from poor countries even at the expense of jobs in uncompetitive industries at home. For this is the kind of adjustment that will be necessary to cope with the realities of an interdependent world.

Unfortunately, government leadership is not offering policies based on interdependence realities. And without such leadership to confront Americans with the choices now before them, a special obligation will be placed on congressional and private leaders to translate the current rising public understanding of interdependence into a willingness to make personal sacrifices. The American public already has demonstrated that it can affect governmental policy. Private leaders, and indeed, the public in general, have an obligation to reject proposals that nations be written off as unsalvageable, and to make clear their response to the arguments of the neo-Malthusians.

A major defect of the neo-Malthusian agrument is its exaggerated view of

[16]Louis Harris, *The Anguish of Change* (New York: W. W. Norton and Company, Inc., 1974), p. 286.

the importance of outside aid in reducing fertility rates. As argued earlier, acute economic insecurity is a major factor in encouraging high fertility rates in developing countries. There is evidence that this economic insecurity can be reduced enough to have a significant downward impact on fertility rates if increased assistance from the outside is paired with appropriately comprehensive development strategies in developing countries. Where this approach has been tried, it has shown encouraging results.

Thus the real choice and challenge before governments and the public in both the rich and the poor countries is whether or not they will address themselves to the real causes of uncontrolled population growth. And in this effort, outside assistance does have an important role to play. What will be the response of the U.S. government and the American people to this historic issue?

A Matter of Perspective

An attempt probably will be made in the fall of 1975 at the U.N. General Assembly's Special Session on Development to secure wider and more meaningful acceptance of the objective that every human should have, as a fundamental right, access to the minimum material conditions required for human dignity. If this issue is presented in understandable form to the American public and escapes entanglement in a North-South power struggle, there is strong reason to believe that the response of most Americans will be clear and affirmative—that they will choose the doctrine that every human being has a right to basic material satisfaction rather than resort to Malthusian principles.

The proposals to turn our backs on the world's poorest people cannot be lightly dismissed—if only because of the stature of some of those who advocate this course. Moreover, the three challenges discussed appear to have a significant constituency. This willingness to accept so inhumane a course of action may stem in large measure from despair that the task of bettering the human condition is not feasible for some countries. So many have said so much about the crises, the ills, and the awesome magnitude of the overall problems of development that the evidence of human *progress* has been lost from sight altogether. But the shocking thing about the admonitions to let death rates rise is that they are based on needless pessimism. Nothing in the record to date—or even in recent trends—warrants such a conclusion. On the contrary, that record encourages us not to tire, for the goal of meeting every person's basic human needs *is* within reach. Astonishing progress has been registered in the past thirty years. Now is hardly the time to abandon this course.

CHAPTER III

Next Steps Toward Global Food Security

Lester R. Brown and Erik P. Eckholm

In 1974 world attention focused on food with an uncommon intensity. Two factors contributed to this. One was a poor crop, which resulted in a decline in world food stocks even below the dangerous levels of the preceding year, as well as in soaring food prices and growing competition among countries for available food supplies. The second was the convening of a major international conference, at the political level, on the short- and long-range implications of the food crisis. The poor crop both heightened interest in and underlined the importance of the conference.

The U.N. World Food Conference, held in Rome in November 1974, outlined the principles for a cooperative global approach to solving world food problems, including objectives to be addressed over the next decade and the institutional structures and means of attaining them. But the accomplishments of the Conference thus far remain largely at the level of rhetoric. This is so despite the encouraging start made in the months following the Conference by the establishment of the World Food Council and the Consultative Group on Food Production and Investment, and by the U.S. decision to increase its food aid by some two million tons. Critically important questions facing the international community in the food area in 1975 include the following: Can substantially increased resources be mobilized to increase food production in the developing countries? Can significant progress be made toward establishing an international system of grain reserves? Will it be possible to reach early agreement to guarantee at least 10 million tons of food aid annually? None of these questions can be successfully resolved without active U.S. participation and legislative action. Meanwhile, as action on these issues is being debated and negotiated, the world in 1975 is more vulnerable to a major new grain shortfall than at any time since World War II.

The 1974 Crop

World grain output almost always rises from one year to the next. Although one or more of the world's major food-producing regions may have a particularly poor crop, the total world food output generally increases as a result of additional investment and technological progress. But 1974 was an exception to this trend. For only the second time in the last dozen years, world output declined from the preceding year. And even while the world had added nearly 70 million people since the last harvest, world grain production dropped by 5 per cent from 1973.

Food output turned downward in three of the world's major food-producing regions—Asia, North America, and the Soviet Union—for a variety of reasons. In North America, the decline was the result of exceptionally poor weather—widespread drought, flooding (which resulted in delayed spring planting in some areas), and early frost (which contributed to widespread crop losses, often in the very areas earlier affected by floods). In the Soviet Union, the crop decline from 1973 to 1974 was simply due to the fact that weather was not as exceptionally favorable as it had been in 1973. In Asia the reasons for the downturn in food output were more complex. In some countries, crop declines were due to unfavorable weather. High prices and inadequate supplies of fertilizer and energy also had a pervasive negative impact throughout Asia. The U.S. Department of Agriculture estimated that the Indian wheat crop was reduced by a million tons, or by 4 per cent, solely as a result of the lack of fuel for operating irrigation pumps.

The decline in the 1974 crop was a precipitous one; it was an even larger drop from the preceding year than had occurred in 1972, when the world food market was thrown into disarray. But another important factor differentiated the 1974 situation from the 1972 experience. In 1972, the world still had substantial reserves of food to draw upon to help cushion the impact of the disappointing harvest. But by 1974, reserves were at the lowest level since the years immediately following World War II, leaving societies everywhere dangerously vulnerable to the weather.[1]

The fall in production meant that world food consumption would necessarily be reduced during 1974 and 1975. The difficult question facing the international community was how the inevitable belt-tightening would be allocated. Would those nations with surplus food and/or money have the will to ensure that the minimal survival needs of the impoverished were met? Or would price and politics serve as the global rationers, dooming millions to premature death? The immediate specter of spreading malnutrition, and in

---

[1] See Table C-7, p. 244.

some regions, outright starvation, lent an unanticipated degree of urgency to the U.N. World Food Conference in November 1974.

The Complexity of the Problem

Perhaps the most striking aspect of the world food problem in the mid-1970s is its incredible complexity, requiring, at a minimum, the insights of economics, ecology, agronomy, meteorology, and political science. The analytical difficulty of the problem is reflected in the failure of agricultural analysts to anticipate the major change in trends in the world food economy during the early 1970s. Very few anticipated that the world fish catch, which had been increasing by nearly 5 per cent per year between 1950 and 1970, would show a three-year sustained decline during the early 1970s. The massive Soviet grain purchase in 1972 also took the world almost completely by surprise, even though political scientists were aware of the Soviet government's growing responsiveness to consumers' demands. And although the U.S. Department of Agriculture, with one of the largest economic analysis units available anywhere, projected an increase of only 3 per cent in food prices during 1973, the increase turned out to be closer to 20 per cent. Few foresaw the possibility that the vast acreage of idled U.S. cropland would be called back into use within a two-year period—and even fewer foresaw that this might not suffice to overcome scarcity, rebuild depleted reserves, and return food prices to more "normal" levels.

The food problem has become so complex that it is at times even difficult to ask the right questions about it. In looking at future food production prospects, for example, it is often asked what the potential is for expanding food production. Viewed in purely technical terms, one can say that world food output can be doubled or tripled, or more, during the next several decades. But this is not really the crucial point. The important question is: At what *cost* can a given increase in output be achieved?

We know that the most productive land in the world is already under cultivation and that, with few exceptions, the most desirable irrigation sites already have been exploited. We know that energy, and therefore fertilizer, is likely to be far more costly in the future than in the past. We know that in the more advanced countries, where crop yields are already high, future production increases will be far more costly than in the past. In order to bring marginal resources into use, world prices for food must rise well above their historic levels, and they are doing so.[2] Unfortunately, however, food prices are rising beyond the purchasing power of several hundred million of the world's poorest people. As a result, the food intake level of millions of low-income people around the world is being pushed below the survival line—in many

[2]See Table B-7, p. 228.

regions reversing the long-term trend of improved nutrition, lengthening life expectancy, and declining infant mortality.

Injecting the cost consideration into our analysis spotlights the necessity for a radical shift in the approach to ending food scarcity. Traditionally, nearly all emphasis has been given to expanding supplies. Although current efforts to raise output remain urgent, an equal emphasis is now needed to slow the growth of demand for food that is attributable to both population growth and rising affluence. If this is not done, the world will be forced farther and farther up the cost curve over time—as even more marginal resources are brought into use. Conceivably, technological progress could offset the effect of diminishing returns from additional resources, but in recent years it has not been able to do so. In addition, far more effort must be devoted to raising output rapidly in the *developing* countries, where major gains still are possible at far less cost than in the more agriculturally advanced countries.

Raising Output in the Developing Countries

Despite all the controversy it generated, the World Food Conference was marked by a surprising degree of consensus on the basic dimensions of the world food problem. No conclusion was more widely shared than the urgency of raising food output within the food-short developing countries. Both the U.N. Food and Agriculture Organization (FAO) and the U.S. Department of Agriculture predict that if the production and demand trends of the last decade were to prevail throughout the next decade, the net grain imports of the developing countries would increase from 16-20 million tons in the period 1969-1971 to 70-85 million tons by 1985. A major global collaborative effort is required if this staggering import deficit is to be avoided.

Expanding food production in the developing countries can help solve several important problems which these countries face, including the lack of food itself, the need for productive employment, and the need to create more economic activity in the countryside to slow the rising tide of rural-urban migration. It can also help create a social climate of progress in which birth rates will fall.

One of the most dangerous misconceptions spawned by the current food crisis is the notion that the race between food and population in many developing countries is a hopeless one—that these countries can never be expected to feed themselves. On the contrary, now that the formerly idle U.S. cropland has been released for production, the world's greatest unrealized potential for expanding food output is in the developing world. Even though soils in Bangladesh are inherently more fertile than those in Japan, rice yields in the former are less than one third those in the latter. India produces 100 million tons of grain on 350 million acres of cropland while the United States, with a comparable area and a somewhat similar rainfall pattern, produces nearly 250 million tons. Corn yields in Brazil are only one third those in the United States.

Furthermore, dramatic production increases in many populous developing countries in the late 1960s proved that rapid progress is possible when the right blend of government policies and technical know-how is available. Peasant farmers—thought by many to be rigidly tradition-bound—were quick to change their practices and to raise productivity when provided the means and incentives for doing so. In India, for example, wheat output soared from 11 million to 26 million tons between 1965 and 1972—an unprecedented increase in production of a food staple that temporarily eliminated India's need for food imports in 1972. The triple shock of droughts, quadrupled energy prices, and a world fertilizer shortage—all largely outside the control of the principal countries now facing food shortages—was an important contributing factor to the reversal of what had generally been encouraging trends. Given the appropriate political will, cooperative endeavors in such areas as building grain reserves, increasing fertilizer output, providing financial and technical aid, and developing labor-intensive agriculture can overcome these detrimental forces.

This is not to say that slowing population growth is not also a key factor, or that failure to properly stress agricultural progress in the poorest countries' development efforts has not contributed to their current unfortunate plight. It is, however, important to keep in mind the tremendous unexploited food-producing potential waiting to be tapped in the developing world—particularly in the face of arguments that the poorest countries be "abandoned" by the rich as hopeless cases incapable of ever meeting their own food needs.[3]

The advantages to the international community of an intensified effort to expand food production in the developing countries become evident when one examines the rates of return on inputs. At a time of scarcity of essential inputs such as fertilizer and energy, it is important that these resources be used in the most productive manner. The additional food that can be produced with an additional ton of fertilizer has dropped sharply in the industrial countries as fertilizer use has increased dramatically over the past generation. In the U.S. corn belt, for example, the use of an additional ton of fertilizer might produce an additional five tons of grain. In a country such as India, however, where fertilizer usage levels are quite low, an additional ton of fertilizer could easily result in the production of an additional ten tons of grain.

The most important action point in expanding food production in the developing countries is within these countries themselves. With few exceptions, all are in desperate need of a) government policies giving greater priority to agriculture, and b) agricultural reforms to both distribute land

---

[3]See also Chapter II.

more equitably among those who work on it and provide the poorer farmers (who are a generally neglected group) with needed credit and other supporting technical services. While many developing countries have been quite prepared to talk about reform at the international level and about the need for a new world economic order, they often have done little to achieve reform at home.

Thus, although a growing body of evidence indicates that the greatest remaining agronomic potential is now in the developing world, this potential will not materialize easily. Agricultural development in the poor countries involves complex social, political, and economic changes. Without a strong commitment to these changes on the part of governments, as well as a willingness to undertake basic reforms in the distribution of power and services at the local level, the needed progress will not occur. Hopefully, the new attention accorded agriculture in the wake of the World Food Conference will result in a new commitment to agricultural progress by developing-country governments. The industrial powers, for their part, need to acknowledge forthrightly that a government willing to, and capable of, restructuring rural societies for broadly based agricultural progress will not necessarily share their world view and economic assumptions—and that the frequently voiced commitment to reducing hunger in the world may involve cooperating with regimes with diverse approaches to international affairs and economic organization.

While outside aid cannot substitute for an internal commitment to reform and agricultural progress, in most countries, agricultural development can be facilitated by technical and financial assistance from the more prosperous countries aimed at promoting small-farm, labor-intensive cultivation. By helping to hold down world food prices, greater international assistance for agricultural development would have beneficial consequences for consumers throughout the world.

One of the more encouraging developments at the Rome Conference that could contribute to the realization of the agronomic potential in the developing countries was the call for the creation of an Agricultural Development Fund. This potential new investment vehicle is being created largely at the behest of the OPEC countries and hopefully will provide a means of channeling some of their surplus capital into the agricultural sectors of the developing countries. Contributions to this Fund are to be voluntary rather than rigidly determined by a quota system. A second important institution created by the World Food Conference is the Consultative Group on Food Production and Investment. This group, whose headquarters already are established at the World Bank in Washington, is intended to identify investment needs and coordinate the aid efforts of traditional bilateral and multilateral aid agencies as well as those of the new Fund and other sources of financing.

There was widespread agreement at the Conference with the FAO estimate that international aid transfers to promote agricultural development need to be raised from the 1974 level of $1.5 billion annually to about $5 billion annually. While much of this resource gap hopefully will be filled by the capital-surplus OPEC countries, these countries have suggested that the level of their agricultural aid contributions may be at least partly contingent upon renewed efforts by the traditional donor countries as well. Since the World Food Conference, the U.S. Congress has authorized an increase in the food and nutrition components of the U.S. bilateral aid program from $291 million to $500 million a year. This was a significant reversal of the downhill trend of the previous several years, but the total remains far short of supporting the interests of consumers everywhere in the world by helping to spur rapid food production gains in the regions with greatest *low-cost* potential. Other means need to be found to increase the flow of resources from the United States for this purpose.

Modifying the Growth in Demand

Perhaps the single most evident weakness of the World Food Conference was its almost exclusive concentration of attention on the supply side of the food supply-demand equation. Despite the growing scarcity of all essential agricultural inputs—land, water, energy, and fertilizer—as well as soaring prices for both agricultural inputs and foodstuffs, there was all too little recognition that a much greater effort must be undertaken to slow the future growth in the demand for food by putting the brakes on global population growth and simplifying diets among the more affluent.

An exception to this criticism of the Conference was the initiative taken by twenty-four developing countries to sponsor a resolution on population and food that declared the importance of the direct relationship between the number of people to be fed in the years and decades ahead and the difficulty in feeding those numbers in the absence of a substantial and immediate slowing of population growth. These twenty-four countries called attention to the decision of the World Population Conference in Bucharest and requested that all governments and peoples "support . . . rational population policies ensuring to couples the right to determine the number and spacing of births freely and responsibly."

World population growth had in fact begun to slow measurably in 1974, but in part for the wrong reasons. In a number of the poorest countries, such as Bangladesh, India, Ethiopia, the Sahelian-zone countries, and other low-income countries, death rates are rising, thus at least temporarily slowing the rate of population growth. But most people would agree that reliance on rising death rates to alleviate food scarcity is neither morally nor, in the long run, politically acceptable. Just as important as the moral argument, but less widely understood, is the accumulating evidence that rising death rates in any case cannot provide a long-term "solution" to the population problem. Many of the "lifeboat ethic" theorists who now suggest that writing off millions of the malnourished is the only possible way the world can survive the food-population crisis have failed to examine what the demographic consequences would be if hunger, manifested in high child mortality, were to continue its recent spread. Available social science research indicates that when parents in the developing countries lose a child, they subsequently tend to overcompensate by having more than one additional child in response. An effective check on population growth will require a frontal attack on malnutrition and infant mortality, as well as the universal extension of family planning services and at least elementary educational opportunities, particularly for women. Properly designed agricultural development programs (emphasizing labor creation and progress on the part of the farmers with smaller holdings) can simultaneously improve both the food and population outlooks by raising food output and elevating the social welfare of many of the world's poorest people.[4]

At the World Food Conference, representatives of governments with rapid rates of population growth were not always enthusiastic about discussing stepped-up efforts to slow population growth, but representatives of affluent countries were even less enthusiastic about focusing on the question of simplifying diets. One of the notable exceptions was the delegation of the Norwegian government. At the Conference, the Norwegians focused attention on malnutrition in the form of overnutrition in the industrial countries. They urged industrial countries to adopt explicit national nutrition policies and to harmonize these with national agricultural policy.

Norway is in fact far ahead of most industrial countries in this respect, and its experience provides an instructive example for other developed countries. A few years ago, Norwegian political leaders asked the medical and nutrition professions to determine an optimum diet for the average Norwegian, given certain statistics—body size, climate, types of work, and other physical activity. One concern prompting this effort was a mushrooming incidence of cardio-vascular disease, believed to be linked to affluent dietary patterns. Once it had been determined at the national level how much wheat, milk, fish, and other foodstuffs would provide an optimum diet, an effort was made to adjust agricultural policies by using various incentives and disincentives to achieve a nutritionally desirable mix of foodstuffs produced. Both public education programs and economic subsidies were introduced to promote the use of lean meats instead of the fattier grain-fed meats, and to increase the direct consumption of grains and vegetables over that of livestock products and sugar.

One of the consequences of this policy in Norway has been the reduction of per capita claims on agricultural resources, since the average individual in Norway—as in other industrial societies—consumes more fat-rich livestock

---

[4]See Chapter IX.

products and more calories than is desirable.[5] Norway's program has also had the incidental effect of reducing Norway's agricultural trade deficit. The harmonizing of agricultural and nutritional policies in Norway is thus having three highly beneficial effects: an improvement in health and life expectancy; a reduction in the amounts of land, water, energy, and fertilizer required to feed the Norwegian population; and an improvement in the Norwegian balance of payments due to the reduction of feedgrain imports. By serving as an example, Norway succeeded in focusing considerable attention at the Conference on the nutritional problem of the affluent—namely, the fact that overconsumption can impair health and reduce life expectancy just as surely as does underconsumption.

In the United States, as well as in Western Europe and Japan, soaring prices of cereals in 1974 did compel a significant cut in the feeding of grain to livestock. It appears quite possible that the historical trend toward higher meat consumption per person in the United States will be slowed, and perhaps even reversed altogether, because of the convergence of economic, health, and moral considerations. It also is quite likely that economic forces will promote a shift in the U.S. beef industry away from inefficient feedlot fattening and toward greater use of rangeland grazing, which is an efficient use of resources. But whether the U.S. government and other governments will perceive the underlying forces and social needs at play *in time* to exercise constructive leadership remains open to question. The U.S. Department of Agriculture is still projecting and promoting a continuation of the historical trend of rising per capita meat consumption through the next decade, once the current economic difficulties of the livestock sector are straightened out. More study is needed of the multiple potential benefits of a shift toward less grain-intensive protein sources for reasons of personal health, battling inflation, and reducing agricultural stresses on the ecosystem.

Reducing Food Insecurity

A major concern of national and global food policies must be the reduction of the instability in the food economy that has left all concerned parties—farmers, consumers, and government policy makers—so insecure and vulnerable. It is difficult to overstate the negative economic, social, and political consequences of instability in a sector so basic to human welfare and economic activity. Soaring prices for wheat, corn, or soybeans not only send shock waves through the food economy, but fuel the fires of inflation in other sectors as well. The tripling of world grain prices in the early 1970s, followed by wage earners' efforts to recoup their lost real income, has been an important driving force behind the double-digit inflation plaguing most

---

[5]See Table A-6, p. 208.

countries—and a force largely beyond the reach of general fiscal and monetary restraints.

With the safety valve of reserves gone, fluctuating supplies and prices of grains have severely disrupted the livestock, baking, and canning industries in the United States. The exercise of political pressure by these and other groups in exporting regions has resulted in unprecedentedly stringent export controls on both foodstuffs and agricultural inputs that are jeopardizing postwar efforts to liberalize international trade. The impact of soaring food prices, rising malnutrition, and food supply insecurity on political stability is impossible to isolate but doubtless profound. The most skillful diplomatic efforts to create a workable world order will be undermined if the institutions and policies necessary to restore some semblance of stability and security to the food economy are not established.

World food security in the mid-1970s has reached the lowest level in more than two decades,[6] and delegates at the World Food Conference were keenly interested in doing something about this situation. Perhaps the most important of their achievements was the agreement reached on the need for a new approach to global food reserve management. Clearing up the confusion left by a year of contradictory statements by high-level U.S. officials, Secretary of State Kissinger himself proposed the creation of a cooperative system of national reserve policies along the lines of a plan earlier developed by A. H. Boerma, Director-General of the Food and Agriculture Organization (FAO). Under this plan, the responsibility for reserve holding is to be spread among major exporting and importing nations. While nations will retain sovereignty over their own reserve holdings and decisions, national policies will be coordinated through periodic meetings. The Conference resolution on the food reserves set a world reserve target of 60 million tons in addition to the approximately 100 million tons considered necessary as basic "working stocks." Key issues yet to be resolved include the following: a) the appropriate division of reserves among the food importers and the principal exporters, who have traditionally held virtually all reserves; b) the extent to which the poorest countries will be assisted with food and money for participation in the reserve system; and c) the rules under which the reserve stocks can be released. The last of these issues is considered most important by American farming interests, which are fearful that reserves will be used to depress farm prices artificially to an increasingly low level.

It is important to set up the reserve machinery quickly, so that the appropriate level of stocks can be built up as soon as food market conditions ease. The potential extra demand created by an international determination to rebuild reserves also can help reassure farmers that the market will support their all-out production efforts in the next two years even if normal commercial demand slackens due to global recession. (By early 1975, many

---

[6]See Table C-7, p. 244.

American farmers were considering a reduced production effort out of fear that a surplus might drive down prices sharply.)

Closely related to the Conference decision on the reserve question was the agreement on the creation within the FAO of a Global Information and Early Warning System on Food and Agriculture. The purpose of the system would be to regularly monitor crop conditions throughout the world during the growing season and to make this information generally available immediately, so that governments could adjust various agricultural, production, trade, and consumption policies accordingly. Central to the success of this initiative, as well as to that of the new reserve system, is participation by the Soviet Union. The importance of this issue derives in part from the size of the Soviet Union as both a producer and a consumer of food, but even more importantly, from the wide fluctuations which characterize that country's food output. Annual fluctuations in Soviet output due to weather, particularly to drought or harsh winters, can exceed the normal year-to-year increases in world food output. The Soviet Union's refusal to cooperate in this effort would greatly reduce the effectiveness of such a system; indeed, the major food-exporting countries may well find it impossible to provide the Soviet Union with any guarantee of market access if it does not participate in the information-sharing and reserve systems. Unfortunately, China also has not shown a willingness to participate in these systems. The consequences of non-participation by the Chinese are not as serious as those of the Soviet Union's non-participation, since China's international food purchases do not fluctuate so dramatically. But China's participation nevertheless is desirable, since over the past several years it has emerged as one of the world's major grain-importing nations.

The information system is intended to monitor not only agricultural crop conditions but also the nutritional status of various populations. Professor Jean Mayer, a Harvard University nutrition expert who attended the Conference, provided a useful suggestion in this area that deserves serious consideration. Professor Mayer recommended that an effort be made to monitor systematically the nutritional condition of infants among the lowest income groups of individual societies. He argued persuasively that this is the most sensitive single indicator of the point at which societies begin to suffer from severe nutritional stress.

Food Assistance

Although the World Food Conference was originally convened to focus on longer-term efforts to solve the world food problem, the enormous worldwide crop shortfall in 1974 necessarily drew attention to the short-term aspect of the crisis. The question which hung over the Conference was how to make it to the next harvest without a massive human tragedy. Unfortunately, the United States, the one country which *could* have been the most responsive to this question, and which by doing so could have helped set the tone for the entire Conference, was not responsive to the pleas made by the most severely affected countries for an immediate, major new program of food assistance.

The Conference did pass a resolution, with U.S. support, calling for a minimum food aid guarantee of 10 million tons per year beginning in 1975. This would be well below the level of several years ago but above the 1974 level. How the total would be allocated among donors and what role cash donations by the OPEC countries would play in meeting this target were not specified. During the food crisis period of the mid-1960s, the United States alone provided as much as 15 million tons of grain per year in the form of food aid to needy countries.[7] In contrast, at the time of the Conference, the United States was publicly planning only about 3.3 million tons of food aid for the fiscal year 1975—a small fraction of what it had provided in others years of dire need.

The U.S. failure to announce an increase of 2-4 million tons in its 1975 food aid program before or during the World Food Conference was a serious blunder, both in terms of American standing throughout the world and in terms of the welfare of the food-short countries. In the weeks leading up to the Conference, the large size of the deficit confronting a number of countries had become apparent, and television screens around the world were filled with images of the starving. The time was clearly ripe for a major new cooperative international effort to provide relief. While two other aid donors, Canada and the European Community, did announce significant food aid increases, there was a strong sense among donor governments that a new program of the required magnitude would not materialize without strong U.S. leadership, given U.S. dominance of world grain markets. In the months preceding the Conference, many observers perceived an opportunity for putting together an international food aid package involving a total sum and a potential impact far greater than the offers that have gradually trickled out from various capitals—had the United States been willing to pledge a sizable food aid increase in that period. With more creative diplomacy and leadership, it even might have been possible to broaden the package to include action by the OPEC countries to reduce the impact of soaring oil prices in the most severely affected countries.

The United States, however, adopted a piecemeal approach. For several months President Ford refused to announce a food aid target for the year, choosing instead to put the program under periodic review. Meanwhile it became apparent that a high proportion of what food was available—perhaps half the total—would be devoted to overtly political uses in countries such as South Vietnam, Cambodia, Egypt, Syria, and Chile—countries generally experiencing a far less acute need for food than those countries actually facing famine. In response, Congress passed a law limiting food aid for "security"—

---

[7]See Tables C-12 and C-13, p. 250.

as opposed to humanitarian—uses to 30 per cent of the total concessional sales program.

In late January 1975, with only five months remaining in the fiscal year and after Congress had restricted the "security" portion of the program, the administration finally made a public commitment to increase food aid for the year, raising the total to 5.5 million tons of grain at a cost of $1.6 billion. This was a welcome and substantial increase in the program, involving an increase of more than 2 million tons of grain and $600 million in expenditures over the previous year's food aid program.[8] However, by its earlier evasive handling of the issue, the United States missed a major opportunity to exercise constructive world leadership. Furthermore, the late timing of the eventually increased food shipments had damaging practical consequences. Major new shipments did not get under way in time for either of the periods of maximum need—the late autumn of 1974 and the spring of 1975—in the drought- and flood-blighted countries of South Asia. As a consequence, there was a major loss of life in the region, as well as an escalation of physiological and mental damage from severe malnutrition. Less than 20 per cent of the food aid for FY 1975 had been shipped by mid-February, seven and one half months after the start of the fiscal year.

Fertilizer Scarcity

The World Food Conference recognized the acute worldwide shortage of fertilizer and the likelihood that it would persist for at least a few more years. In response to this, the United States delegation sponsored a resolution recommending an effort to temporarily curtail non-essential fertilizer uses, such as the fertilizing of lawns, cemeteries, and golf courses. The U.S. Department of Agriculture reports that non-essential fertilizer use in the United States approaches 15 per cent of total use, which is approximately the amount used on farms in India. Unfortunately, however, no program to implement this idea was set in motion by the U.S. government.

Short supplies and high prices of fertilizer will continue to constrain food output in the developing countries during 1975. The principal obstacle to achieving adequate fertilizer supplies in the poor countries is the financial one. With aggregate global supplies short of the global demand, fertilizer prices have been bid up to record levels; in some countries, the combination of soaring energy, food, and fertilizer prices has depleted foreign exchange reserves, leaving them unable to purchase their fertilizer needs.[9] In addition to the difficulties of procuring supplies internationally, the tripling or quadrupling of fertilizer prices has put great pressure on limited credit

---

[8]See Tables C-12 and C-13, p. 250.
[9]See Tables B-7, p. 228 and B-8, p. 230.

resources in the rural areas of many developing countries, making it even more difficult for the poorest farmers to obtain fertilizer.

Increased international financial aid for fertilizer purchases is one form of assistance needed to help alleviate this situation. For the longer term, there is no alternative to the rapid, worldwide expansion of production at the lowest possible cost. A large number of fertilizer factories are being constructed now throughout the world, and many experts feel that within a few years the problem of shortages will be eliminated. However, the investment needs this implies for the next decade are far from committed at this time.

The shortage of nitrogen fertilizer is particularly serious; at the same time, however, a major opportunity exists to expand nitrogen fertilizer supplies at a relatively low cost. The natural gas now being wastefully flared at oil wellheads in the Middle East and other oil-surplus regions could, if combined with capital and technology, provide vast quantities of nitrogen fertilizer. Nitrogen fertilizer synthesis is a highly complex process, and production in most of the countries with abundant natural gas will not materialize without the technical cooperation and capital equipment of advanced U.S. and European firms. Unfortunately, the large fertilizer-manufacturing companies of the Western world so far have been reluctant to commit themselves to building new plants in the Middle East at the rapid pace required—apparently out of fear that political and economic instability in the region might threaten their investments. Many of the energy-surplus countries, for their part, have not yet shown an urgent interest in investing new capital in nitrogen fertilizer production to supply the soaring needs of the developing countries, which to some do not appear to offer promising commercial markets. A cooperative global effort to combine available raw materials, capital, and technology is required to meet the fertilizer needs of the future.

To alleviate the current crisis, a crash effort is also needed to increase the efficiency of existing nitrogen plants in developing countries, many of which are producing at less than two thirds of their theoretical capacity. This situation has many causes, including unreliable supplies of raw materials and electric power, difficulties of obtaining spare parts and rapid repairs, labor troubles, and many other technical and managerial problems. Increased international efforts to provide technical assistance for plant management and repair could help mitigate the current shortage.

Evaluation of the Conference

Many have asked how successful the World Food Conference was. There are at least two ways of assessing its contribution. First of all, it was enormously useful as a global public education exercise. By providing an opportunity for the media to focus on the food problem, it raised the level of awareness of food-related issues throughout the world and helped to create the climate of public understanding needed to support the major new initiatives and reforms required. More than 1,200 journalists were accredited to the Conference.

A second way to gauge the Conference is in terms of its accomplishments on the institutional and policy sides. A definitive answer to this question cannot yet be given, but the stage was set for progress and institution building in some important areas. Edwin Martin, the coordinator of the U.S. participation in the Conference and now head of the new Consultative Group on Food Production and Investment, has summed up the thinking on this point well:

> It was the first effort to map out a global food strategy. It will take some time to organize and get into operation the follow-up institutions created. . . . It will be especially important also to test what happens if we have 2 or 3 years of good harvest. Will complacency take over? Hence 5 years seems the very earliest point at which it would be fair to conclude that the Conference succeeded or failed.[10]

This disarray in the world food market of the last three years has no parallel in the entire period since the late 1940s and is one important sign of the broader economic and political discontinuities that mark the turn from the third to the final quarter of the twentieth century. The World Food Conference was one of the first major efforts to design the new international institutions demanded by a changing world order. It must now be followed up by strong, far-sighted political leadership—from national governments, from the new World Food Council established at the Conference to oversee progress in meeting the food problem, and from an informed world public that makes enlightened policies good politics.

---

[10]Edwin M. Martin, "Spurring Greater Production," *War on Hunger* (January 1975), p. 16. Published by the Office of Public Affairs, U.S. Agency for International Development.

CHAPTER IV

Trade Initiatives and Resource Bargaining

Guy F. Erb

Traditionally U.S. trade policy has concentrated on relations with the industrialized countries of Western Europe, and more recently also with Japan. The developing countries of Africa, Asia, and Latin America have been at the margin of U.S. trade concerns. The last major international negotiations on trade liberalization—the Kennedy Round of the mid-1960s—brought only limited gains to developing nations, which did not at that time exert much influence on the trading interests of rich countries. But for several years now, developing nations have been challenging the past U.S. approach to its trading relations with them. New products, such as electronic goods and machinery, have been added to the primary products and light manufactures, such as textiles and shoes, that have long been the principal exports of these countries. Indeed, rapidly growing U.S. imports from developing countries have already aroused considerable domestic reaction against further changes in U.S. trade and production patterns to accommodate this inflow.

Although imports of manufactures from developing countries have been rising, primary products (excluding petroleum) still account for over half of all U.S. imports from Africa, Asia, and Latin America. The fluctuations in commodity prices during 1973-74[1] highlighted the instability of the markets for primary products as clearly as they demonstrated the interdependence of developed nations with suppliers of essential commodities. Both producers and consumers have an interest in arrangements that would ensure adequate prices to producers and secure access to supplies for importing nations. Producer nations are demonstrating a strong intent to meet their commodity

---

[1]See Table B-7, p. 228.

trade objectives; their policy decisions and the possibility of an upsurge in demand for commodities—with a consequent recurrence of price rises—mean that the United States can no longer assume that cheap and easy access to unlimited supplies of primary products will automatically be made available through the operation of "market forces."

Thus negotiations on trade policies concerning industrial products, agricultural goods, and raw materials will be necessary to meet the goals of developed countries for a more open trading system and the goals of developing countries for greater—and more secure—access to rich-country markets for their old and new exports. The heavy borrowing by many developing nations in the wake of the fuel and food crises lends greater urgency to their trade needs. More than financial assistance and recycling of oil surpluses[2] will be required to ensure the satisfactory participation of these countries in the international trade and monetary systems. The credit-worthiness of developing nations ultimately rests on their earnings from exports. Consequently, improved access to the import markets of the United States and other rich nations is essential to their participation in financial and monetary systems. Therefore liberalization of tariff and non-tariff barriers to trade and new U.S. policies toward commodity arrangements are two major aims of the international negotiations that are now under way.

However, the recession in industrial countries greatly complicates the task of negotiating trade liberalization and new "rules of the game" for trade policies. U.S. domestic interests—in particular influential labor and industry groups—oppose the reduction of U.S. barriers on the ground that the already weak U.S. economy will be adversely affected by new imports and by further shifts of production overseas. Indeed, most Western industrialized nations face demands that they revert to trade restrictions. This is why policy makers in industrialized nations now have come to view multilateral trade negotiations as a restraint on protectionism and as an essential support for international economic systems. More open U.S. trade policies and a generally constructive stance in the negotiations will depend on strong, full-employment policies at home and effective programs to facilitate adjustment by U.S. workers and firms to economic changes brought about by freer trade.

U.S. trade policy is now poised between increased protectionism and the continued dismantling of trade restrictions that has characterized the last thirty years; it could go either way. The Trade Reform Act of 1974, which is the basis for U.S. negotiations with all countries during the trade talks, empowers the President to protect U.S. domestic interests and to facilitate the adaptation of the economy to trade flows as well as to reduce trade barriers; it contains the authority to liberalize or to protect, to negotiate or to retaliate, to adjust or to resist change. Debate between the domestic interests behind these opposing tendencies is certain to mark the five-year life span of the Trade Reform Act that was signed by President Ford in January 1975.

---

[2]See Chapter V.

Increasing protection for U.S. labor and industry clearly is one trade policy option before the U.S. Administration and Congress. Negotiated compromises seeking to meet the trade and employment requirements of all nations are an alternative option. The focus of the public debate over these issues will be in Congress, which reasserted its trade policy role in its preparation of the Act, and which is actively participating in the domestic and international aspects of U.S. trade policies—including trade negotiations.

The Multilateral Trade Negotiations

The major parties in the negotiations that are now under way in Geneva are the industrialized nations. Indeed, Europe and Japan—which, together with the United States, seek a continuation of the trade liberalization that supported their export drives of the 1960s—waited for the U.S. Congress to approve the U.S. negotiating authority before they began to bargain in February 1975. But the multilateral trade negotiations and related negotiations on arrangements for commodity trade also offer the United States opportunities to set new directions in its policies toward trade with developing nations in both manufactured goods and raw materials.

Since the multilateral trade negotiations formally opened in September 1973, bringing together both members and non-members of the General Agreement on Tariffs and Trade (GATT) for wide-ranging trade talks, the world economy has suffered the shocks of the food and fuel price rises and the economic downturn that now grips most industrialized countries. Thus the meetings that began the actual negotiating phase in early 1973 took place in an atmosphere unfavorable to trade liberalization. The trading interests of all nations depend on the maintenance of a trading system that is strong enough to weather fluctuations in economic output. The negotiations are as important to ensuring the long-run adaptability of trade rules as they are to lowering trade barriers. Consequently the United States needs to look beyond the short-term economic situation in this country as it prepares for these trade negotiations. Any tariff concessions granted by the United States during the negotiations can be staged over ten years. Furthermore, any non-tariff liberalization will be subject to adequate import safeguard provisions as well as to procedures agreed upon within trade policy codes. Protection for U.S. interests will also result from the program of adjustment assistance contained in the Trade Reform Act. It is therefore definitely possible to envisage a positive outcome from the interaction of Congress, officials responsible for formulating U.S. trade policy, and other participants in the negotiations.

U.S. Trade Goals. Now that the U.S. negotiating authority is assured and the multilateral trade negotiations have begun in Geneva, it is possible to assess U.S. trade policy objectives and the means available to achieve them. In line with its own objective of obtaining further tariff reductions, the United States is at present negotiating to reconcile its desire for an across-the-board tariff cut with the European Community's concern that this method might not sufficiently reduce many relatively high U.S. tariff rates while it might deprive the Community of protection in the many cases where its own tariffs are already relatively low.

The United States also seeks to reduce, harmonize, or eliminate non-tariff barriers in the negotiations. Together with other developed nations, it has made some progress in identifying non-tariff barriers that should receive priority attention in the multilateral trade negotiations—notably, product standards, export subsidies, and government procurement practices.

In an area that promises to be one of the most contentious in its negotiations with the European Community, the United States will attempt to negotiate liberalization of trade in agricultural products in conjunction with industrial-sector trade.

Another U.S. objective is the negotiation of an international agreement on the use and surveillance of import safeguards designed to temporarily ease the impact of foreign trade on domestic economies.

Although developed nations dominated the debate of the above issues during the technical preparatory work of the "pre-negotiation" phase of the trade talks, these issues are also of great importance to developing countries. It is important for them, for example, that any tariff-cutting formula should be flexible enough to reduce rich-country duties on individual export items of developing nations. They also maintain that an import-safeguards agreement should not be another form of long-run protection against emerging traders.

The leverage which the developing countries can exert on industrialized nations is still limited, but there are areas where the achievement of U.S. objectives is dependent on negotiations with developing countries. *First*, given U.S. concern about the political-economic implications of "North-South" trade arrangements (such as the one recently signed by the European Community and forty-six developing nations from Africa, the Pacific, and the Caribbean) and about the attempts of raw-material producers to form cooperative groups or cartels, the United States will try to demonstrate that multilateral trade liberalization offers more secure gains than discriminatory or cartelized trade patterns.

Second, like the developing countries, the United States also seeks to reform the GATT. U.S. negotiators have a congressional mandate to seek changes in the GATT to make it reflect better the "balance of economic interests" in the world economy. This objective has generally been interpreted as a desire of the United States to wield more influence within the GATT. But it also could lead to a recognition of the growing trade of developing areas. For example, the developing nations (excluding members of OPEC) account for about one quarter of U.S. exports and imports[3]; in 1974-75, a drop in purchases of U.S. agricultural exports by certain Asian countries prompted a governmental mission to bolster U.S. trade. Thus far U.S. policy makers have been unimpressed by the trade growth achieved by the developing countries or by the capacity of the latter to bargain effectively in the multilateral trade negotiations. But achieving the U.S. goal of revising GATT rules where they are now inadequate and extending them to areas where they are not at present governing trade practices will depend on a broad measure of support for such changes on the part of other national delegations to the GATT, including those from developing nations.

Third, although the pursuit of some of the above goals within the group of industrialized nations will place U.S. policies in conflict with the negotiating aims of many developing countries, the United States nevertheless remains committed to improving the trade prospects of Africa, Asia, and Latin America. To this end, it has agreed, following other developed nations, to implement a generalized system of tariff preferences (or duty-free entry for certain developing-country products) and to negotiate the liberalization of barriers to tropical products and other export items of developing nations.

The Trade Reform Act of 1974. The Act's very significant tariff-cutting authority allows the elimination of tariffs of 5 per cent or less and the reduction of other duties by up to 60 per cent. U.S. non-tariff trade barriers, such as industrial standards and customs procedures, also may be liberalized, subject to congressional approval. This authority, together with the provisions granting tariff preferences to developing nations, could open the U.S. market to more foreign trade.

Although the House and Senate modified the original Administration trade proposals in ways designed to liberalize access to the U.S. market, the alternative of resorting to protection is also present in the legislation—in the eased provisions concerning import relief, the tightening of anti-dumping and countervailing-duty provisions, and in its expectation of private-sector and congressional involvement in the negotiating process. As Senator Long— Chairman of the Finance Committee that prepared the bill for the Senate— stated, the Act "contains hundreds of provisions which provide protection in one respect or another for various segments of American labor and industry."

Congressional involvement in these trade talks will be much more intensive than ever before. Its oversight and review of the negotiations stem from, and will also contribute to, an increased public interest in U.S. foreign economic policies. The domestic implications of trade policy and the congressional views expressed during the debate on trade issues will make it necessary for the Executive Branch to reconcile its negotiating objectives with Congress. This undoubtedly will complicate the U.S. negotiators' tasks in Geneva. Nevertheless, greater public understanding of and participation in foreign economic policy will contribute to the formulation of viable U.S. trade policy commitments by ensuring that support exists for any measures adopted.

Nowhere is the issue of congressional oversight more clearly drawn than in the Act's approach to the reduction or elimination of *non-tariff barriers.* Any U.S. trade agreements that alter American non-tariff restrictions require

---

[3]See Table B-2, p. 222.

affirmative congressional approval. This provision has already caused concern among European and Japanese negotiators who remember the unsuccessful attempts to get congressional approval in the 1960s for liberalization of the "American selling price" regime (which provides significant protection to parts of the U.S. chemical industry); in that case, the fact that no time limit had been specified in existing legislation allowed indefinite postponement of congressional action. However, the present Act calls for a yes or no vote on results of non-tariff barrier negotiations within sixty days of the submission of a trade agreement to Congress. While this procedure strengthens the role of Congress in the negotiations, it also provides U.S. negotiators and other trading nations with the certainty of an early decision as to whether or not the United States will liberalize specific non-tariff barriers.

Negotiating with the Developing Countries. The main objectives of developing countries in the trade negotiations will be: 1) to obtain some modification of the structure of developed-country tariff policies, which at present sharply "escalate" the degree of protection according to the degree of processing of imported commodities—thereby discouraging the growth of processing industries in the developing countries; 2) to ensure that new most-favored-nation tariff concessions—which will tend to erode the benefits of existing preferential tariff systems—are matched by the introduction of improvements in these preferential systems; 3) to gain acceptance by developed countries of the principle that relative underdevelopment justifies special or "differential" treatment in any trade policy codes that are agreed upon during the negotiations; 4) to obtain agreement to negotiating procedures which ensure that developing countries receive a fair share of the benefits from any tariff-cutting formula agreed upon and from non-tariff barrier agreements.

What are the prospects that these goals can be achieved? In spite of the low priority assigned by many U.S. policy makers to trade policies toward developing countries, the manufactured exports of many developing nations give them a place at the negotiating tables as "principal suppliers" of numerous items imported by developed countries. There are other areas as well in which the negotiating strength of developing countries may be enhanced by the fact that some developed countries share the same interests or concerns. To illustrate, U.S. representatives have already emphasized the common interests of North and South American food exporters in lowering European barriers to agricultural trade. Sustaining such a mutual interest would be easier if the United States met some of the trade objectives of the Latin American food exporters in other areas of the negotiations by, for example, offering to liberalize the U.S. market for the manufactured exports of such countries.

Another opportunity for bargaining may arise from the convergence of developed-country concern about reliable and reasonably priced access to the raw materials of developing countries and developing-country concern about easier access to rich-country markets for manufactured exports. Here again conflicts will arise as raw-material exporters seek to reduce barriers to *processed* forms of their main exports. But even allowing for such divergent interests, it should be possible for bargains to be reached across the various sectors of the negotiations, taking account of the issues important to developed- and developing-country negotiators.

The prospective negotiations of course have been greatly complicated by the U.S. reaction to the impact of the price rises by the Organization of Petroleum Exporting Countries and of the embargo imposed by Arab petroleum exporters. The demand pressures, high prices, and scarcity situations that arose in other commodity markets in 1973 also aroused great concern in the United States about American reliance on imported raw materials and the likelihood of coordinated market intervention by the producers of other essential commodities. Largely because of these developments, the Trade Reform Act goes beyond the traditional preoccupations of U.S. trade policy to include specific guidelines and recommendations on access to raw-material supplies. For example, the Act calls for international negotiations on supply access and clearly recognizes that only a process of give-and-take will result in a viable bargain between consumers and raw-material exporters.

These provisions of the legislation leave the way open for the developing countries to attempt to bargain for better market access for their manufactured exports and price stabilization schemes for their primary exports, in exchange for some assurance of developed-country access to supplies of raw materials. But the prospects for such a bargain across economic sectors may be hampered by the Act's authority to penalize nations withholding supplies or raising prices. The strong reaction of the Executive Branch and Congress to the oil-price increases and subsequent events such as Venezuela's announced support for the price of coffee exports of certain Latin American nations, is reflected in the Act's stipulation that the OPEC countries are ineligible for the U.S. tariff preferences. Under the new legislation, members of other producer groups also may be denied the preferences. This retaliatory restriction was both unfortunate (because of its adverse effect on the atmosphere for constructive negotiations with many developing countries) and inappropriate (since tariff preferences are not policy instruments that can significantly influence the actions of petroleum exporters). While the restriction may arouse some second thoughts among the producers of primary products about the wisdom of resorting to future cooperative measures, it is not likely to have much impact, since their long-run interests in adequate earnings from commodity exports will far outweigh the generally small trade losses which might result from denial of tariff preferences.[4]

---

[4]For a discussion of the limitations of the U.S. preference scheme, see Guy F. Erb, "The Developing Countries in the Tokyo Round," in James W. Howe and the staff of the

So far, however, the fact that the preference schemes extended by most developed nations are greatly limited by various protectionist measures has not diminished the insistence of many developing countries on obtaining further non-reciprocal concessions. Developed countries, in particular the United States, regard reciprocal negotiations as the only way to ensure secure and long-term trade concessions. It may well be in the interest of the developing countries not to overemphasize the tariff-preference issue, since the main long-run effects of the negotiations will be found in other areas. Most-favored-nation tariff cuts; liberalization of non-tariff barriers; international agreements on import safeguards, subsidies, and countervailing duties; the reform of the GATT; and possible liberalization of trade in agricultural and tropical products have far more important long-run implications for Africa, Asia, and Latin America than any temporary preferential tariff system. Moreover, insistence by developing countries on non-reciprocal gains from the negotiations might cause the developed countries to turn "inward." Limited groups of "key" nations might very well opt to negotiate almost exclusively among themselves, leaving only minimal preferential gains for poor nations.

To minimize the possibility of such key-country groupings, negotiation of mutually acceptable concessions is preferable to insistence by developing countries on non-reciprocal benefits from the trade talks. But U.S. negotiators must recognize that the developing countries seek more favorable treatment from industrialized countries than the latter accord one another because of the vast gap between the economic situations of rich and poor nations. In the mandate for the multilateral trade negotiations (the Declaration of Tokyo), developed countries did agree to provide "differential" measures to developing countries which would give them ". . . special and more favorable treatment in the sectors of the negotiations where this is possible and appropriate." This wording clearly leaves much room for disagreement between developed and developing countries as to when differential treatment is "possible and appropriate." Notwithstanding the formal acceptance of differential treatment for developing nations by the industrialized countries, problems remain in the interpretation and application of this principle during the negotiations. U.S. responses in this area will be facilitated by Section 102(f) of the Trade Reform Act, which permits U.S. participation in non-tariff barrier agreements that differentiate between the rights and obligations of developed and developing nations.[5]

By placing both requests and offers on the negotiating table, the developing countries would both strengthen their position vis-a-vis developed na-

---

Overseas Development Council, *The U.S. and The Developing World: Agenda for Action, 1974,* published for the Overseas Development Council (New York: Praeger Publishers, Inc., 1974), pp. 89-90.

[5]Committee on Finance, U.S. Senate, *Trade Reform Act of 1974,* Senate Report No. 93-1298, November 20, 1974, p. 77.

tions and enhance the possibility of mutually beneficial bargains. Their concessions might include: simplifying their import formalities and customs procedures; binding (freezing) existing tariff levels; participating in codes for trade policies (e.g., codes on standards or subsidies), including acceptance of obligations—possibly less stringent ones than those applied to developed countries under such codes; participating in commodity arrangements involving multilateral purchase and supply contracts or other forms of assuring consumer countries of reliable access to raw-material supplies; setting fixed limits on export taxes applied to raw-material exports, or on the relationship between taxes on a raw material in its crude and processed forms; and either immediate tariff cuts (where protection levels are unnecessarily high and cutting is feasible) or the staging over a five-to ten-year period of those concessions which would significantly reduce the protection offered domestic supplies.

The possibility of negotiating on trade in industrial goods on a *reciprocal* basis is an option available to only the more advanced developing countries. Moreover, obtaining access to markets in return for the supply of primary commodities is possible only for those supplying countries which control a significant proportion of world trade in certain commodities. For the poorest of the developing nations, those which cannot bring significant "cards" to the negotiating table, trade concessions should be made available during the negotiations without insistence on reciprocity. Certain other nations in Asia, Africa, and Latin America could provide limited reciprocity to qualify for trade gains from the negotiations. Clearly the larger and more advanced developing countries will have to face up to their strengthened position in the world economy and accept the responsibility of negotiating on a reciprocal basis—even if they do not accept the obligations of fully developed countries. The United States and other developed countries should adopt an imaginative and positive approach to this issue. Forms of reciprocity and differential treatment acceptable to all parties, including the U.S. Congress, must be sought and applied during the negotiations.

Trade Codes. Agreements on codes governing the use and surveillance of certain trade barriers will be an important part of the negotiations. There is a danger that such codes will be limited to major industrial countries—the "key" nations—and will pay inadequate attention to the trade strengths and aspirations of relatively new major exporters—for example, Singapore, Korea, Brazil, and Mexico. There is indeed a very real possibility that industrialized countries might establish codes for use of certain trade policy instruments to protect their economies from the expanding export capacity of developing nations.

Several trade policy codes have already been drafted within the GATT. For the most part, developing countries did not participate actively in the formulation of these draft codes and may well object to certain of their provisions. Some developing countries have already presented suggested modifications of these codes. Consequently, initial skirmishes have taken place on, for example, the issue of differential treatment for developing countries in the determination of permissible export subsidies. The United States has called for as rapid an advance as possible on those codes on which considerable progress already has been made. The intent apparently is to bring forth specific agreements during the process of negotiating instead of attempting to tie together a total package of concessions, agreements, and liberalization at the end of the negotiations. While this is probably a wise objective—given the difficulty of maintaining momentum in trade negotiations that continue over a long period—it should not be pursued at the expense of hearing out the objections of developing countries to specific aspects of trade-policy codes. In most cases, viable codes cannot be prepared without providing for the widest possible participation. If large numbers of trading nations were left outside the scope of such agreements, economic conflicts between members and non-members would be frequent and in all probability disruptive of the aims of the code.

U.S. Adjustment to Trade. The long-term adjustment of the American economy to changes in world production and trade will hinge upon the U.S. capacity for adapting domestic production to economic growth in foreign countries. Both the House and the Senate introduced significant improvements to the Administration's initial proposals for adjustment assistance to workers and firms severely affected by imports. The result of the congressional changes is a complex and lengthy set of adjustment assistance measures that could provide significant help to workers, firms, and communities; about $300 million in federal funds will be allocated to this program in fiscal year 1976.

Under the adjustment assistance program, a worker can receive 70 per cent of his or her average weekly wage for one year (or longer if the individual needs time to complete training or is over sixty years of age). In addition to federal or state assistance for retraining, workers affected by imports may receive assistance in their search for new jobs or help in relocation. A firm in difficulty because of imports may, if it does not have access to private capital markets, receive technical and financial help under the adjustment assistance provisions of the Trade Reform Act. Communities that are adversely affected by imports may seek both assistance under the provisions of the Public Works and Economic Development Act of 1965 and loan guarantees for working capital or for constructing or modernizing productive facilities.

Before passage of the Trade Reform Act, much of the U.S. labor movement opposed the adjustment assistance provisions as being inadequate. Many saw quantitative restraints or increased tariffs as the only satisfactory response to rising U.S. imports. The Act does make it easier to resort to import-restraint measures; yet there is an important gap in these provisions. Although they are fixed for five years (subject to a three-year extension) and will also phase out over time, they are not linked to long-run domestic adjustment. Such a link between import relief and adjustment assistance, although not favored by most developed countries, should be part of an adequate U.S. response to shifts in world trade and investment. It remains to be seen whether the assistance provided under the Act will meet the demands of labor and other U.S. economic interests. If it does not, a major, long-run conflict will prevail between those interests and the trading aims of other nations.

Policy Recommendations. The overall objective of the United States in the multilateral trade negotiations should include the more effective participation of developing countries in the world economy through a reduction in the trade barriers that now place their exports at a disadvantage in the markets of industrialized countries. This general objective serves the interests of the U.S. economy, in particular American consumers, and will also support U.S. goals for multilateral economic systems. It should be sought through such specific steps as the following.

The retaliatory restriction denying U.S. tariff preferences to OPEC—and potentially to other groups as well—should be deleted, altered, or interpreted so that it does not pose an obstacle to fruitful negotiations with developing nations, particularly those of Latin America.

U.S. policies to attain its own trading objectives with the developed world should include acceptance of significant differential treatment for developing countries as regards their concessions and obligations under trade liberalization procedures and trade policy codes.

As experience is obtained in the operation of the new adjustment assistance program, it may be necessary to improve the benefits to American workers, firms, and communities. The Administration should be ready, if necessary, to enlarge the funds available for adjustment assistance or to amend the Trade Reform Act to improve benefits from adjustment assistance programs.

Commodity Policy

The adverse effects of commodity-price fluctuations are not new to international policy makers. Over thirty years ago J. M. Keynes wrote in an official memorandum that, under conditions of wide price fluctuations, "an orderly program of output, either of the raw materials themselves or of their manufactured products, is not possible." "The whole world," he observed, "is now conscious of the grave consequences of this defect in the international competitive system."[6]

Yet no lasting solutions to commodity-trade problems have been achieved since those words were written in 1942. In the past, the United States has relied on "market forces to provide it with imports of raw materials,

---

[6]J. M. Keynes, "The International Control of Raw Materials," reprinted in *Journal of International Economics* 4 (August 1974), pp. 299-315.

although from time to time it also has participated in commodity arrangements. The developing countries do not, however, see "market forces" as abstract and benevolent mechanisms for the global distribution of financial resources and production, and they have begun to ask forcefully: Whose market forces are at work, and for whom?

Although reliance on commodity markets in the past may have seemed to serve U.S. purposes, the free market has been found wanting by many other producer countries whose export receipts have fluctuated widely and whose overall earnings have remained at unsatisfactory levels. During the 1973-74 "commodity boom," the prices of many commodities exported by developing-world producers rose markedly. Since then, however, commodity prices—notably those of industrial raw materials—have fallen drastically.[7] For example, both copper and rubber are now close to being produced at a marginal loss in some producing countries. Rubber, which provides the means of subsistence for some twenty-five million people, has dropped in price by about 30 per cent in the past year. By the first week of December 1974, the price of copper on the London Metal Exchange had fallen 59 per cent from its April high, gravely affecting the four main exporters: Chile, Peru, Zambia, and Zaire.

The trade and production of several commodities is controlled by a few large firms. This "vertical integration" has resulted in a narrowing of the range of price fluctuations or in regular upward adjustments in prices. To illustrate, the price of nickel is largely set by a few multinational corporations according to the costs of production. Thus the nickel price increased—by 12 per cent between April 1974 and early 1975—in spite of the recession. The divergent experience of managed and other commodity markets cannot escape the notice of the exporters of primary products.

Developing countries' persistent interest in commodity arrangements stems from the fact that although their exports of manufactured goods have been increasing rapidly, trade in raw materials still represents the most significant source of foreign exchange for most developing nations. As a whole they still rely on exports of raw materials for 75-80 per cent of their total export earnings.

Recent downward fluctuations in the prices of primary commodities seem to have diminished developed-country interest in formulating cooperative measures to govern commodity trade, but they have caused renewed interest and concern in developing nations. Prices of some industrial raw materials (especially those traded on the world's free markets, such as base metals, cotton, rubber, and fibers) have collapsed. The prices of commodities other than petroleum have declined by 50 per cent since last year. The export earnings of non-oil-producing developing nations probably

---

[7]See Table B-7, p. 228.

will fall by about $8 billion in 1975 as a result of the decrease in commodity prices and the declining volume of purchases due to industrial recession.

Thus the terms of trade, as compared to a few years ago, have shifted back in favor of manufactures, and consequently the purchasing power of the earnings of raw-material exporters of goods other than oil and grain—that is, the earnings of *most* developing countries—has been hit particularly hard. Developing nations regard both the fluctuations in their earnings and the deterioration of the purchasing power of their exports as serious obstacles to their economic growth. To better comprehend their point of view, we need only recall the outrage of many Americans when they perceived the loss this country suffered because of the sale of wheat at low prices to the Soviet Union in 1972.

U.S. Commodity Objectives. In the past, international trade negotiations within the GATT have traditionally focused on tariff barriers and on trade among industrialized nations, but events in commodity markets have provoked a change in that approach. The United States and the European Community now advocate the inclusion of commodity policy issues in the multilateral trade negotiations. A code on use of export controls, guidelines for commodity arrangements, and the negotiation of arrangements for specific commodities could therefore be the subjects of negotiations. Within the United Nations Conference on Trade and Development (UNCTAD), moreover, developed as well as developing countries are now examining possible new approaches to commodity trade.

In opposition to the traditional lukewarm U.S. attitudes toward commodity agreements, some policy makers now perceive that achievements of American commodity goals require an adaptation to new trade realities. In April 1974, at the U.N. General Assembly's Special Session on raw materials and development, Secretary of State Kissinger stated that "the optimum price is one that can be maintained over the longest period at the level that assures the highest real income. Only through cooperation between consumers and producers can such a price be determined."

The U.S. policy on primary commodities is to ensure *adequate, continuous,* and *reasonably priced* access to foreign supplies. These goals were threatened by the commodity boom of 1973; the April statement by Secretary Kissinger was in good part a reaction to the challenge posed to U.S. policies by rising commodity prices. In 1974, however, commodity prices tumbled, easing the pressure on the United States and other industrialized consumers to adapt to producer aims, and at the same time weakening the attempts of producer countries to obtain the rapid introduction of new commodity policies in industrialized countries.

At least two factors justify a reexamination of U.S. commodity policies at this time. The *first* consideration is the possibility that expansionary policies may bring all of the more industrialized countries out of their present slump at about the same time, leading to a recurrence of strong demand and a resulting upward pressure on commodity prices. Although the economic slowdown in industrialized countries that has followed their nearly simultaneous economic expansion in the early 1970s has brought a downturn in commodity prices, the problem of price instability will undoubtedly reemerge. The *second* consideration is the U.S. need to respond to the current series of developing-country initiatives in dealing with their problems in the present commodity slump. The developing countries have recently demonstrated considerable political cohesion and a willingness to cooperate in producer groupings. Some of their efforts may receive financial support from oil producers. Indications of developing-country cooperation are evidenced by the following developments among others:

(a) The recent meeting on raw materials, held in Dakar, Senegal, where one hundred non-aligned nations supported the recovery of full control over their natural resources and also drew up a plan to maintain the prices of primary-product exports;
(b) The participation of many countries in producer groups for bananas, bauxite, cocoa, coconuts, coffee, copper, iron ore, mercury, pepper, rubber, and sugar;
(c) The March 1975 OPEC summit conference, which, while stopping short of a commitment to provide immediate financial support for developing-country commodity aims, did insist on discussion of raw-material questions during the conference with consumers.

International Commodity Proposals. In the past, the negotiation of price-stabilization agreements for specific commodities has been the major form of international response to commodity problems. The limited effectiveness of this approach is a partial explanation of the current lack of enthusiasm in developed countries about the possibilities of international cooperation on commodities. However, several approaches to commodity policy are possible: the negotiation of specific arrangements, such as the one which previously governed coffee trade; the establishment of new agreements within the multilateral trade negotiations or in conferences that are related to those trade talks; the formulation of codes on such issues as export controls or trade agreement guidelines within the multilateral trade negotiations; the negotiation, by groups of developing countries, of mutually supportive arrangements for exchanges of marketing and investment information; and, finally, negotiations on one or more aspects of the commodity proposals now under study within UNCTAD.

The UNCTAD proposals include the following main points:

1. International stocks of certain commodities might be established to assure importing countries of adequate supplies and to help restrain excessive price movements. The manager of the stock would buy the commodities when prices fell and sell them when prices rose. To find such stocks, a financial

reserve could be established on the basis of loans from individual countries and international financial organizations. OPEC members as well as developed consuming nations might contribute to stock financing arrangements. The critical aspect of the funding of international stocks is the problem of ensuring an adequate return on the operation of the stock. Without such a prospect, it is doubtful that contributions from oil exporters would be forthcoming. One way around this difficulty would be to assign the management of buffer-stock financing to the International Monetary Fund, which already has a facility to assist nations forming buffer stocks and which has also successfully attracted significant inflows from OPEC members. An alternative source of financing—already used successfully by coffee and cocoa producers—might be a levy on production or exports applied by producers themselves.

2. Another form of intervention in commodity markets might be multilateral contracts for a number of commodities. The purpose of these contracts would be to ensure suppliers of a market and purchasers of adequate supplies within an agreed price range. Thus an importing country would commit itself to purchasing a certain quantity of the commodity in question and the suppliers would in turn undertake to supply at least that amount.

3. Loans to assist primary-product exporters in bridging the gap caused by shortfalls in their export earnings long have been undertaken by the International Monetary Fund, which is now considering improvements in its Compensatory Financing Facility. Other compensatory arrangements might also be required if the operation of buffer stocks or multilateral contracts were unable to secure adequate price and production relationships.

While the above proposals aim at stabilizing commodity prices at satisfactory levels, they fall short of directly linking commodity prices to those of industrial goods. Such an approach has been advocated by the oil producers, who have called for the indexation of the prices of their commodities and those of manufactured goods. Their proposals would establish an automatic link between the unit prices of exports from developing countries and the unit prices of their imports of manufactured goods from industrialized countries. A precedent of indexation is provided by the Commonwealth Sugar Agreement's price guarantee systems. The prices under the Commonwealth Sugar Agreement (CSA) were negotiated to cover three years at a time. The pricing scheme was related not to the import prices of the sugar exporters, but rather to reasonable returns to efficient producers. It thus kept the prices of participating producers above levels prevailing outside the U.S. quota system and the CSA system. Another example of an indexation scheme is provided by the parity system that is applied within the United States to maintain the purchasing power of U.S. farmers.

Serious objections have been raised against indexation on the grounds that it would "institutionalize inflation." The complexity of administering an international scheme of this nature also is a serious obstacle. To guarantee prices based on a link to an index of prices for exported manufactured goods, the developed countries would have to regulate import trade (with the risk that the increased degree of regulation might be used to the disadvantage of developing countries). Agreement would have to be established on which manufactured goods would be included in the index as well as on the levels of prices of primary products relative to manufactured goods to be guaranteed under the scheme. Nevertheless, the United States is considering floor-price proposals and indexation in the case of petroleum, as part of its search for a means of ensuring development of alternative sources of energy as well as adequate inflows of foreign petroleum until alternate energy sources are fully available.

Although implementation of some of the above proposals would present novel challenges, experience has already been gained with some types of commodity arrangements. Thus the tin buffer stock offers an example of an international stock arrangement that has functioned adequately for twenty years. The International Wheat Arrangement included systems of multilateral contracts, and the operation of the IMF's Compensatory Financing and Buffer Stock facilities illustrates some of the issues in financing arrangements related to commodity trade.

Future international actions in the commodity area are also likely to be influenced by the example of an initiative recently taken by the European Community, which drew up a trade and aid pact with forty-six developing countries from Africa, the Pacific, and the Caribbean.[8] An important component of this agreement is a program of export-revenue stabilization to compensate primary-product exporters when falling prices reduce their export earnings. Under this arrangement, the Community will compensate raw-material exporters when falling prices reduce their export receipts. Products to be included in the compensation scheme include cocoa, timber products, cotton, tea, raw sisal, and iron ore. The approximately $450 million that has been set aside for the scheme can provide up to nearly $110 million per year for the beneficiaries. The amounts transferred will not bear interest, and recipient countries are to decide on their own how to utilize the funds received. While the "poorest" beneficiaries are not required to reimburse the fund, other countries are expected to repay if their export earnings recover.

Negotiating Commodity Arrangements. The case for official intervention in commodity markets rests on the assumption that cooperation among traders and governments can result in greater price stability, adequate earnings for producers, and security of access for consumers. But intervention schemes have been hampered in the past by the complexity of commodity markets which involve relationships among buyers, sellers, and speculators. Other difficulties encountered with commodity agreements and other types of

---

[8]Of these forty-six nations, twenty are in the group of the "least developed" and "most seriously affected" countries discussed in Chapter I.

commodity arrangements in the past include the following: favorable prices may encourage excess production, and the consequent accumulation of stocks may make it necessary to impose production controls; inadequate stocks in years of production shortfalls may cause prices to break through the agreed maximum price levels; setting prices within a fixed range reduces the degree of assurance that long-term export earnings of producers will keep up with world inflation; all consumers, including poor nations, bear the additional costs of primary commodities when prices are supported.

The solution of these and other problems would require flexible administration of any commodity arrangements and, consequently, a willingness to compromise on the part of both producers and consumers on such issues as price ranges and their modification, sharing the burden of financing stocks, and use and surveillance of production controls.

Given that the United States seeks three main objectives—adequate, continuous, and reasonably priced access to commodities—what measures must it consider to achieve these goals? Dealing with the new attitudes among raw-material suppliers is the first step toward meeting U.S. commodity objectives. Taking that step will depend on the abandonment by the United States of its visceral reaction against producer-country cooperation. Too often, the hostile reactions toward producer groupings appear to be based on the premise that cooperation among producing and exporting countries is prejudicial to U.S. interests. This is not so, since the main objective of such groupings is more likely to be collective bargaining than confrontation with industrialized countries.

For the developing countries, collaboration among themselves is an essential contribution to strengthening their bargaining power vis-a-vis the industrialized countries and large corporations. Their cooperation includes exchange of information on prices, contractual arrangements for investments and sales transactions, and market information. Among the developing countries there are of course advocates of strong cartel action as well as of more limited producer-country cooperation, but duplicating the oil-exporters' action is not a likely outcome for most other raw-material exporters. Whatever the technique, however, all producers share the objective of increasing their capacity to obtain greater returns from the production, processing, and export of primary commodities. The interest of Australia, for example, in cooperation with other bauxite and iron-ore producers, suggests that the industrialized countries will find that even countries once considered as "safe" sources of raw-material supplies will engage in cooperation with producers to ensure satisfactory earnings from their resource exports.

The U.S. Congress pointed the way toward a flexible approach to producer-country cooperation in Sections 106 and 108 of the Trade Reform Act. Section 108 sets as a "principal United States negotiating objective" the establishment of trade agreements to assure the United States of "fair and equitable access to reasonable prices" to supplies. To achieve such agreements, the Congress called "for reciprocal concessions or comparable trade obligations, or both, by the United States"—clearly foreseeing a bargain between raw-material producers and consumers on a multilateral basis, if possible.

At the same time, however, Sections 106 and 108 of the Act raise an alternative possibility, namely bilateral accords on resources between the United States and individual developing countries. As attractive as such agreements may seem under certain conditions, they would give a "divide and rule" tone to U.S. policies and might only serve to coalesce groups of producer countries around their opposition to such tactics. A further drawback of such bilateral arrangements is their adverse impact on consumer-country cooperation as industrialized nations try to safeguard their interests without taking adequate account of the concerns of their allies.

Commodity Policy Recommendations. Traditional U.S. objections to commodity arrangements—or, for that matter, interagency wrangling within the Executive Branch about an appropriate commodity policy—should not impede a positive and imaginative look at possible solutions to problems of commodity trade.

A constructive contribution by the United States to the multilateral formulation and management of new arrangements is now necessary. Any revival of a U.S. stockpiling policy, for example, should be undertaken by responding to multilateral guidelines within an international framework rather than by attempting to influence commodity markets unilaterally should prices rise in future. Moreover, consideration of international buffer-stock negotiations should include the possibility of funding buffer stocks through the International Monetary Fund.

Policy coordination within groups of producer nations is not an obstacle to effective commodity arrangements but rather a *prerequisite* of viable arrangements involving consumers as well. Consequently, the United States should actively seek negotiations with such groupings instead of resisting their joint actions. The United States should act on the authority of the Trade Reform Act, meeting producers halfway in an attempt to agree on new forms of international management of commodity trade.

There is a risk that ambitious commodity proposals will meet with such complex institutional obstacles and substantive delays that no progress will be achieved. But the choice before the United States and other nations is not "all or nothing." Movement on one or more of the various commodity proposals should be made within the next twelve to eighteen months, starting, for example, with international buffer-stock proposals and intensive work on one or two commodities for which arrangements are ready for negotiation. At the same time, work could continue on other aspects of commodity policy. Certainly it is in the interest of the United States to move beyond its present position of mere willingness to examine proposals "with an open mind."

CHAPTER V

Petrodollars and Multilateral Development Financing

Guy F. Erb

High rates of inflation, declining economic growth in both rich and poor nations, and serious balance-of-payments problems are the main economic issues of 1975. These difficulties are the results of stagnation in industrialized economies, which dates from the second half of 1973—and from the 1973-74 increases in petroleum and food prices.[1] In the United States, the domestic problems of high unemployment and the choice of policies to restore dynamism in the economy are rightly receiving top priority. At the same time, however, the *international* factors which affect the U.S. economy—including approaches to trade, monetary, and investment issues require urgent attention.

The United States appears to be taking for granted multilateral institutions and economic systems that evolved slowly in the post-World War II period. The environment for international cooperation is the result of many policy decisions, some of which may be of little importance if taken individually. At the present time—when an unsettled international monetary system, widespread recession, changing relationships between rich and poor nations, and the petrodollar crisis threaten the world's economy—the cumulative effect of decisions of this kind is especially important.

The recent multilateral initiatives designed to overcome short-run balance-of-payments problems due to the oil price rises are in this category of decisions. Thus, for example, the industrialized nations have acted quickly to create mechanisms to deal with their own energy and financial needs. Other proposals in this area that should be helpful to developing countries are

---

[1] See Table B-7, p. 228.

encountering obstacles or are still under study. The implementation of these proposals depends on decisions by developed countries to commit resources as well as on negotiated compromises among themselves, the oil-exporting countries, and prospective recipient countries. If these negotiations fail, the framework for multilateral cooperation in this and other areas will be greatly weakened.

Maintaining a cooperative approach toward trade with other industrialized nations is no easy process, but frequently the shared interests of developed countries can be relied upon to prevail over narrow national interests. It is even more difficult to shape such an approach toward developing countries, since their interests and perceptions often differ widely from those of developed countries, and since their leverage over world economic systems is still limited. However, the leverage of these countries is growing and is already dramatic in the case of petroleum exporters. An adequate U.S. approach to the maintenance of multilateral systems must therefore implement policy decisions which recognize the changing role in the world economy of the countries of Africa, Asia, and Latin America. Without such an approach, the United States will see piecemeal erosion of its influence within the very multilateral systems it helped to create.

The Petrodollar Crisis

The oil embargo of 1973 and subsequent price increases added to the economic woes of industrialized and developing nations and disrupted established patterns of international relations. The rise in petroleum prices increased the export earnings of members of the Organization of Petroleum Exporting Countries (OPEC) by over $80 billion in 1974. After their 1974 expenditures of over $50 billion on imported goods and services, these countries retained a current-account surplus estimated at $50 billion. A similar surplus is expected during 1975. Over the long run, this current-account imbalance between oil exporters and importers can be reduced or eliminated by trimming the growth in demand for OPEC oil as alternative sources of oil become available. Long-term balance also involves finding substitutes for oil, lowering oil consumption, increasing the demand for imports in the petroleum-exporting countries, and encouraging long-term investment by the oil exporters in the oil-importing nations. At the moment, however, huge surpluses are still being accumulated by the oil exporters, even though the recession and a consequent decline in demand for oil are holding down the imbalance.

The existence and growth of these surpluses is a key issue confronting international economic policy makers for two reasons. First, the oil exporters' long-term investments, purchases of imports, and short-term placements of funds do not match the current-account deficits of individual oil-importing countries; the surplus earnings of oil exporters have to be transferred, or "recycled," to the oil-importing countries with inadequate foreign exchange to pay for their petroleum imports. Second, the size of the financial holdings of oil exporters has altered political-economic relationships between a major part of the developing world and the industrialized nations.

Recycling. Thus far, the United States has received a large proportion of the oil exporters' total surplus. But there are many other countries, both developed and developing, with urgent needs for financial support. The interrelationships between the United States and these nations make it impossible to shield the U.S. economy entirely from the deflationary impact of declines in foreign economic activity. The impact of events in other industrial countries is particularly important for the United States, but a widespread economic recession in the countries of Africa, Asia, and Latin America also could have significant repercussions on its economy. Failure to reallocate financial resources to enable individual nations to meet their oil import requirements is likely to lead to restrictions on non-oil imports. Such measures are under discussion in the United Kingdom and already have been applied in several developing countries in response to soaring import bills. Other possible developing-country reactions to their balance-of-payments disequilibrium with serious portent for the developed world include foreign-exchange restrictions, exchange-rate changes, and demands for the renegotiation of external debt.

Power and Income. A second key problem raised by the petrodollar surpluses for U.S. policy makers is that international power relationships have been upset as a result of the rise in OPEC influence and the impact of oil price increases on living standards in rich countries. Talk of military intervention has resulted from these perceptions of power loss. Certainly OPEC action did cause a significant shift in international power relationships and introduced many political-economic uncertainties. But the fact that development and growth in the Southern hemisphere are bringing about changes in the world economy needs to be faced by developed-country policy makers. Resort to threats of military intervention or economic reprisals is less a sign of U.S. strength than an indication that more constructive approaches may be precluded by the U.S. neglect of possible multilateral solutions.

The other factor confronting U.S. decision makers—the loss of income resulting from the oil price rise—must be evaluated in the light of domestic economic policies in industrialized economies. In oil-consuming countries, the oil price increase had the effect of a significant rise in indirect taxation. It transferred funds from oil consumers to oil exporters and thus added to the recessionary pressures that were already gathering force in industrialized countries. The oil price rise was not, however, the major cause of the recession. One estimate put the maximum one-time income loss of OECD countries due to high prices for oil and other commodities at 2 per cent—an amount comparable to about six months' income growth (at moderate rates) in these countries.[2] This amount appears relatively modest in comparison with the recessionary impact of the restrictive fiscal and monetary policies followed by most industrialized countries since mid-1973. In response to these policies, the growth of the combined real gross national product of six OECD countries—Canada, France, Germany, Italy, Japan, and the United Kingdom—declined at an annual rate of 0.5 per cent from the second half of 1973 to the first half of 1974. This contrasts with their 9.5 per cent annual growth rate for the first half of 1973.[3] In the United States, the downturn in domestic demand began in the second half of 1973 and the downturn in GNP in the third quarter of that year—before the large oil price rises occurred. The embargo—which began at that time—had only a limited impact on U.S. economic activity.

Recycling Policies

During early 1974, it was by no means evident that the deficit of the oil-importing countries could be successfully absorbed by the world economy. Cassandra-like predictions of international financial collapse abounded. By early 1975, however, it was apparent that private banks and official mechanisms had surmounted the first year's difficulties satisfactorily. One third of the oil deficit in 1974 was financed directly by the oil-exporting countries. More than half of the overall oil deficit was financed directly or indirectly by the international operations of private banks. Thus the private sector received a large share of the inflow from the oil-exporting countries.

By mid-1974, the strains placed on the private banks by the size of the recycling operation, together with gaps in the distribution of funds, led to a decision by the Executive Directors of the IMF to set up an official recycling facility. Borrowing directly from the oil-exporting countries, the IMF reduced some of the problems created for the private banking system by the necessity of handling very large OPEC-country deposits with short maturities. The Fund siphoned off some of these surpluses into its new Oil Facility, and provided a source of supplementary funds for nations lacking ready access to capital markets, thus contributing to the restoration of confidence within banking and financial circles.

Both developed and developing countries were eligible for drawings under the Oil Facility, and the latter had received some $2 billion from this Facility as of February 1975. This assistance relieved the difficulties of numerous countries. The strong external position of many other developing countries eased their adjustment during 1974 to the oil price rise. During 1973 and part of 1974, developing countries benefitted from an upsurge of commodity prices and a consequent buildup of their foreign exchange

---

[2]Hollis B. Chenery, "Restructuring the World Economy," *Foreign Affairs,* Vol. 53, No. 2 (January 1975), pp. 246-7.

[3]"Inflation and Stagnation in Major Industrial Countries," *Federal Reserve Bulletin* (October 1974), pp. 683-4.

reserves. In addition, some were able to draw upon private capital markets, and others received about $2.5 billion in direct financial support from oil-exporting countries.[4] International organizations and bilateral assistance programs also provided significant transfers of resources. Nevertheless, the total current-account deficit of developing countries in 1974 was three times that of 1972—over $20 billion—and it is expected to rise to over $30 billion in 1975.

Meeting that deficit calls for major private and official transfers. The allocation of funds to individual poor countries is as critical an issue as the total transfer itself. Given the world recession, the prospects for 1975 and 1976 are unfavorable compared to those that many developing nations faced in 1973 and 1974. The reserves of these countries are now being drawn down, and in some cases the full impact of the oil price increase is just being felt. Developed countries also face major economic and balance-of-payments problems in the years immediately ahead. For these reasons, by late 1974, industrialized nations were calling for two additional inter-governmental measures to complement the recycling operations of private capital markets: the first was the "safety net" proposal of U.S. Secretary of State Kissinger and Secretary of the Treasury Simon for an OECD-based system of financial support; the second, which came from the European Community, advocated expansion of the IMF's Oil Facility. Negotiations in January 1975 resulted in the adoption of modified versions of both these suggestions.

The "Safety Net." The Kissinger/Simon proposal for channeling funds to developed countries in balance-of-payments difficulties is designed primarily to help an economically viable, politically cooperative Western alliance to manage its oil deficits. Together with the developed-nation International Energy Agency, the "safety net" is intended to be an element in the emerging contest between OPEC and the OECD over the international power and influence which the oil exporters will wield in the future.

The Finance Ministers of the Group of Ten major industrialized countries agreed to make available the "solidarity fund" to members of the OECD as a lender of last resort for a period of two years. All participants will contribute to the fund according to quotas which will also determine the borrowing rights of each country seeking to finance serious balance-of-payments difficulties. The total of all participants' quotas will be about $25 billion. When the United States made the original proposal for such a "safety net," it also suggested a separate fund for assistance to developing countries, but the current agreement makes no direct provisions for the needs of countries outside the OECD.

The IMF Oil Facility and Subsidy Account. The compromise within the OECD countries also resulted in an enlargement of the IMF's Oil Facility for 1975, although the amount was less than that originally advocated by the IMF

---

[4]See Chapter VII.

Managing Director and the European Community. The target figure for borrowing from oil-exporting countries—which had been set at 3 billion IMF special drawing rights (SDRs) during the Facility's initial phase—was raised to 5 billion SDRs, or over $6 billion.[5] In addition to seeking contributions from OPEC members, the Fund hopes to tap the resources of non-oil-exporting members who are in strong reserve and payments positions. The conditions governing the loans made by the Facility are to be less stringent than normal IMF transactions because of the unusual circumstances generated by the oil price increases. Furthermore, according to a precedent-setting decision by the Interim Committee on the International Monetary System, the IMF is establishing a special account, which will be used to subsidize interest payments on the Oil Facility drawings of the most seriously affected countries. The subsidy account will be established with contributions from oil-exporting countries and industrial countries, as well as from other Fund members in a position to contribute. Should contributions fall short of the amounts necessary to provide an adequate interest subsidy, the sale of small amounts of IMF gold holdings could be used to add to the subsidy account.

Oil and Development Financing

The oil price rises had particularly severe effects on developing countries. Long-run balance-of-payments problems made it nearly impossible for many of these countries to meet their current needs without outside support. Yet they could not repay short-term credits without adding further strains to their already overburdened economies. Consequently, the IMF, the World Bank, and the IMF/World Bank Joint Ministerial Committee on the Transfer of Resources to Developing Countries (the Development Committee) are considering other proposals for concessional transfers of resources to developing nations. The suggested mechanisms are intended to complement the operation of the Oil Facility and subsidy account by providing funds on longer terms than those available from the IMF, but, if introduced, will only be operational about the time the Oil Facility closes its doors. The first proposal is a trust fund that would provide loans to the poorest countries for periods of up to ten years. The second is a proposal that the World Bank open a third lending window whose resources would be lent at terms softer than current bank lending, but harder than the interest-free credits available from the International Development Association (IDA). In addition to these official measures private financial mechanisms also have been suggested.

The Trust Fund Proposal. Originally proposed by the United States, the new trust fund would be based on two sources of finance: voluntary contributions from oil-exporting nations and other countries in a position to

---

[5]At this writing, SDR 1.00 = $1.22.

contribute and sales of gold held by the IMF. Revaluation of the price of gold has brought the IMF a large windfall gain; its gold holdings now are worth about $30 billion. Thus the IMF could sell gold in private markets, reimburse countries for their gold contributions at the official price, and use the balance for the operations of the trust fund. Sales of gold and voluntary contributions could raise between $1.5 billion and $2 billion for the trust fund's first year of operation. The terms proposed for the trust fund's loans are a ten-year period of repayment, a four-year grace period, and interest rates below those currently applied to IMF operations. IMF quotas could determine limits of borrowing from the trust fund.

The proposal is something of a hybrid, mixing relatively long-term loans with IMF lending criteria, which are related to balance-of-payments considerations. Consequently the objectives of the trust fund need better definition: Is the fund to provide short-term balance-of-payments support to the most seriously affected countries during the next two or three years? That is, will it serve as a successor to the IMF Oil Facility? Or will the aim of the fund be the provision of long-term development finance to developing countries over a period of several years? Obtaining agreed answers to these questions may well take interested governments most of 1975.

Many developing countries are not in favor of the proposed trust fund. Their lack of interest may be due to several factors. First, the operations of the trust fund—as proposed by the United States—are limited to the poorest IMF members, which would exclude many developing countries. Second, many countries would prefer to see any benefits from IMF sales of gold holdings transferred to them directly rather than to the trust fund. A third developing-country objection may be the proposal's provision that the trust fund be managed by the IMF, whose priorities are often considered to be less related to long-run development than those of the World Bank. A final factor behind the proposal's lack of support among developing countries is its apparent substitution by developed countries for the "link" between SDR creation and resource transfers that has long been advocated by the developing countries themselves. The link, however, is dependent upon IMF allocations of SDRs—which are not likely to take place in a world awash with petrodollars and revalued official gold reserves unless SDRs are substituted for gold or for other reserve assets. Thus within the IMF the link remains "under active study," but "other ways" of transferring real resources to developing countries, perhaps the trust fund, are being considered as well.

The IMF Oil Facility is scheduled to terminate at the end of 1975, and the United Nations Special Programme of assistance to the most seriously affected countries will complete its work even earlier, in May 1975. Consequently, developing countries may well need to take another look at the proposed trust fund as a means of obtaining a share of the IMF's windfall gain from the revaluation of gold. For its part, the United States should consider the extension of the trust fund's operations to countries other than the poorest

IMF member countries, as well as other suggestions that may be made to broaden the support for the proposal.

A Third Window. The proposed third window would allow the World Bank to charge lower interest rates on its loans to poor countries. Regular Bank loans channel resources raised on private capital markets to member countries. Interest rates on these loans are dependent on the market rate the Bank itself pays to purchasers of its bonds. Currently, Bank loans bear an interest rate of 8.5 per cent per year, a high charge for countries at low levels of development that already face heavy burdens of debt. In order to lower the interest burden for certain Bank members while maintaining the Bank's return, an interest subsidy has been proposed for third-window loans. A fund of about $200 million could lower the interest rate to 4.5 per cent on $1 billion of 30-year World Bank loans. Resources for the additional loans would be raised as needed on private capital markets. The U.S. share of such an interest subsidy fund during the one-year period proposed for initial third-window operations would be only about $20 million.

Several issues still need to be resolved regarding this proposal. One involves deciding which countries are to be eligible to use the facility: Should its funds be lent principally to those nations that now qualify for IDA credits (countries with per capita incomes of less than $375 per year)? Or should they be available to a wider range of countries? Another important issue is whether the facility's decision-making authority will be separate from the World Bank's existing procedures. This last question has little relevance if the third window is to be closed after its one-year trial period. This time limit has been suggested partly to avoid jeopardizing the fifth replenishment of IDA. Closing the window would result in a weakening of the World Bank's lending program: it would not be able to meet adequately the requirements for concessional finance of the countries not eligible for IDA credits.

A Private Proposal. Private individuals have recommended plans ranging from discussions between a few "key" oil producers and consumers (namely, Saudi Arabia, Kuwait, Iran, the United States, and Germany) to a multilateral negotiation based on the equal participation of three groups of countries: the oil-exporting, the industrialized oil-importing, and the non-industrialized oil-importing countries. The authors of the latter proposal, which appeared in the January 1975 issue of *Foreign Affairs,*[6] recommend a comprehensive approach to the present imbalance in the global balance of payments. Their proposal goes beyond the scope of either the Kissinger-Simon "safety net" or the IMF Oil Facility in that it considers both the short-term problem of financing the oil-induced trade deficits and the long-term management of the oil revenue surplus. The authors recognize that a transfer of real assets from oil-importing countries to OPEC members will inevitably

---

[6]K. Farmanfarmaian, et al., "How Can the World Afford OPEC Oil?," *Foreign Affairs,* Vol. 53, No. 2 (January 1975), pp. 201-222.

occur as the latter absorb more goods and services. Such a transfer is implicit in the regaining of a current account balance. This process will require a considerable expansion of the productive capacity of the oil-importing countries if their level of consumption is not to decline. Surplus OPEC oil revenues are the logical source of the needed new investment capital. But the available capital must be channeled into productive investments which are attractive to OPEC investors. Because private foreign investment is a very sensitive political issue, the authors recommend a privately managed investment fund to handle some of the OPEC investments so that the implications of direct OPEC control of a nation's productive assets do not become a political issue.

Sensitivities about OPEC investment are on the rise in the United States and other developed nations. Several bills have been introduced in the U.S. Congress which would require special reporting procedures for foreign investments and which would, under certain conditions, empower the President to rescind any deal made between a U.S. firm and foreign interests. The Administration opposes such controls on the grounds that they might result in new limitations on U.S. investors abroad. Clearly the potential investment of a part of the oil surplus in U.S. industry has dramatized for Americans their own sensitivities in an area where there have been numerous conflicts between the United States and developing countries. Review or control procedures for foreign private investment adopted by the United States would undoubtedly contribute to the introduction of more stringent controls by developing countries on U.S. investment.

A private "buffer" between OPEC investors and developed or developing recipients of capital might assuage some host-country concerns. Such an investment fund, however, could manage no more than a relatively small portion of the total accumulated surplus of oil exporters, which is expected to be between $200 billion and $300 billion in 1980. Furthermore, the efforts of such a private body notwithstanding, investments in less developed areas will generally remain less attractive than those in industrialized nations. Thus multilateral institutions, which can handle large capital transfers and at the same time provide an adequate return to OPEC investors, are necessary to ensure the transfer of an adequate proportion of accumulated oil surpluses to those countries most in need of development capital.

Neither Rich Nor Poorest

While relations with oil producers dominate the headlines, and considerable attention is devoted to the emergency needs of the nations most seriously affected by the rise in prices of food, fertilizer, and petroleum products,[7] another group of about fifty developing countries—neither the newly rich oil

---

[7]See Chapter I.

exporters, nor the critically affected "Fourth World"—is in danger of being neglected. Most of Latin America is in the intermediate category, along with many Asian and some African countries. This group of countries faces the prospect of diminishing concessional assistance and unfavorable export prices as recession slows demand in industrialized nations. Among international measures now being considered, the trust fund is not primarily designed for their use, and the potential beneficiaries of the third window have not yet been determined.

But the stake of these intermediate countries in the international trade, monetary, and financing systems is high, and their links with these systems are important. For example, their Eurocurrency borrowings in 1973 amounted to $4.8 billion, or over 60 per cent of the total Eurocurrency credits obtained by developing countries. In 1974 their use of Eurocurrency markets reached $6.2 billion, or 87 per cent of total developing-country credits from this source. Yet even within this group of countries, access to private capital markets was highly concentrated. Thus in 1974, Mexico, Brazil, the Philippines, and Argentina accounted for 69 per cent of total Eurocurrency borrowings by intermediate nations.[8] Access to the national capital markets of industrialized countries is also limited for most developing nations.

Thus private capital markets do not yet provide broad enough access to financial resources for numerous developing nations. One way to rectify this situation would be through loan guarantees or interest-subsidy mechanisms. These could operate through an international intermediary, as in the proposed third window of the World Bank, or through bilateral programs. At this time, the Development Committee of the IMF and the World Bank is studying means of promoting increased access to capital markets by developing countries through these and other means. At the national level, the U.S. Agency for International Development has proposed a system of guarantees to facilitate the access of many of the more advanced developing countries to the U.S. capital market. Such a scheme would provide additional concessional finance and would make minimal demands upon the U.S. budget.

The official external debt of the intermediate countries reached $47 billion in 1973, or 53 per cent of the total debt outstanding of developing countries. Debt service of $4.4 billion in 1972 placed a heavy burden on their economies.[9] However, many of these nations apparently prefer improved long-term access to private capital markets to international consideration of widespread renegotiation of debt.

The intermediate countries also account for a significant portion of world trade. In the case of the United States, they provided 18 per cent of U.S. imports and took 22 per cent of U.S. exports in 1974. Already the threat of an

---

[8]See Table D-13, p. 267.
[9]See Table D-17, p. 274.

economic slowdown in these countries has prompted concern about U.S. agricultural exports to such nations; for example, in some Asian nations, demand for U.S. cotton is falling off in the face of recessionary tendencies which have reduced imports of textile products by industrialized countries.

A Challenge to Multilateralism

Recession and inflation threaten the multilateral economic systems that evolved during the 1950s and 1960s. These developments come at a time when the developing countries are seeking greater fundamental changes in international economic relations which, in their view, are dominated by the industrialized world. They want greater participation in multilateral decisions and, specifically, a greater voice in the operations of international financial institutions.

The IMF was the first institution to recognize formally the need to make changes, when it decided to double the share in total quotas held by oil-exporting members. This change will be made by reducing the share of industrialized nations' quotas while maintaining those of non-oil-exporting developing countries. Hence, OPEC members and developing countries will account for about one third of Fund quotas. This is not an easy change for developed countries to contemplate, and their jockeying for position as quotas are adjusted has been intense. The United States, for instance, has refused to give up its 20 per cent share of total quotas, which represents veto power on certain important IMF decisions.

As painful as such changes may appear in developed-country capitals, they are necessary to the construction of a truly multilateral framework for international economic policies. Moreover, willingness to adapt international decision-making arrangements to new political-economic realities is only part of this effort. If developed and developing nations are to maintain viable international economic institutions, they must include greater and more equitable participation by developing countries. U.S. actions to further this goal should include support for the multilateral financial and monetary arrangements which will help solve the balance-of-payments crisis facing many countries. Each individual measure—for example, the trust fund or the third window—may appear relatively small, and, consequently, not essential when considered alone, but when all are taken together they can make an important contribution to ensuring the support that multilateral institutions need from all their member countries.

There is, furthermore, a long-run structural difficulty facing *all* countries that use oil-financing arrangements. In the short run, financial support gives rise to claims upon the resources of oil-importing countries. Exports of goods and services to oil-producing countries represent a real resource transfer. For the industrialized countries, these claims are being liquidated rather more rapidly than has been expected through increased imports by oil-exporting countries. Most of the expanding import demand of oil producers will be directed toward developed countries, which are the main source of armaments, high-technology goods and services, and other manufactured goods.

In the short run, the capacity of the industrialized economies to absorb the impact of the oil price rise could permit a relatively rapid return to the uneasy relations between underdeveloped and developed countries that prevailed prior to the oil price rise. If delays or failures meet the efforts of developing countries to establish additional sources of financial support and improved trading opportunities, it will have been demonstrated once again that, by assigning high priority to their own narrow interests, developed countries are able to safeguard their economic health without significantly altering their financial, trade, and investment relations with developing countries. Such temporizing only bottles up the pressures that created and perpetuate the sense of grievance that links oil-exporting countries with poorer nations.

Recommendations

Recent reports of shortfalls in the amounts received by the IMF Managing Director for the operation of the expanded Oil Facility and of a lack of U.S. support for the third window and IMF subsidy account are of great concern. The United States—by virtue of its size and past leadership position in international economic affairs—exerts a crucial influence over the decisions of other nations regarding multilateral financial assistance. Without a firm indication that the U.S. Executive Branch and Congress back all three of these measures designed to benefit the developing countries—the subsidy account for the Oil Facility, the trust fund, and the third window—other developed nations may reduce their own contributions to the subsidy account, and the oil exporters may well hesitate before they back the Oil Facility to their full capacity.

The United States should support the IMF Oil Facility with contributions both to the Facility itself and to the subsidy account. The first round of IMF requests for contributions to the Facility this year yielded about half the authorized total. The first priority is therefore to bring total contributions during 1975 up to the authorized level. Furthermore, the United States should be prepared to support an expansion of the IMF Oil Facility if it becomes evident that balance-of-payments deficits cannot be adequately covered by funds available through the Facility and other sources of finance. The U.S. contribution to an adequate subsidy account for the Oil Facility would be very modest, perhaps $10 million. This amount should be provided as soon as possible.

In the international discussions of the IMF trust fund, the United States should adapt its original proposal to meet the concerns of other nations. In particular, the coverage of this scheme should be broadened to include all of the countries in the most-seriously-affected and least developed categories.

Broad international support for the subsidy account and the trust fund will depend upon bilateral and multilateral measures to meet the need of the intermediate countries that are neither most seriously affected by the current crises nor newly rich from petroleum exports. Consequently, U.S. programs to guarantee, or lower the cost of, greater developing-country access to the American capital market should be introduced as soon as possible.

The multilateral third window now under consideration in the World Bank should also be fully supported by the United States, since it would entail only a small contribution to the interest subsidy fund.

The third window is not, of course, a substitute for the World Bank's International Development Association or other sources of concessional transfers that now operate through regional development banks and other institutions. They too, will need the support of the U.S. Executive Branch and Congress in coming years. There is no doubt that obtaining congressional approval for the U.S. contribution to the fifth replenishment of IDA and the $1.8 billion proposed by Secretary of State Kissinger for the Inter-American Development Bank is a difficult task. But these funds are also essential to the successful management of international economic systems.

It is possible that other nations will support multilateral financial measures without U.S. participation. Letting others "bear the burden" in this way may seem attractive to a United States beset with a balance-of-payments deficit and domestic recession. But the costs of such an approach would be a diminution of the U.S. voice in the operation of international economic systems and an increase in the likelihood of confrontations over economic policy between the United States and developing nations.

CHAPTER VI

The New Interdependence: From Hierarchy to Symmetry

Ali A. Mazrui

The first three quarters of this century have come to a close. Nineteen seventy-five is a year of reflection about whether the remaining quarter of a century will witness that level of international economic justice which the rest of the century had thought about and talked about—but never found the will or even the inclination to pursue.

At the heart of this question is the old issue of equality, which in history has always been linked to the tensions of interdependence. The degree to which men have needed each other has been at the core of their interrelationships. Theories about the consequences of the division of labor, and about the origins of caste, class, and hierarchy, essentially have been concerned with issues of equality and issues of interdependence. It is quite clear from both the history of social institutions and the history of social ideas that interdependence could either create or destroy equality. The critical factor concerns the precise nature of that interdependence.

Ever since the energy crisis hit the headlines of the world press, a new agonizing reappraisal of interdependence among nations has been under way among both scholars and policy makers. Discussions have gone on between the European Community and the Arab oil producers concerning the possibility of exchanging European technology for Arab oil in a bid for mutually induced economic development. The U.S. government has explored ways of strengthening relations between Western Europe and the United States in search of a new economic basis for the Atlantic partnership. The United Nations has discussed the problems of raw materials in relation to international trade, and one eminent speaker after another has called for a new definition of international interdependence.

But what was central to all these discussions and debates was an ancient moral problem: the problem of equality—at once simple and taxing, at once topical and perennial.

In this paper, three stages of interdependence are distinguished: primitive, feudo-imperial, and mature. The *first* of these stages, primitive interdependence, exists in conditions of rudimentary technology and limited social horizons. In most parts of the world, primitive interdependence within individual societies is a matter of the past, with only a few residual elements surviving to the present day. But there are small societies in the developing world that are still characterized by very limited and narrow social horizons, and by very rudimentary and primordial technology. To the extent that their members are mutually dependent for the fulfillment of their needs, such societies do exhibit precisely what we here mean by primitive interdependence.

The *second* stage is feudo-imperial interdependence, which seeks to combine some of the characteristics of feudalism and some of the attributes of imperialism. A central characteristic of this kind of interdependence is *hierarchy*, and hierarchy is of course founded on the premise of inequality.

The *third* stage of interdependence is one which combines sophistication with symmetry. The sophistication comes from enhanced technological capabilities and expanded social and intellectual awareness; the symmetry emerges out of a new egalitarian morality combined with a more balanced capacity for mutual harm. The different parties in this stage of interdependence must not only need each other—their different needs also must be on a scale that enables serious mutual dislocations in case of conflict. The combination of an egalitarian ethic and reciprocal vulnerability within a framework of wider technological and intellectual frontiers provides the essence of mature interdependence.

Technological Change and Social Imbalance

Relations among nations in the first three quarters of the twentieth century have been primarily feudo-imperial or hierarchical—without either the kinship solidarity of primitive interdependence or the sophisticated symmetry of mature interdependence. One of the most important questions confronting the last quarter of the twentieth century is whether the human race is at last about to evolve a genuine pattern of mature interdependence before this momentous century comes to a close.

The most basic factor behind the West's rise to imperial preeminence was the technological revolution in Europe. The rise of new techniques of production and the utilization of new forms of energy and mechanical

119

implements set the stage for the West's expansion and territorial colonization. A basic paradox soon revealed itself. While the industrial revolution in Europe prepared the way for domestic equality within each country, it at the same time established the basis of major international disparities between the industrialized world on the one hand, and much of the rest of the world on the other. From the eighteenth century onward, technology helped to lay the foundations of a more egalitarian England and an even more egalitarian America; yet that same technology, by increasing the inventive and productive capabilities of these societies way beyond those attained by others, initiated a process of massive disparities of income and power among the nations of the world.

At the global level, the United States grew to become the richest and most industrially developed country. The distance between the United States and a country like Niger, Mali, or Tanzania in terms of affluence and technological sophistication illustrated the powerful tendency of modern technology to widen disparities far more than was conceivable a few generations ago. These levels of affluence had their repercussions on the global plane. The Northern hemisphere as a whole consumed a staggeringly disproportionate share of the scarce resources of the world, conducted the bulk of international trade, controlled much of the world's finance, and enjoyed the highest standards of living as yet attained by man. Asia, Africa, and Latin America were overshadowed in both living standards and outright power.

To some extent, this world order did involve a form of interdependence. Primary producers contributed raw materials and oil and other sources of energy to the manufacturing and industrial plants of the Northern hemisphere, and they received processed goods and products of highly sophisticated technology in return. It was claimed that this was indeed a sound basis for partnership between the poorer societies of the world in Asia, Africa, and Latin America, and their more affluent neighbors to the North. Copper from Zambia and Chile, coffee from Brazil and Uganda, oil from the Middle East and Venezuela, tea and jute from Pakistan, rubber from Malaya, uranium from Niger, cloves from Zanzibar, and cocoa from Ghana all provided a pattern of contributions from the Southern hemisphere to the life style and methods of production of the people of the North. Back from the North came radios and bicycles, typewriters and train engines, knives and forks, padlocks and tractors. A partnership was presumed to have grown out of the natural processes of economic and industrial change. It was indeed a system of interdependence, but the interdependence was once again feudo-imperial. The richer countries seemed to be getting richer still; the poorer seemed to remain in indigence. "Nothing prospers like prosperity"—so the international system of the world seemed to affirm. An old adage thus discovered a new and ominous vindication. Under the impetus of technological success, the North was widening more than ever the gap existing between itself and the less fortunate sectors of the human race.

120

And then one day the term "energy crisis" entered the vocabulary of international affairs. A developing-country poet might have written, as William Wordsworth did of the French Revolution:

> Bliss was it in that dawn to be alive
> But to be young was very heaven!

Economic Power and New Strategies

The October 1973 war in the Middle East helped the process of reawakening in the developing world. The war was fought at two levels—the military and the diplomatic. From the point of view of the Middle East, both levels were perhaps equally important. The relatively modest military successes of the Arabs were politically important beyond their military significance. They certainly helped to restore Egyptian and Syrian morale, and contributed toward destroying the belief in some circles of the world that Israel was invincible.

But while these military factors were quite fundamental to the Middle East itself, it was the *economic* war waged by the Arabs that fired the imagination of the developing countries. From the point of view of the rest of Asia, Africa, and the Middle East, it was neither the tank battle in the Sinai nor the air battle over the Golan Heights that was basic to their own destiny. Rather, it was the utilization of oil as a political weapon, with all its implications for relations between the affluent industrial world and the primary producers of the Southern hemisphere.

From this economic point of view, the term "October War" is somewhat inaccurate. The Arab *economic* war for the restoration of Arab lands lasted for several months longer than the Arab *military* challenge to Israel. In a sense the use of Arab economic power in order to recover those lands still continues.

What the Arab economic war revealed were two potentially critical strategies for creating a new economic order in the world: the strategy of *counter-penetration* by the Southern countries into the dominant countries of the North, and the strategy of *inter-penetration* between the different sections of the South itself. Before examining these two approaches in greater detail, another school of thought should be mentioned that has many adherents in the developing world: the strategy of disengagement.

Disengagement: An Elusive Dream

Those who promote a strategy of disengagement seek to explore the maximum possibilities of "emancipation" from the international capitalist system. But here one must distinguish between domestic and international capitalism. There are developing-world theoreticians who assume that by eliminating capitalism at home, they would necessarily "disengage" from the international capitalist system. What they overlook is that a country can abolish private enterprise and even private property at home and still be wholly dependent on the vagaries of trade with the capitalist countries and the fluctuations of the capitalist monetary system.

The Soviet Union, domestically socialist in at least economic organization, has been groping for ways to strengthen its links with the capitalist system. It has negotiated the involvement of Japanese firms in the exploitation of mineral resources in Siberia and has sought Japanese expertise in related economic endeavors. It likewise has been keen on expanding trade with the United States. The attainment of most-favored-nation status, which signifies eligibility for concessions gained by all participants in international trade negotiations, has been one of the Soviet Union's economic ambitions in the process of consolidating detente with the United States. Even the 1971-72 grain deal between the Soviet Union and the United States was envisaged by both sides as a step toward strengthening Soviet links with U.S. private enterprise. In that grain deal, Soviet commercial skills in the art of "maximizing returns" were impressively revealed. What all this meant was that a superpower like the Soviet Union, while committed to domestic socialism, might nonetheless find it moral and prudent to strengthen its links with international capitalism.

A similar trend is discernible in the economic attitude of the People's Republic of China. It is true that China pursued a policy of isolation for over twenty years, yet its isolation did not take place entirely by choice. The United States took the leadership for that period in ostracizing the People's Republic. When, under former President Richard M. Nixon, the United States at last decided to end its policy of ostracism, and to court Chairman Mao's China instead, the latter did not resist the overtures. Since then China has begun to respond to economic explorations from Japanese and Western European as well as from American business firms. China has not yet moved as enthusiastically as the Soviet Union to strengthen links with international capitalism, but the trend is in that direction.

If "disengagement" from the international capitalist system is difficult even for such socialist giants as the Soviet Union and China, it is bound to be an elusive dream for most developing countries.[1]

The Strategy of Southern Counter-Penetration

As already mentioned, one of the two major strategies for changing the existing international economic order is that of Southern counter-

---

[1]The strategy of disengagement should not, however, be confused with yet another important school of thought in some developing countries which counsels developing countries not to imitate the values, methods, and institutions of the North but to design or discover and adapt indigenous ones. This school does not seek to isolate or disengage the South from economic transactions with the international capitalist system.

penetration. In 1975 the oil producers will have many billions of dollars available for investment abroad. Should they use it for investment in the developing world or in the Northern hemisphere? The answer would seem to be that they should do *both*—since their increasing investment in the European Community and in the United States clearly will advance their objective of counter-penetration.

Japanese counter-penetration of the United States is an illustration of how a former appendage of American capitalism became a serious economic rival to the United States. Japanese businessmen have recently been manipulating aspects of the American economy almost as effectively as American businessmen once manipulated Japan. The strategy of counter-penetration in Japan's relations with the West so far has been dramatically and convincingly vindicated.

Compared with Japan's capabilities for counter-penetration, those of the developing countries still seem very modest; yet the oil producers may help to create a kind of leverage that could one day transform the world economic order. Disengagement from the capitalist system would only weaken countries such as Libya, Iran, Nigeria, and Saudi Arabia. Moreover, it is their potential influence within the system that much of the rest of the South really needs. Parts of the Northern hemisphere are beginning to feel the countervailing power of parts of the South.

Even as the Arab world celebrated the first anniversary of the October 1973 war, two trends were already discernible among the industrialized nations. One was a campaign to get the petrodollars recycled—a campaign led by the United Kingdom, which was eager to persuade the oil producers to invest their surplus capital in countries such as itself. This approach had already met with some success. Both Iran and the Arab world were evolving an aggressive commercial enthusiasm and had begun widespread soundings for new investment opportunities. Chancellor Helmut Schmidt of the German Federal Republic announced in November 1974 that a Middle Eastern government had bought a substantial share of the Daimler-Benz Corporation, the manufacturer not only of Mercedes cars but also of some military vehicles. It later transpired that the government concerned was Kuwait, which had acquired a 14 per cent interest in the firm. A few months earlier, Iran had acquired a 25 per cent interest in the steel division of the massive Krupp Enterprises. Other industrial and commercial enterprises in the Western world which had entered, or were reported to have entered, into discussion with oil producers included Lockheed Aircraft Corporation in the United States, Pan American World Airlines, and Grumman Aerospace Corporation.

But precisely because the oil producers were beginning to take seriously the Western invitation to recycle and reinvest their dollars, a second trend was also discernible in the West—a groping for ways to "contain the threat of excessive foreign investment." At a news conference early in December 1974,

Secretary of State Henry Kissinger indicated that the U.S. government wished to study "the implications of substantial investments" by the oil-producing countries in the United States, "how we can keep track of them," and the identification of the "dangers against which we must guard."[2]

More specifically, the American government was becoming concerned that some oil-producing countries might attempt to take over financial control of critical defense industries. The anxieties were partly an outgrowth of Iran's summer 1974 offer of a loan to help financially troubled Grumman Aerospace Corporation. Iran's offer originally envisaged the acquisition of a potential equity position in the company. A controversy flared up, influenced by the fear that some oil-producing countries might attempt to take over control of industries that are critical to American defense needs. The Defense Department resolved the Grumman case by insisting that Iran should not be given equity control of this traditional producer of fighter planes for the U.S. Navy. A full-scale study was ordered a few months later by the Ford Administration about the wider implications of this new wave of foreign investments into the United States. A distinction was beginning to be made behind the scenes between investment from military allies such as Western Europe and Japan, and investment from non-aligned developing countries with different political and economic imperatives. In the words of a December 1974 report in the *The New York Times*:

> In contemplating a possible invasion of Arab oil money, the Defense Department finds itself trying to walk a line between an over-all Administration policy of welcoming foreign investments and a desire to protect the defense sector against foreign control. In the past year, there have been some rumblings of discontent in the Congress over foreign investment in American industry—faint echoes thus far compared to the cries in Canada and Europe over alleged domination by American investments. . . . At a news conference last Friday, James R. Schlesinger, Secretary of Defense, said his department would examine any attempt by a foreign government to acquire a major or controlling interest in an American contractor doing classified work "with great caution and on a case-by-case basis."[3]

If the strategy of counter-penetration achieves nothing else, it should at least increase American understanding of the fears of those who have previously expressed anxieties about the U.S. economic presence in other lands. Such a fundamental reexamination by the United States of the role of

[2]See *The New York Times*, December 8, 1974, and December 10, 1974.

[3]*The New York Times*, December 10, 1974. Consult also Paul Lewis, "Getting Even: A Redistribution of the World's Wealth," *The New York Times Magazine*, December 15, 1974, pp. 13, 76-93.

foreign investment in world affairs could itself have far-reaching implications. Yet that would only be the beginning. The long-term potential of counter-penetration lies in creating conditions which would help to force the creation of a new international economic order.

What should be borne in mind is that counter-penetration consists of more than just the recycling of petrodollars into the developed world. An even more fundamental aspect of the strategy is the conversion of developing-country resources from their oil role as sources of dependency to a new role as sources of power. Part of this conversion is merely a change in the level of political consciousness and economic astuteness. For as long as the Arabs did not realize that their oil was a potential source of immense power, their oil became a pretext for their own exploitation by others. But as the oil producers attained new levels of economic awareness and political consciousness, they first began demanding bigger percentages of profits from the expatriate oil companies. As they obtained larger and larger percentages of the profit, and as the consumption of oil in the developed world increased, an awesome realization dawned upon the consciousness of the oil producers. If they were united, they could transform their dependency into power. The Organization of Petroleum Exporting Countries (OPEC)—originally conceived primarily as an instrument for pressuring the foreign oil companies—was soon to enter the mainstream of world economic diplomacy. Without their realizing it, the age of counter-penetration by the South had begun.

In addition to these two aspects of counter-penetration (recycling petrodollars and converting primary resources from a symptom of dependency to a tool of power), the strategy of counter-penetration also requires a sensitivity to the implications of the international monetary system. The immense foreign reserves in the hands of the oil producers should be used to force changes in the international monetary system in the direction of easing the burdens of the developing countries. The potentialities of this monetary power in the hands of oil-producing countries was illustrated in December 1974. A major oil company almost casually revealed that Saudi Arabia no longer wanted to be paid in sterling for its oil. Until then, Saudi Arabia had received about a quarter of its oil revenue in the form of the British pound. The new decision created consternation in London. The pound descended to an all-time low in Western markets, and the stock exchange in London reverberated with gloom. The Bank of England had to supply millions in support of the pound. The only silver lining of that cloud was the possibility that Saudi Arabia would continue to invest in Great Britain, even when it no longer accepted pounds for its oil. The future of sterling as a world currency was briefly under cloud simply because one Arab country was unilaterally reconsidering its financial options. The world thus caught a glimpse of the potential power of the oil producers to force major changes in the international monetary system.

Finally, the counter-penetration strategy also has a demographic element

125

related to population distribution. The "brain drain" from the developing into the developed world could one day become a source of Southern influence within the North—comparable in principle to the role played by Jewish intellectuals and businessmen in Europe and North America in defense of Israeli interests. Given that Israel has been so dependent on the United States, especially for economic and military support, and therefore has been deeply penetrated by America, the Jewish presence within the United States is a case of demographic counter-penetration. There are other examples of such demographic counter-penetration in the United States, including the political influence of Irish Americans made evident in varying degrees since the last quarter of the nineteenth century. The more recent influence of Greek Americans on U.S. policy in the Mediterranean is another case in point.

As for the more humble migratory patterns from poorer countries to richer countries, these too might one day serve comparable purposes. The world of the future will include interlocking population centers—Blacks in the Americas and Europe, Whites in Africa, Jews in North America and the Middle East, Arabs in Africa, East Indians in the Caribbean, and perhaps one day even Chinese in Australia. Some population exchanges will be symmetrical, for example, Blacks in the White world "in exchange" for Whites in the Black world. Other demographic migratory patterns might be less symmetrical—for example, the Chinese in Malaysia. Where there is lack of symmetry, or where the immigrants are more privileged than the indigenous peoples, tensions are inevitable. But despite some examples to the contrary, such as General Idi Amin's expulsion of Asian ethnics from Uganda, the central long-term world trend is toward the emergence of an interlocking population system between now and the end of the twenty-first century. Demographic counter-penetration from the Southern into the Northern hemisphere would be only one aspect of such a system.

Inter-Penetration Within the Developing World

Clearly relations between the Southern and the Northern hemispheres are only part of the quest for a new economic and political order. In matters of migratory patterns, as well as in other areas of international life, relations among different parts of the South itself are equally important.

The birth of developing-country solidarity came as a result of a marriage between two movements—Afro-Asianism and non-alignment. Solidarity between Africans and Asians started as a racial assertion, but by the late 1960s it was based less and less on the sentiment of being colored peoples and more on the recognition of shared economic and diplomatic weaknesses.

The non-aligned movement was also changing its emphasis—away from preoccupations about keeping out of the "cold war" and refusing alliances with the major powers, and toward a struggle to try to create a new economic order in the world. Issues of race continued to be central as long as southern

Africa continued to be dominated along racial lines. A conference of non-aligned countries was held in Lusaka, Zambia, partly to dramatize the commitment of the movement in support of the remaining wars of national liberation. But both the Lusaka conference in 1970 and the Algiers conference in 1973 clearly revealed that the non-aligned movement had become more committed to the cause of economic justice in the world than in the old days of Tito, Nehru, Nasser, and Nkrumah, and less preoccupied with issues of avoiding military alliances—since the superpowers themselves were now pursuing a policy of detente.

As Afro-Asianism became "deracialized" and non-alignment demilitarized in emphasis, a new synthesis emerged based on the concept of the Third World, or the "Group of 77" developing countries. This synthesis provided a transition from "pan-pigmentationalism," an affinity based on color, to "pan-proletarianism," an inchoate solidarity based on shared indigence and underdevelopment. While Afro-Asianism had by definition limited itself to two continents, the Group of 77 also encompasses Latin America. It is thus a tricontinental phenomenon, forging a limited interdependence among underdeveloped countries in Asia, Africa, and Latin America. Although this interdependence is relatively rudimentary for the time being, it is once again transnational and still provisionally influenced by an egalitarian ethic among the constituent countries, and increasingly conscious of the possibilities of cooperation in the future.

Developing-world transnationalism has found expression in a variety of sub-movements, ranging from the radical left-wing tricontinental movement to the United Nations Conference on Trade and Development (UNCTAD). Also increasingly significant have been the alliances of primary producers, ranging from the Organization of Petroleum Exporting Countries to the new informal arrangements among producers of copper. Most of these primary producers are competitors and thus vulnerable to tactics of divide and rule. Yet in their relationship to the consumers of their primary products, there has been growing a sense of solidarity, however fragile and inchoate it is for the time being.

The doctrine of equality among developing countries is also fragile and uncertain. Technological imbalances are important not only in relationships between the North and the South, but also in relationships among the Southern countries themselves. Countries such as Brazil and India are technologically in a different category from countries such as Libya and Uganda. The weight and leverage exerted by the technologically and demographically more powerful developing countries carries the risk of feudo-imperial influences among them.

Brazil has long had a vision of a leadership role—first in Latin America and then in the developing world as a whole. It has seen the establishment of a constituency of influence within the South as a step toward the attainment of superpower status. For some time, Brazil even appeared to entertain the possibility of sharing a feudo-imperial role with Portugal in Africa. The Portuguese colony of Angola briefly seemed to be developing into a condominium under the joint hegemony of Portugal and Brazil.

There were occasions when some developed countries sought to influence Portugal's policies in Africa through the intervention of Brazil. Brazil's former Ambassador to Washington, Roberto de Oliveira Campos, claimed soon after the coup in Portugal in the spring of 1974, that in 1963 the Kennedy Administration—apprehensive about the possibility of a repetition in "Portuguese Africa" of the chaos that had befallen the former Belgian Congo on attainment of independence—had offered financing for Brazilian welfare and economic projects in Angola, Mozambique, and Guinea-Bissau. According to Campos, the United States was reluctant to approach Portugal directly, fearing a negative reaction from Lisbon that might shake the Atlantic alliance. The Kennedy initiative, if Campos's report is correct, failed partly because Brazil was unsure about the wisdom of the American initiative, and partly because Portugal was predictably unenthusiastic once the danger of a Congo-type collapse had receded.

By 1963, Brazil was already sensing the broad difficulties of feudo-imperialism in the modern period but still continued to play a role basically supportive of Portugal. By the end of the 1960s, however, its shift from serving as a co-imperial power in an informal sense to serving as a developing-world partner in Africa began to be discernible. While it was still reluctant to be associated with African liberation movements as such, it nevertheless sought to establish new economic relations not only with the countries still under Portuguese control, but also with countries in the independent sector of the continent. On the one hand, Brazil's economic and technological development was widening the gulf between itself and many of the other developing countries. On the other hand, the new policies pursued by Brazil in the developing world emphasized a spirit of egalitarian solidarity and seemed to lay the foundations for a new developing world transnationalism.

The Arab world was also exploring possibilities of enhanced solidarity with African states and the Moslem world. Some of these movements could conceivably split the Group of 77 along continental, religious, or ideological lines. But they could also be seen as additional manifestations of the new mood of transnationalism among the poorer and weaker countries of the globe.

The new interdependence of Arabs and other developing countries continues to be fitful and inconclusive. The Arab oil producers have been reluctant to concede special concessions in oil prices to fellow developing countries. In the case of the African states, the only commitment undertaken by the Arab oil producers was to provide development aid and subsidies from a new Arab fund for Africa, but even this aid fell far short of meeting the extra costs of increased oil prices.

There was a possibility of special concessions to Moslem countries from

Arab oil producers, but the Islamic Summit Conference of Lahore in 1974 failed to realize such a spirit of economic generosity and solidarity between the haves and the have-nots. What all this means is that the struggle for an effective and operational developing-world transnationalism has only just started. There are enormous obstacles in the way of its fulfillment. These obstacles range from a residual dependency complex among those developing countries dominated by their former metropolitan masters to excessive greed among those developing countries which have become staggeringly rich without evolving a commensurate scale of developing-world solidarity.

The bulk of economic interaction in the world so far has been between the Northern industrial nations themselves (upper horizontal relations). Next in importance has been interaction between the industrial North and the less developed Southern hemisphere (vertical relations). The least significant has been interaction within the Southern hemisphere itself (lower horizontal relations). Because of this latter deficiency, the bonds among developing countries have been weak. Until recently, there was only a very limited sense of interdependence and little awareness of each others' problems. A strategy of increased mutual economic penetration between developing countries, ranging from trade to technical assistance, could raise their level of interdependence and enhance the possibilities of an organic solidarity among them.

In the economic domain, a form of partnership based on interlocking economic systems may be defined as "organic solidarity." An alliance for purposes of collective bargaining with a third party may be defined as "strategic solidarity." The developing countries have already discovered the virtues of strategic economic solidarity against the industrial North. Most developing-country economic dealings are with the industrial North rather than with other developing countries. By "ganging up" against the industrial powers in forums such as the U.N. General Assembly's Special Session on raw materials, or the U.N. Conference on Trade and Development (UNCTAD), the Group of 77 has begun to develop some skills of strategic solidarity. But only effective inter-penetration among developing-world economies could create a solid organic form of interdependence.

In the new era of counter-penetration, there is need to use petrodollars for investment in such efforts as irrigation in the Sahel or in Sudan, not only in Daimler-Benz and International Business Machines (IBM). The oil-exporting developing countries must be the vanguard of the Third Development Decade, as well as the remainder of the Second. They are in a position to demonstrate that what could not be accomplished under Northern economic leadership in the 1960s can be accomplished with the imaginative initiatives of the Organization of Petroleum Exporting Countries in the 1970s and the 1980s. The South's underprivileged status in relation to the industrial North may at last be transcended as the developing world itself creates a genuine organic and symmetrical solidarity among its own members in the South.

But what is likely to be the balance between vertical counter-penetration (from the South into the North) and horizontal inter-penetration (among Southern countries themselves)? For a while, the oil-rich developing countries will be tempted to invest much more in the industralized countries than in less developed nations. This is partly because of the tempting short-term returns of investing in Western Europe and North America, and partly because the industrialized countries can in any case *absorb* more capital than can the less developed economies.

But investment by developing countries elsewhere in the developing world will nevertheless grow and expand. So will foreign aid from resource-rich developing countries into resource-poor less developed economies. There are already strong indications of such a trend, in spite of all the skepticism one finds in the North. In the words of the Washington correspondent of *The Financial Times* of London:

> For the very poor [countries], there is no alternative to charity. The O.P.E.C. countries are starting to face up to their responsibilities here, although their reaction has been slow and they often show a preference for the Islamic poor over the rest. All the same, their development aid is already up to the target level set by the United Nations—something which cannot be said for the rest of the industrial world and particularly for the United States, which is not only the world's richest nation but its meanest. As yet O.P.E.C. aid may be insignificant in terms of the size of the difficulty the oil-price rise has created for the very poorest countries such as India and the Central African nations, which have neither oil nor many other marketable commodities. But the fact that they are making some kind of an effort helps them maintain the political support of the rest of the Third World, and there is some fragmentary evidence thàt they may already be doing rather more than appears in any of the figures.[4]

Among the oil-rich developing countries, some differences in orientation are inevitable. Investment by the conservative oil-rich regimes is more likely to fit the pattern of vertical counter-penetration than that of horizontal inter-penetration. Kuwait, Saudi Arabia, and Iran will either favor Western Europe and North America or give priority to fellow Moslems. Algeria and Libya, on the other hand, may prefer developing-world solidarity to profits gained in Europe or America. They may still show a preference for helping fellow Moslems, but are also likely to show sensitivity to the needs of other developing societies in Africa and Asia. Therefore, while conservative regimes such as Kuwait and Saudi Arabia enhance the process of vertical counter-

---

[4]Paul Lewis, "Getting Even," op. cit., p. 84.

penetration, radical or militant regimes such as Algeria and Libya should in time accelerate the process of horizontal inter-penetration among the Southern countries themselves. What should be borne in mind is that these are predictions about probable future behavior rather than interpretations of the aid record so far.

But neither kind of regime is likely to limit itself to only one direction of investment and general economic activity. Destiny has placed on the shoulders of the oil-rich developing countries an historic role in the transformation of the world's economic order.

Policy Options for the United States

It is in the enlightened self-interest of the United States, as well as of other powers, that the age of feudo-imperial or hierarchical interdependence should come to an end. *How can the hierarchy come to an end without also destroying the interdependence?*

For a while the West will experience an immense temptation to maintain the hierarchy. The energy crisis could provide the pretext for either gunboat diplomacy or outright resurgence of full imperial annexation. President Ford's hard-line speech at a Detroit conference and the speeches of Secretary of State Kissinger at the United Nations and the University of Chicago in the fall of 1974 were widely interpreted as implying the threat of military intervention in the Middle East should the energy situation reach economic "strangulation." Both speakers have denied that they ever intended such a threat, but official denials in matters of this kind are not adequate proof of lack of calculation in that direction.

One scenario involves an initiative by Israel with tacit Western encouragement or in outright collusion with the West. The precedent of 1956 when Israel was encouraged by France and Britain to launch an attack against Egypt in the hope of overthrowing President Nasser is still widely remembered. Israel's warning in November 1974 to countries such as Kuwait, Libya, Iraq, and Saudi Arabia that sending token contingents to Syria and Egypt in the next war would be taken by Israel as a declaration of war upon itself was interpreted in some developing-world circles as a diplomatic preparation for the invasion of oil-rich Arab countries in the next war. Israel might not be able to maintain control over such newly occupied distant oilfields for very long, but the new situation which this would create could enable the major powers to define new conditions for the price and availability of oil in return for the restoration of the oilfields to their Arab owners.

Such a scenario assumes that the Soviet Union would limit itself to making noises of protest without directly intervening on the side of the Arabs. If by any chance such military options are being considered by some of the back-room scenarists in the State Department and the Pentagon, they should be abandoned speedily. First, such options raise the risk of a nuclear war—

should either the Soviet Union or the United States miscalculate about the intentions of the other. Second, they risk the widespread sabotage of oil installations in the Arab world, causing for at least a short while a more devastating energy crisis than anything experienced so far. Third, they risk ruining the chances of a Middle East settlement for the rest of this century. And fourth, they risk hardening the lines of confrontation between the developing world as a whole and the West for at least another generation.

One realistic initial response by the United States would be to pursue further the implications of the Shah of Iran's suggestion that oil prices should be related to world prices of manufactured products, food, and other commodities. The Shah has argued that oil prices account for only 2 per cent of the total inflation of 20 per cent in the world—much of the rest of the inflation (18 per cent) having been caused by domestic factors in the industrial world. He has further argued that there is little likelihood of reduced oil prices for as long as the other causes of inflation in the industrial world are left unchecked. The projected collective discussions and negotiations between oil producers and oil consumers in 1975 should provide a useful forum for airing and beginning to resolve this issue.

A second potentially profitable response by the United States would be to encourage more emphatically the whole strategy of recycling petrodollars. The United States is no longer as negatively oriented toward the strategy as it was at the beginning of 1974, but the Ford Administration still shows considerable skepticism and caution.

If counter-penetration is partly designed to make the North as vulnerable to economic pressure from the South as the latter is to the North, why should the United States not remain cautious, skeptical, and even hostile to such a trend? One answer lies in the principle of *reciprocal vulnerability*. Two trends in December 1974 were potentially mutually negating. One trend was captured in the Charter of Economic Rights and Duties of States adopted by the General Assembly of the United Nations in that month—a new international doctrine virtually legitimizing future nationalization without compensation of any foreign industry in the developing world. The other trend was the increasing readiness of oil-rich developing countries to invest heavily in Northern industry. The General Assembly's Charter seemed to threaten Northern investment in Africa and Asia—while Arab and Iranian investments in the North were at the same time providing alternative safeguards for the future.

In the past, Northern investments abroad had to rely primarily on overall Northern domination of the world for security. In the future, however, Northern investment will increasingly need to rely on reciprocal investment by others in the industrialized world. If Saudi Arabia today acquired a large stake in Northern industry, and if tomorrow a socialist revolution took place in Saudi Arabia, the new government would be circumspect about nationalizing foreign firms in Saudi Arabia without compensation. The principle of reciprocal economic vulnerability would help to consolidate genuine symmetrical interdependence. The price of such interdependence is the ability to harm each other as genuine equals. The fear of such reciprocal harm should help to deter irresponsible and one-sided ventures. The industrialized world should therefore not only continue to encourage the oil-rich developing countries to bank their billions in the North, but it should also promote a genuine interlocking world economy by permitting massive Southern investment in their own industries. Just as the Northern hemisphere has a direct stake in many of the economies of the developing countries, so some of the latter should establish a direct stake in the economies of the industrial giants.

A third factor in promoting an interlocking world economy is to link food, energy, and technology policies. The European Community has already started exploratory discussions with the Arab League about a system of exchanging European technology for Arab oil. The discussions were interrupted as a result of the Arab desire to include the Palestinian Liberation Organization as a participant in the negotiations, but this interruption is likely to be of relatively short duration. A technological "quid" for an oil "quo" seems destined to be the basis of future economic relations between Europe and the Arab world.

A particularly critical area of convergence for the three elements of technology, energy, and food production would lie in such ambitious projects as the containment of the Sahara desert. How can areas like the Sahel be saved from the Sahara's expansion? How can countries bordering or encompassing the desert be made more productive? An alliance linking Arab petrodollars, Western technology, and African endeavor could help in finding positive answers to such ominous questions. Petrodollars *earned* in the deserts of Arabia could help *transform* the deserts of Africa. In the difficult enterprise of making the Sahara bloom, the developing world might find one project worthy of inter-penetration—made the more effective with the technological expertise of a more responsive Northern hemisphere.

But until the Sahara does bloom, there are lives to be saved from starvation. At the World Food Conference in Rome in the autumn of 1974, the American delegation was split over tactics and over immediate action to be taken for the alleviation of drought and famine. The official position of the Ford Administration was far behind countries such as Canada, Norway, and Australia in readiness to meet the food aid challenge. Canada committed over 15 per cent of its food production for the next three years to food aid. If the United States would like to see the oil producers become more sensitive to the problems of others, the United States itself, as the world's largest food producer, should display a similar sense of global responsibility. Those who consume resources on a per capita scale greater than anybody else should learn to make commensurate contributions to the alleviation of human misery. The United States has yet to rise to that challenge.

Perhaps the conference of oil producers and oil consumers in 1975 can be used as an occasion for American commitment on food supplies, as well as OPEC commitment on energy prices. A formula does need to be found not only to enable oil prices to float with the prices of other commodities, but also to link the energy crisis to the broader crisis of basic human survival.

What is at stake is indeed the belated but still sorely needed transition from an interdependence based on hierarchy and Western charity to an interdependence based on symmetry and mutual accountability. The last quarter of the twentieth century stands a chance—modest, but still a chance—of traversing the remaining distance toward such a world order.

CHAPTER VII

The OPEC Nations:
Partners or Competitors?

James P. Grant

A new group of nations with great economic influence, the Organization of Petroleum Exporting Countries (OPEC),[1] has emerged on the world scene in the mid-1970s. The more than fourfold increase in the price of oil decreed by these nations in 1973 is leading to the biggest sudden shift of financial resources from one group of nations to another that history has ever witnessed. OPEC's oil revenues in 1974 surpassed $100 billion, a 500 per cent increase over its 1972 revenues. While poor oil producers such as Indonesia were able to use most of their increased revenues for additional imports, the richer oil producers, particularly those of the Persian Gulf and Venezuela, had surplus on current account totalling over $50 billion for 1974. The import needs of these countries as a group probably will not match their export earnings until about 1980, by which time they will have accumulated a capital surplus of somewhere between $200-$300 billion. This chapter describes the key issues raised by this massive resource shift, assesses the major new assistance efforts launched by the OPEC countries, and explores briefly the issue of how the United States and other industrial market-economy countries should relate to this great new power on the international stage.

Even before the OPEC price intervention, the world faced a long-term energy crisis comparable to, and in many ways even more severe than, the

---

[1]The states with full membership status in OPEC (those with the right to vote, right to veto, and the obligation to abide by OPEC policies) are: Algeria, Ecuador, Indonesia, Iran, Iraq, Kuwait, Libya, Nigeria, Qatar, Saudi Arabia, United Arab Emirates, and Venezuela. Gabon is an Associate Member with the right to vote but no veto power. Trinidad, Tobago, and Peru have Observer Status which must be renewed prior to each OPEC meeting.

global food situation. Reserves of cheap oil are limited, and by the 1980s, the world will need to find alternate energy sources that may cost 25 to 50 times as much as the production of oil in the Persian Gulf. Much higher energy costs were in the cards for the not too distant future; the only question was *when* this would happen. Given this energy prospect, the developing oil producers— particularly the poorer countries, such as Indonesia and Nigeria, and those with relatively very limited reserves, such as Venezuela—of course considered a higher price for their non-renewable resource long overdue.

The United States bears a major share of the responsibility for OPEC's new power role. The average American uses more than two times as much energy as the average German, and nearly 100 times as much energy as a South Asian, making the United States by far the world's largest user of oil; until recently, however, the United States was able to meet almost all of its demand from domestic sources. It was the major entry by the United States into the international oil market in the early 1970s—after it was no longer able to meet most of its rapid annual *increase* in demand from domestic supplies— that virtually doubled the growth in demand for oil from developing-country producers, thereby in a sense overloading the world's oil-producing and marketing system.[2] The U.S. move converted the world oil market from one favoring buyers to one favoring suppliers—suppliers who, in this instance, had major outstanding grievances with the principal buyers over the low price of oil and the dispute with Israel.

Both the need for developing alternate energy sources—at much higher costs—by the mid-1980s and the shift from a buyers' to a sellers' market in the 1970s had been sensed if not fully foreseen by knowledgeable experts. What these analysts did not anticipate, however, was that Arab frustration over U.S. policy toward Israel and the price grievance shared by all developing-country oil producers would be sufficient to convert OPEC into an effective oil cartel. Indeed, the OPEC cartel is made up of as unlikely a group of economic partners as can be imagined: it includes radical and feudal Arabs, traditional antagonists such as Iran and Iraq, tiny but rich Kuwait and vast but poor Indonesia, white Venezuela and black Nigeria, and (from the U.S. point of view) friends such as Indonesia and Saudi Arabia and radical critics such as Algeria and Iraq. Despite its varied membership, OPEC's cohesion appears likely to continue for at least several years, particularly now that the long-standing border dispute between Iran and Iraq has been settled.

OPEC's policies require two responses from the world community: *first*, a comprehensive long-term global energy strategy comparable to the one now being hammered out with respect to food, and *second*, a quick solution to the short-term balance-of-payments and other problems raised by the abruptness of the 1973 oil price increases. Unfortunately, the fourfold energy price rise

---

[2]See Chapter VIII.

struck the world scene in the controversial context of the Middle East war in late 1973. The initial OPEC policies of harsh confrontation have tended to elicit a similar response from the United States, which for one year explored the use of virtually every lever short of force to roll back oil prices and sought to unite the OECD behind a common response. A certain amount of counter-organization among consumers is obviously necessary to avoid unbridled additional price increases and to reduce the vulnerability of the OECD countries at a time of continued Arab-Israeli confrontation. Planning for conservation, development of alternate energy sources, and oil price negotiations are likewise useful. As yet, however, there appear to be no official U.S. policies for responding to long-range energy needs in a *global* context— or for addressing the need of the poorer developing countries to develop alternative energy sources—on any scale comparable to the plans for meeting the world food insecurity problem. U.S. efforts to mobilize consumers have tended to exclude major oil-importing developing nations such as Brazil and India while including relatively minor "old rich" oil importers such as Luxembourg and Denmark.

Old Rich–New Rich Cooperation

The question of cooperation between OECD nations and OPEC nations arises on a number of important fronts. The *first* is the issue of how OPEC and OECD resources can best be channeled to help the countries most seriously affected by recent price rises. A related *second* issue is the desirability of the "old rich" and the "new rich" joining in a global cooperative developmental effort, including special programs for food, fertilizer, and hopefully energy production and distribution. There is a need for a global approach to ease the transition to higher production costs of energy over the next ten years. A *third* set of issues relates to ensuring that OPEC resources are recycled in a way that will ease the balance-of-payments straits for the most seriously affected industrial and developing countries;[3] a key question here is who will bear the risk of loss in the event of default by the poorest credit-risk nations. Agreement on oil price is a *fourth* issue. Oil producers (like American farmers and raw-material producers everywhere) want to be assured of a fair price and an acceptable floor. The oil importers want to bring the price down, and— even more important—they do not want it to go up further. A vital *fifth* issue involving the Arab producers is, of course, the Arab-Israeli conflict and its resolution. *Sixth* is the challenge of creating an investment climate that encourages the OPEC countries to invest their resources for domestic as well as world developmental purposes—a climate that encourages them not to squander their great but finite inheritance unnecessarily on arms, or on

---

[3]See Chapter V.

excessive consumption—just as Argentina did when, in a few years of consumerism, it wiped out the large reserves it had acquired during World War II. Finally, there is the range of issues involving the future relationship of the richer OPEC countries with the advanced industrial market-economy countries and the question of whether—and if so, how—the former will be treated as members of the OECD "club" in terms of their investments, participation in private financial councils, and role in the dominant institutions of the market-economy world.

So far this set of issues has not been approached comprehensively or collectively by the OECD countries. Confrontation has been the order of the day on the issue of the oil price, with the United States, in particular, acting as though OPEC were a belligerent in the new "cold war"; it has been marshalling allies, urging oil conservation to reduce demand, seeking a major price rollback, and generally failing to engage in a dialogue with producing nations until it is in a much stronger bargaining position. At the same time, all the industrial countries have been competing vigorously to sell goods of varying usefulness (or potential harm) to the new rich, with the United States clearly the "winner" in terms of arms sales and private contracts for technicians and equipment in the expanded development efforts of the OPEC nations.

OPEC Nations as Aid Providers

Hard figures on OPEC aid commitments and disbursements are virtually nonexistent. Data provided by the OECD, other multilateral institutions, and the press tend to differ widely. There are many reasons for these discrepancies, including varying definitions of aid and military assistance and differences in the time periods concerned. It is nevertheless clear that the OPEC countries became major aid providers in 1974, rivaling and in some ways exceeding the performance of the advanced countries and far surpassing in all respects the aid efforts of the communist countries. Faced with pleas for help from the developing countries sorely hurt by the price rises of 1973,[4] and needing continued diplomatic support in their confrontations with the United States, which was adamantly insisting on a sharp oil price rollback, the OPEC nations in 1974 committed approximately $10 billion and disbursed more

---

[4]The short-run balance-of-payments outlook for oil-deficit developing countries is one of sharp deterioration in 1974, compared to 1973. An even further deterioration is likely in these countries in 1975 as their exports decline (in response to the lower rate of expansion in the OECD countries) and as the prices of their essential imports remain high. Preliminary analysis by the OECD indicates that about half of the deterioration in the external payments situation of developing countries in 1974 can be attributed to oil price increases and about half to higher prices of imports of manufactured goods and food imports. As one illustration, India's import bill increased from $3.2 billion in 1973 to an estimated $5 billion in 1974. The cost of petroleum and related products increased from $447 million to $1.3 billion; fertilizers more than tripled in cost, rising from $205 million to over $600 million; and agricultural imports increased from $605 million in 1973 to $1.2 billion in 1974. India's exports increased in value from $2.96 billion in 1973 to around $3.85 billion in 1974, primarily because of higher prices for its sugar and tea exports.

than $2 billion in aid to other developing countries.[5] New reciprocal as well as common interests have created the strongest coalition of developing countries to date—with the more numerous poorer members providing diplomatic support for their OPEC brethren, and the latter providing the rest with both economic aid and political support for their demands on the industrial countries for increased economic equity.

How Much? From Whom? For Whom?

Bilateral financial aid commitments from OPEC nations are estimated to have totalled approximately $11 billion between 1970 and 1974, beginning modestly in 1970 and rising to approximately $2.7 billion in 1973 and $7.2 billion in 1974 (see Table D-8, p. 262). An additional $3.6 billion was committed between 1970 and 1974 ($2.4 billion in 1974 alone) to international agencies to be used for multilateral assistance. In addition, during 1974, $3.2 billion was offered to the IMF in connection with its new Oil Facility and over $1 billion was made available to the World Bank. Thus the total assistance pledged by OPEC countries on concessional to near-market terms in the first nine months of 1974 amounted to $13.7 billion.[6] Disbursements were of course at a much lower level, totalling approximately $4.5 billion from 1970 to 1974, of which $2.6 billion is estimated to have been disbursed in 1974. While comparisons need to be made with care, it might be noted that the DAC countries in 1973 disbursed $7.2 billion of concessional aid directly and $2.2 billion through multilateral agencies; their 1974 commitment figure was somewhat higher, approximately $11 billion.

The largest OPEC donors are Saudi Arabia, Iran, Kuwait, and Venezuela. During 1974, Iran and Saudi Arabia made large commitments— primarily through bilateral channels—totalling $3 billion each. Kuwait committed $1.3 billion, mostly for bilateral programs. Venezuela pledged $750 million, over 95 per cent of which was committed to multilateral mechanisms. Indonesia and Nigeria, with per capita incomes well below $250 even with their new oil revenues, are not major aid providers.

A useful insight into the evolution of the program of one major donor, Iran, has been provided by the chairman of the Development Assistance Committee (DAC)[7] of the OECD following his discussions with Iranian officials in Teheran in January 1975:

In March 1974, Iran began to commit to foreign assistance and investment that part of its earnings from oil which it was estimated

---

[5]Most figures in this section are from Working Document DD-403 of the OECD, December 6, 1974. See Tables D-8 and D-9, pp. 262-63.
[6]These figures exclude most military assistance and related economic support for defense purposes to several Middle East countries. Also not counted are the concessional oil sales agreements between a few developing countries and OPEC countries.
[7]See also pp. 193-94.

would be in excess of Iran's capability to absorb through greatly increased imports for its domestic programmes. The excess for foreign transactions is estimated at $14-$16 billion for the four-year period from March 1974 to March 1978. This estimate was agreed upon within the Iranian government after intensive efforts had been initiated to assure maximum feasible expansion of Iran's import capacity.

Iranian authorities reported that by December 31, 1974, they had made commitments of some $9 billion of their projected surplus—$4 billion for developing countries and $5 billion for developed countries. The $5 billion to developed countries for "assistance" in recycling is in deposits with central banks of industrial countries, investment in industrial firms and other purposes.

The $4 billion resource flow to developing countries includes over $1 billion for the purchase of World Bank bonds and as funds for developing countries through the IMF oil facility. About $3 billion will be provided directly to developing countries in projects and programmes, mostly through five- to ten-year loans at concessionary rates (one half to two and a half percent). Disbursements on the $4 billion of commitments will reach at least $1.5 billion (3.6 per cent of GNP) by March 1975, the end of the first year of Iran's aid programme. Disbursements of official development assistance (ODA) on DAC criteria will be about $600 million or 1.4 per cent of GNP.

By any standard, in a brief few months, Iran has launched a remarkably diversified and effective programme of project and programme financing. Major recipients are India, Pakistan, Sudan, Egypt, Syria, and Sri Lanka. Projects totalling over $60 million have been assisted with grant aid in Morocco, Afghanistan, Senegal, Jordan, and Pakistan, and there is a loan to Bangladesh as part of the consortium.

Venezuela, on the other side of the world, has concentrated primarily but not exclusively on its immediate region, having agreed to provide funds over a several-year period through the Inter-American Development Bank ($500 million, of which $100 million in 1974, $50 million in 1975), the Caribbean Development Bank ($25 million, of which $5 million in 1974), the Central American Bank for Economic Integration ($40 million, of which $10 million in 1974), and the Andean Development Corporation ($60 million, of which $20 million in 1974). The terms of Venezuela's assistance vary widely. Thus the special, $500-million trust fund to be loaned by Venezuela to the Inter-American Development Bank for loans to its least developed members carries an interest rate of 8 per cent, whereas another $100 million is being lent to the Bank at highly concessional rates. The funds made available to the Caribbean and Central American Banks have a maturity of up to 25 years, a grace period of up to seven years, and a 2-6 per cent rate of interest. Venezuela also allotted $500 million to the World Bank, through January 1975, at an interest rate of 8 per cent and an average maturity of 11 years; $540 million[8] to the International Monetary Fund's facility for financing oil imports; and $100 million to the United Nations Emergency Fund for the countries most seriously affected by the recent price rises.

Venezuela has also committed $20 million for use in Central America and the Caribbean through bilateral arrangements and is considering financing a $200-million refinery in Costa Rica. In addition, it reportedly plans to contribute about 70 per cent of the funds needed by the Central American countries for a coffee stockpile to stabilize and support coffee prices. One Venezuelan program now being implemented is a five-year arrangement permitting the Central American republics to borrow back, on a long-term basis, up to half of the money they pay for their oil imports from Venezuela. Under this arrangement, part of the purchase price of imports is to be paid directly to Venezuela, and part is to be deposited at interest in a local bank account in the importing country. The principal is to be paid to Venezuela at the end of the fifth year—unless it is used in the interim for a mutually agreed development project, in which case it can be repaid at 8 per cent interest over a period of up to 25 years. The funds deposited by Venezuela in a country participating in this arrangement can be used either for projects approved directly by Venezuela or for projects in which the World Bank, the Inter-American Development Bank, or AID are participating and whose soundness they have certified.

Given their limited management capacity, most OPEC donors have made extensive use of special development funds patterned after the prototype of the Kuwait Fund for Arab Economic Development (KFAED), which has lent some $500 million in its twelve-year life. The Arab Fund for Economic and Social Development, with an initial capital base of $340 million, was set up in 1972 as a multilateral version of KFAED. Saudi Arabia has launched and provided much of the financing for the $900-million Islamic Development Bank, which has also received contributions from Libya, the United Arab Emirates, and Kuwait, among others. OPEC assistance to poor African countries is being channeled mainly through the $200-million Special Arab Fund for Africa, the African Development Bank, and the KFAED.

As suggested above, the reason why the OPEC countries so far have resorted mainly to arrangements of this type is that most of their governments and private sectors still lack the capacity to assess projects on any significant scale. Only Venezuela and Kuwait have some capacity in this area, and even

---

[8]Of which $270 million was disbursed in 1974.

they are relying extensively on others. This means that for project development, appraisal, and implementation the OPEC countries—unlike the DAC countries, which tie their aid heavily to the use of their own technicians and equipment—have to rely on third-party capabilities. There is a major new opportunity here for both private-contractor initiatives and for useful cooperation between OPEC donors and other aid donors, multilateral and bilateral, with additional project-development and implementation capacity.

As for the direction of OPEC assistance, approximately one third of OPEC-country 1974 bilateral commitments, or $2.7 billion, went to the most seriously affected Fourth World countries and over $4 billion to other developing countries; the bulk of the latter sum went to Egypt, Syria, and Jordan. Prior to 1973, aid disbursements by the Arab oil producers were directed overwhelmingly (83 per cent) to these three countries, mostly in forms analogous to American economic security assistance to Israel and to the countries of Indochina. Thus the OPEC countries have been diversifying their assistance to include some of the Fourth World countries, although Egypt, Syria, and Jordan still receive a majority of all OPEC bilateral aid (60 per cent of both bilateral commitments and disbursements in 1974).

The principal Fourth World beneficiaries of OPEC 1974 bilateral commitments appear to be Pakistan ($957 million), India ($945 million), [9] Mauritania ($153 million), Malagasy Republic ($114 million), Sudan ($107 million), Sri Lanka ($86 million), Somalia ($82 million), Yemen People's Democratic Republic ($14.2 million), and Bangladesh ($82 million). The commitments to Fourth World countries exceeded somewhat the additional cost ($2 billion) of their oil purchases; their disbursements (over $700 million), however, were still at a far lower level (see Table D-9, p. 263).

Burden Sharing

By existing international standards, the OPEC nations are doing well at sharing the development assistance "burden" with other donor countries. As *The Economist* aptly summed up the situation in its report of February 15: "The oil exporters are mainly poor but generous" (see Table D-7, p. 261). The official U.N. target for transfers of concessional resources from developed to developing countries is 0.7 per cent of donor-country GNP. OPEC 1974 disbursements of $2.6 billion—out of a collective GNP of less than $200 billion for nearly 300 million people—are nearly double that target. The figure for 1975 almost certainly will be higher, given the much higher 1974 commitment level. The DAC countries, which in 1974 disbursed approximately $11 billion—out of a collective GNP of $3.5 trillion for nearly

---

[9]Approximately $230 million is expected to have been disbursed as of March 31, 1975, in the form of concessional sales of oil (similar to U.S. concessional sales of food under P.L. 480) from Iran and Iraq.

750 million people—are providing aid at a level of 0.3 per cent of GNP. The U.S. level is estimated to be 0.2 per cent of GNP in 1974. The current level of OPEC disbursements also exceeds the combined net flows of $750 million provided by the U.S.S.R. (0.16 per cent of GNP) and the $500 million provided by China (0.3 per cent of GNP).

The combined oil earnings of the United Arab Emirates, Qatar, Kuwait, Libya, and Saudi Arabia account for about 50 per cent of total OPEC earnings from oil exports. The total population of these countries is almost 13 million; their combined oil revenue is approximately $50 billion, or almost $4,000 per capita—somewhat less than the OECD per capita GNP average of $4,735. Like the OECD countries, the richer of the OPEC countries can well afford to extend concessional credits and grants to poor countries.

The rest of the OPEC countries, however, are not in a comparable position to afford aid. The eight countries that account for one half of total OPEC oil revenues have a per capita GNP averaging less than one twelfth of the OECD per capita income average. Even if populous Nigeria and Indonesia are excluded, the per capita GNP of the remaining six OPEC countries is one fifth that of the OECD countries.

Future Prospects for OPEC Aid

Disbursements of OPEC aid can be expected to rise in 1975, 1976, and 1977 because of the high aid commitments in 1974. New aid commitments, however, may well be smaller in the next three years than in 1974 for reasons discussed below. Any analysis of the duration and size of OPEC aid needs to take into account two principal factors: financial ability and motivation. The liquidity of many of the OPEC countries will decline rapidly later in the 1970s. Several authorities have predicted that, by 1980, the OPEC countries as a whole will be running a current-account deficit. Indeed, Iran's concessional lending can be expected to drop sharply by 1980—when it is again expected to become a net importer of capital and when its per capita income still will be very substantially below the OECD average. Other OPEC countries—Saudi Arabia, Libya, and some of the small Persian Gulf states—will then still be accumulating very substantial surpluses and may be expected to remain major sources of development assistance. However, by 1980, all of the OPEC countries, and particularly those with limited petroleum reserves, such as Venezuela, will be even more conscious of the fact that their oil revenues will ultimately run out, making them totally reliant on their income from petrodollar investments at home and abroad.

Each OPEC nation's foreign policy context over the next few years also will be a major determinant of the scale of its aid. If the Arab-Israeli confrontation is still intense, and if the OECD countries are still vigorously attempting to obtain an oil price rollback, the OPEC nations may find it valuable to distribute concessional aid widely to help hold together their

Table 1. OPEC Petroleum Reserves, Petroleum Production, and Population

	Estimated Petroleum Reserves (billion barrels)	Production, 1973 (million barrels/day)	Reserves at 1973 Production Rate (years)	Population, mid-1975 (millions)
Saudi Arabia	140.8	7.7	51	9.0
Kuwait	72.7	3.1	66	1.1
Iran	60.2	5.9	28	32.9
Iraq	31.2	2.0	44	11.1
Libya	25.6	2.2	32	2.3
United Arab Emirates	25.5	1.5	45	0.2
Nigeria	19.9	2.0	27	62.9
Venezuela	14.2	3.5	11	12.2
Indonesia	10.8	1.3	22	136.0
Algeria	7.4	1.0	20	16.8
Qatar	6.5	0.5	31	0.1
Ecuador	5.7	0.2	78	7.1

SOURCES: Oil figures are from *Business Week*, January 13, 1975, p. 80, and population figures are from Population Reference Bureau, "1975 World Population Data Sheet."

present broad base of developing-country support on these two issues. On the other hand, if international economic and political tranquility is restored (especially if there is a resolution of the Arab-Israeli dispute), OPEC's concessional aid levels may be expected to decline to the level of the U.N. target of 0.7 per cent of GNP. If the aid levels prevailing among DAC aid givers in 1980 are as low as the World Bank now projects (between 0.2 per cent and 0.3 per cent of GNP), this will be a further incentive for OPEC aid to decline.[10]

It is possible, however, that OPEC assistance might, even in such an increasingly tranquil world setting, remain high; this might prove true, for example, if OPEC members maintain or develop strong ties with other developing countries similar to Algeria's present support for the Group of 77, or Saudi Arabia's ties with Moslem countries, or Venezuela's and Iran's links with their respective neighbors. Some OPEC countries also might have a

[10]See Table D-4, p. 258. The World Bank's GNP forecasts for 1980 are $411 billion (in 1980 dollars) for the 300 million people of the OPEC nations, and $8 trillion (an increase over the $3.1 trillion in 1973) for the 750 million people in the OECD countries. If the OPEC countries, excluding Nigeria and Indonesia, were to honor the U.N. official development assistance target of 0.7 per cent of GNP, total OPEC official aid would be at the $2.5 billion level; if these countries were to follow the DAC example, however, the total might be well under $1 billion.

particular interest in making quasi-concessional investments in commodities or production facilities in developing countries. For example, the Persian Gulf countries might have a strategic or other special interest in stepping up fertilizer and food production in South Asia, the Sudan, and Sahelian Africa, particularly in areas with large Moslem populations.

There is as yet no comprehensive institutional mechanism for linking the development cooperation programs of the OPEC nations with those of the OECD nations or the multilateral institutions—nor have the OPEC countries created a cooperative mechanism for coordinating their own programs. Yet there should be room for greatly increased cooperation between the OPEC nations and the OECD countries and the multilateral institutions, since the OPEC countries are heavily dependent on the programming, managerial, and implementation skills of others for the success of their programs. With imaginative leadership, there should be substantial prospects for involving the "old rich" and the "new rich" in coordinated programs under the leadership of multilateral structures such as the Consultative Group on Agricultural Production and Investment recently established on the recommendation of the World Food Council.

There is a special danger that, as OPEC liquidity diminishes and its aid commitments also diminish later in this decade, Fourth World countries will be among the first to be hurt. The longer-range development needs of poorer countries are all too often sacrificed to short-run political objectives—as evidenced recently by the priority being given by the United States and the Arab OPEC countries to assisting countries involved in the Arab-Israeli conflict. To avoid this situation, there is need for a joint OECD-OPEC multi-year agreement to provide—in approximately equal amounts from the "old" and the "new" rich—an additional flow of some $4 billion annually over the next five years to the Fourth World countries. The U.S. share of this undertaking should be about $1 billion.[11] To the extent that such aid is channeled through multilateral institutions, there is a need to give the OPEC countries a say in policy more commensurate with their financial contribution—through measures such as the establishment of the Agricultural Development Fund proposed by the World Food Council and through appropriate adjustments in existing multilateral funding mechanisms.

---

[11] This additional billion dollars might be made up of increased food aid (as described in Chapter III of this volume) and expanded grants and concessional loans (as suggested in Chapter I). In addition, a significant portion could come from the proposed Export Development Credit Fund approved by both the House Foreign Affairs Committee and the Senate Foreign Relations Committee in 1973. This Fund would use repayments of old aid loans to pay for part of the interest charges on credits furnished U.S. exporters to encourage them to export to markets in the poorest countries—markets that have been denied U.S. exporters for lack of suitable export credits. This arrangement would not only furnish goods and services badly needed by the Fourth World countries on terms they can afford, but would also create jobs in the United States in a time of recession. See Tables B-3 and B-4, pp. 223-24.

OPEC Nations and the International Economic Order

The United States in early 1975 had not yet evolved a longer-range vision of how the newly powerful OPEC nations might relate to the existing international economic order. There is now a unique opportunity for nearly 300 million people (a population equal to that of Western Europe, North America, or Latin America) to progress developmentally at a rate never before seriously considered possible for so populous a group of heretofore poor nations. There is also an urgent need to reduce and avoid the obvious frictional problems that normally characterize the emergence of major new powers. Certain OPEC nations are becoming new power centers, either within their regions (as is true of Venezuela, Nigeria, and Indonesia) or even globally (Saudi Arabia, Kuwait, and Iran). Mention need only be made of Germany before World War I, of Japan and Italy before World War II, and of the Soviet Union and China more recently—and of the oil embargo and price shocks of 1973—to illustrate the point that adjustment costs can be very high. However, as we learned after World War II in our relations with Japan, Germany, and Italy, accommodation and economic cooperation can have highly beneficial results for all sides. The longer-run stakes involved are very large indeed; and if the rapidly progressing OPEC countries can establish a new and more symmetrical interdependence with the "old rich," all or most developing countries should benefit to some degree, and new patterns of accommodation and cooperation that could be of great value for the future may be established.

Iran as well as Kuwait and Saudi Arabia apparently desire a closer economic relationship with the OECD nations—a greater interdependence on the basis of greater economic equality. Subject to a further de-escalation of the Arab-Israeli conflict, it is possible to envisage the advanced market-economy countries welcoming such countries into the "system," much as Japan has been integrated into it in the past twenty-five years. Algeria, Libya, and to a lesser extent Venezuela have, on the other hand, seen themselves as leaders of the Third World in a broad confrontation with the "old rich" designed to hammer out a new international economic order.

If the industrial market-economy countries decide to take a comprehensive global approach to all or most international economic issues analogous to that being followed in the case of food, this distinction between the Middle East oil producers and other oil producers is not particularly important—again assuming the Arab-Israeli conflict is solved or brought under long-term control. But if a long period of confrontation were to emerge between the North and the South or parts thereof, or if the Arab-Israeli dispute were to flare anew, it is likely that the industrial countries will instead seek bilateral relationships with selected developing countries. If a more acute North-South confrontation were to emerge, a major effort addressed to "welcoming" the richer oil producers—including maximum encouragement of OPEC investments in the advanced economies—would undoubtedly be considered. This would not be true, however, if the Arab-Israeli controversy were to continue at or above present levels of intensity; the industrial market economies, and particularly the United States, might then seek stronger ties of cooperation with non-Arab oil producers, as well as with developing countries generally, in order to reduce the likelihood (or effectiveness) of another Arab oil embargo.

OECD Cooperation in the Development of the OPEC Nations

As noted earlier, the United States has been slow to develop its thinking as to the desirable longer-range relationship between the OPEC countries and the industrial market-economy countries. This has been due to its prolonged (and unrealistic) effort to obtain a substantial oil price rollback as well as to the continuing uncertainties of the Arab-Israeli conflict. The former, hopefully, is no longer a serious issue, and the latter should not preclude a strategy of long-range accommodation with the many non-Arab OPEC nations.

Part of any successful long-range accommodation must necessarily include effective development cooperation. Despite their present highly favorable financial position, all of the OPEC countries except Venezuela lack adequate industrial know-how and skilled manpower and are seeking to acquire advanced technology to accelerate their development before their oil resources are depleted. For Venezuela, this may be a limited period of eleven years; for Iran, it may be somewhat longer, perhaps twenty-eight years. For populous Indonesia and Nigeria, with their relatively limited years of reserves at current rates of production and their low per capita incomes, this is a highly valuable and fleeting opportunity to develop forward momentum that will carry them out of poverty. It would be a tragedy if any of these countries were to expend much of their oil inheritance on needless arms, inefficient investments, and overconsumption before establishing alternative viable productive capabilities for themselves.

As of early 1975, the United States had taken only some preliminary steps toward encouraging the development and ultimate viability of the OPEC nations by its decisions to participate in joint bilateral commissions with Saudi Arabia and Iran. It was, moreover, still opposing the efforts of multilateral institutions to assist the development efforts of such poor OPEC nations as Nigeria and Indonesia. There was also still debate about the extent to which the OPEC countries should be encouraged to invest their billions of surplus funds in the United States—even though the benefits of this potential inflow seem to far outweigh its disadvantages. The United States has long asserted the valuable contribution of its investors to the economies of other countries, yet Congress is at present considering legislation to limit foreign

147

investment in the United States. It would seem that the possibility of any harmful side effects of foreign investment in this case, as in others, could be minimized through the surveillance of such investments under laws and regulations that clearly state the permissible limits of foreign control. Massive investments by the OPEC countries would not only provide needed capital, but would give the OPEC investors a stake in the health of the U.S. economy and in establishing international standards for host-country treatment of foreign investors.

Conclusion

The relationship between the OPEC nations and the industrial countries for the first eighteen months after the oil price rises of 1973 has reflected a general "winners-losers," or "zero-sum game," approach. The opportunity to create a more positive and cooperative relationship to the long-run mutual benefit of the United States, the OPEC nations, and the rest of the world is not yet lost.

Realists have claimed that the world never changes until it is compelled to do so by force or threat of force, leading (at best) to negotiation. But there have been occasions—the current global campaign against hunger may be one—when the world has changed because statesmen have perceived a common interest in solving a common problem to the benefit of all parties. Such a perception should guide U.S. policy makers in shaping U.S. relations with the OPEC countries.

CHAPTER VIII

Systems Overloads and World Transformations

James P. Grant and Robert H. Johnson

These are times of a great global transformation. On the one hand, the dissolution of the last of the great colonial empires and the continuing advance of science and technology offer the prospect of meeting the minimum requirements for a decent life for all mankind. On the other hand, the world faces a set of problems which already have created, or could create, severe crises that would undermine these prospects for progress. These threatening problems include inadequate food supplies, the energy crisis, stagflation, disruptions in the world's monetary and trading systems, and unsatisfactory distribution of income and wealth within and among nations.

In part, these problems are the product of temporary factors such as severe droughts in several areas of the globe in 1972 and 1974, the global economic boom of the early 1970s, and the Middle East war. More basic forces, however, also have been at work. Foremost among these has been the unprecedented secular increase in rates of economic growth. The annual global growth rate, which was 4 per cent in the late 1940s and early 1950s, rose gradually to almost 6 per cent by the early 1970s. Over the same period, a $1 trillion world economy became a $3 trillion economy ($5 trillion in current dollars), and the world's population grew from 2.5 billion to 4 billion. Meanwhile, the international economic institutions that had been created in the immediate postwar period increasingly confronted a set of problems beyond their scope and power to manage. Traditional economic and political concepts likewise have proven grossly inadequate for understanding both our domestic and international problems of the 1970s.

Three points are increasingly clear. *First*, the world can no longer confidently extrapolate a growth pattern for the next twenty-five years similar to the trend line of the 1950s and the 1960s. (If the world experienced serious problems as it went from the second trillion dollars of gross global product to the third trillion, what is going to happen in the balance of this century as the world economy quadruples again—as it would if it were to maintain the global growth rate of the past ten years?) But slower economic growth rates will raise serious political problems in an era of high population growth rates and raised expectations for material well-being. *Second*, the problems we confront cannot be managed within traditional intellectual parameters.[1] *Third,* there is an urgent need for creating new institutions (or strengthening old ones) which are more responsive to the problems we face.

The Problem of Systems Overloads

The basic underlying problem is less one of physical limits to growth than one of institutional, technological, and conceptual limits. We are experiencing systems overloads from the unprecedented rates of growth in output of recent years. Like the short circuits in an overloaded electrical system, a rash of institutional breakdowns is threatening to overload various world systems such as the food, monetary, and ecological systems.

As we have moved to the $3 trillion economy, global systems have shown increasing signs of stress. The world has begun to suffer ecological overload: pollution, eutrophication of lakes, and declining global fish catches due to overfishing. The unprecedented increases in population and affluence of the 1960s and early 1970s have so expanded demand that the demand-supply relationship for a growing list of commodities (most conspicuously oil) shifted to a sellers' market from what for many years had been a buyers' market. Formerly weak sellers are utilizing their new power to settle longstanding economic and political grievances. Increased demand has also led to multi-year shortages of a few critical commodities, notably food and fertilizers. Moreover, remedial efforts in one sector have frequently aggravated problems in another; thus, for example, measures to protect the environment both slowed the supply of energy (e.g., the campaign against the Alaska pipeline) and increased demand (e.g., antipollutant devices on cars which increase gasoline consumption). As growing demand has outrun the easier, customary sources of production, and as most nations, including the United States, have become heavily dependent upon each other for continued economic progress, the response of world economic and political structures repeatedly has been slow and inadequate. Disruptions have been a consequence.

---

[1]As Walter Heller, the outgoing president of the American Economic Association, said after surveying the wreckage of economic forecasting for 1973: "We [economists] have been caught with our parameters down."

The problem of systems overloads can be illustrated more specifically by a brief examination of three problem areas: stagflation, food, and energy. In the early 1970s, all of the world's major national economies were booming simultaneously. All the market economies—including, for the first time in any substantial degree, the U.S. economy—were very vulnerable to international economic forces. There was, however, no effective international machinery for coordinating fiscal and monetary policies, and there were no international institutions for dealing adequately with the sudden crisis imposed by the oil embargo, the fourfold increase in petroleum prices, and growing food shortages. The consequence of the lack of effective global machinery was a disastrous aggravation of the inflation-recession problem. The combination of interdependence and inadequate international institutions helped lead to a simultaneous inflationary overheating of national economies followed by a simultaneous nosedive into recession. National institutions were simply not equipped to handle existing international interdependencies.

Similarly, the growth in demand for food has imposed almost unbearable demands upon the existing international food production and distribution system. At the turn of the century, the global demand for food increased annually by 4 million tons; by the early 1950s, it was rising at an annual rate of 12 million tons; and in 1972, by 25-30 million tons. Global demand is projected by the U.N. Food and Agriculture Organization to rise from approximately 1.2 billion tons in 1969-1971 to 1.7 billion tons in 1985. Roughly half of the current annual increase is accounted for by developed countries, where the rate of population growth is relatively low but the rate of increase in affluence is high. The other half of the increase occurs in developing countries, where high population growth is its principal cause.

The traditional means of expanding output in the developed world are being rapidly exhausted. The United States put the last of its idle cropland back into production in 1974. Moreover, in the developed countries, all water readily available for irrigation is already being utilized, and additional applications of fertilizer now bring sharply diminishing returns.

The principal longer-term means available for meeting the overall world supply gap and at the same time alleviating the problem of an inadequate supply of food in the developing countries is to increase production in those countries. In some developing countries, there still is idle land that can be developed if a variety of natural obstacles (for example, the prevalence of the tsetse fly in Africa) can be overcome. Most developing countries also have considerable unutilized potential—at present world grain price levels—for employing greater quantities of inputs such as water and fertilizer. (It would require increases in grain prices to make such increased use clearly economical in most developed countries.) Densely populated land-scarce countries such as India and Bangladesh also have a major potential for increasing yields (at lower costs than in developed countries) by implementing more labor-intensive, small-farm-oriented agricultural development strategies. But existing governmental and private services are not reaching the small farmer—who generally lacks access to basic health and education services as well as to the financial credit required to increase his production. If India's yields per acre equalled those of the United States, it could readily double its present production of about 100 million tons annually.[2] Utilizing labor-intensive techniques now prevalent in Japan, Taiwan, and South Korea, its annual production could total over 300 million tons.

The world, and particularly the United States, has been slow to recognize—and to respond through policy and institutional changes—to the developing overload of the world food production and distribution system. The United States, for example, failed to anticipate the large Soviet grain purchases of 1972; it restricted fertilizer exports to the detriment of global output in 1973-74; and in 1972 and 1973 it deliberately sought to liquidate government-held grain stocks through such means as withholding millions of acres from grain production (20 million in 1973).[3] The results have been shortages and soaring food prices. Food-price increases contributed as much to global inflation in 1973 and 1974 as the petroleum price rise. The price rises—along with drought—have also led to a maldistribution of the world's existing food supplies, with many of the poorest countries suffering most.

At the World Food Conference in 1974, a truly global response to this global problem was finally begun with the leadership and support of the United States. The Conference identified and initiated action to deal with the critical issues: increased assistance for food production in developing countries; establishment of an international system of grain reserves; reform and expansion of food aid; and commitment by developing countries to rural reforms designed to assist the poor majority of small farmers. Implementation of the Conference proposals would effect a major overhaul of the world food production-distribution system. With appropriate action, the world could feed over twice as many people as it does today.

Unfortunately the global energy problem has not yet been similarly addressed. In this case, too, the difficulties have been created by rapidly rising demand, although the basic supply problems are of a longer-term character. Knowledgeable experts had foreseen the shift of the mid-1970s from a buyers' to a sellers' market for petroleum and the need to develop alternative, higher-cost energy sources by the mid-1980s. Even they, however, did not anticipate the Arab oil embargo or the cohesion among all oil producers (including traditional friends of the United States) that led to the fourfold increase in prices in 1973. Nor did they anticipate the impact of environmental measures on supply and demand. The new era of increased energy interdependence and high energy prices has created a need for improved global resource, monetary,

---

[2] See Lester R. Brown with Erik P. Eckholm, *By Bread Alone* (New York: Praeger Publishers, Inc. for the Overseas Development Council, 1974) p. 213.
[3] See Chapter III.

and investment management to meet both immediate and long-term needs. Instead, there has been a tendency toward a new "cold war" between the "old rich" and the "new rich" oil-producing countries.

These three cases of systems overloads demonstrate that while the market is an essential economic adjustment mechanism, there is a serious need for new values, institutions, and rules to provide a new frame within which market forces can continue to operate if adequate growth is to be maintained and high rates of inflation avoided. For example, with respect to trade in commodities—including food, fertilizer, and petroleum—there is a need for new rules for access to supplies; new reserve stocks for goods in potentially short supply; new assurances on floor prices; and development of new sources of production.[4] The resolutions of the World Food Conference do not imply abandonment of the market system as a regulatory mechanism. They do call for action that would increase food production in the countries of greatest need and comparative advantage, reduce price oscillations, and reduce the inequalities produced by simple reliance upon the existing market mechanism. To achieve such ends, the World Food Conference resolutions recommend utilizing such familiar means as increased development assistance and reserve stocks of grain.

Emerging Historic Transformations and New World Issues

The basic problems we confront as we look to the future will involve not only the creation or rebuilding of institutions, but also an ability to make a number of major adjustments to emerging transformations in world economics and politics. Some of these adjustments will be forced upon us by basic shifts in the directions of major trends; others will be desirable if we are to assure cooperation rather than confrontation in our approach to future world problems.

First, *growth rates for the production of material goods will probably slow sharply* for the mid- and late 1970s, and very likely for the balance of the century, *unless the world can develop new systems, or improve existing ones, for managing areas of scarcity and tension.* Assuming that other sources of the present recession can be dealt with satisfactorily, such tensions and scarcities will reemerge as the condition of relatively full employment that has been characteristic of the past ten years in the developed countries is once more approached. As suggested earlier, the limits to growth are more closely related

---

[4]Means must be found to increase production of commodities that are in chronically tight world supply by utilizing the comparative advantage that many developing countries have for the production of such commodities (e.g., by using the flared natural gas of oil producers for fertilizer production; by developing grain production in countries where increases in agricultural inputs will produce proportionately large marginal increases in outputs; and, quite possibly, by developing low-cost alternative energy sources such as solar energy for pumping water for irrigation.)

to conceptual, technological, and institutional constraints than they are to physical constraints on finite supplies.

Second, supply-demand imbalances in some important areas will have to be met by reduced rates of growth in demand as well as by increases in supply. This, in turn, will force *changing patterns of demand and changing life styles.* Less wasteful life styles in the rich countries can in many cases benefit both rich and poor countries. They can benefit the rich by improving the quality of life. Thus, for example, lower speed limits mean fewer highway deaths, and a more efficient use of food could increase life expectancy. Less wasteful consumption of goods (and increased emphasis upon services) will also reduce the likelihood of irreconcilable conflicts between rich and poor countries by providing the basis for a more equitable sharing of the world's resources between the rich and the poor.

In an increasingly interdependent world of rising expectations among the poor, a third likely shift is *much more attention to issues of distribution within and among nations.* The implicit social compacts that were shaped within and among societies during the past generation were based upon a sharing of the benefits of high world growth rates between rich and poor. If growth rates slow down, there will be greatly increased pressures to devote attention to the distribution of the reduced benefits. Such pressures may grow within societies; more predictably, they will grow between societies.

Emboldened on the one hand by the success of the OPEC initiative, and conscious on the other of the growing dependency of the rich nations on the resources and cooperation of the poor, the developing countries will press far more insistently and with greater power for changes in North-South relationships. At present, it is still very uncertain whether the rich countries will treat such issues as a zero-sum game—as a North-South cold war—or whether they will approach them on the assumptions of mutual interests and benefits—as the United States did, to its great gain, in many of its relationships with Western Europe and Japan since World War II.

It would be a serious mistake to see the North-South conflict as posing a revolutionary challenge comparable to that which appeared to be posed by the communists in the cold war. The developing countries are not aiming to change the *internal* systems of other countries; they are instead avidly seeking reform of the global economic order to provide greater equity and sharing among nations. Like American industrial workers who in the first half of the 20th century sought the right to organize and bargain collectively, the developing countries are attempting to organize in order to ensure that they will be treated by the industrial countries on the basis of greater equality—on a basis that is analogous to the way that the industrial countries generally treat each other.

A fourth likely trend will be that *inflation rates will be significantly higher over the next fifteen years* than in the 1960s. As the poor nations (and masses) of the world press for greater material well-being, the already affluent will very probably be slow to change their consumption-oriented values or to reduce their expectations. In a situation of institutional inadequacies and supply scarcities, this dual set of demands will increase prices. The likelihood of such pressures puts a special premium on implementation of programs—such as those for increased world food production and world food reserves—which can simultaneously improve the well-being of the world's poor through increased participation in production and keep down prices through expanded supplies and better supply management.

A fifth major shift now taking place is that some economic and therefore some political *power is being transferred from those countries depending primarily upon high technology to those which are resource-rich.* Those countries that have substantial resources and technology, such as the United States, will continue to have relatively great power. At the other end of the spectrum, those countries of the Fourth World with few resources and little technology will lose some of the little power they have. In the middle, countries such as Japan, with its high technology but very limited natural resources, will have a less commanding position than they once appeared to possess—while countries such as Saudi Arabia, which has little technology but great resources, will have increased power. The United States as the world's greatest producer and exporter of raw materials, as well as the world's technological leader, has greater economic preeminence vis-a-vis other industrial countries with market economies than it had two or three years ago. Therefore we are having new responsibilities thrust upon us at the very time when we have become less inclined to assume a world leadership role. Without American leadership and participation, however, effective new or improved systems for organizing the international economic order will be difficult or impossible to achieve.

Finally, it is evident that *the concept of the security of the United States must be broadened beyond political and military security and beyond the balance of power.* The concept of security has always embraced the idea of access to essential raw materials, but with growing U.S. dependence upon imported materials, such access has greatly increased in importance. Moreover, our security now depends upon the effective operation of a whole series of world systems—the trade, investment, monetary, food production and distribution, and ecological systems.

Conclusion

The preceding discussion indicates that an historic transformation is indeed now in progress. It is affecting the international economic order, global politics, and, potentially, human values so fundamentally that it can truly be said that a change is occurring in the molecular structure of the world order.

The world achieved progress without historical parallel in the past thirty years because of an unprecedented willingness to change institutional and power structures to accommodate new forces and needs. To an unusual degree, many nations adopted an enlightened view of national self-interest. In the post-World War II era, the recollection of post-World War I chaos, the Great Depression, and fascist agression; the sense of threat from communism; and common support of national independence and freedom all helped create the consensus underlying the Bretton Woods institutions and the Marshall Plan and legitimized the struggle for independence of many colonial territories.

A new set of changes of comparable magnitude is necessary if man is to successfully overcome the new problems he currently faces in his interface with nature and his fellow man. Changes are required to adjust to slower growth rates, to implement new development strategies encompassing the majority in the poor countries, to create new relations between various groupings of countries, and to shape new life styles among the more affluent. None of these changes will be easy, but all are possible and no more difficult to achieve than those of the post-World War II era that is now passing. While the recent disasters and near-disasters do not provide us with an impetus to action comparable to the challenge of a world destroyed by war, we should still be reminded by the progress achieved in the past twenty-five years of what can be achieved through policies of cooperation and sharing.

The developing countries have been seeking, with very little success, to engage the industrial countries in general, and the United States in particular, in a comprehensive dialogue on the structural changes that will be required if our increasingly interdependent world is to be managed effectively and with a greater degree of justice. For reasons already suggested, the United States need not fear such a dialogue and could benefit very substantially politically and economically by undertaking it.

The responsibilities of American citizens and leaders are particularly great. As at several historical watersheds in this century, the course of human progress cannot avoid mammoth setbacks without major affirmative action by the United States. The times require that those Americans in positions of trust in government, business, academia, labor, and the churches provide leadership; and that informed, concerned citizens make it good politics for them to do so.

CHAPTER IX

The Emerging Challenge: Global Distribution of Income and Economic Opportunity

Roger D. Hansen

The 1970s are likely to be remembered as a decade during which a host of issues and problems concerning existing patterns of domestic and international distribution of income and economic opportunity rose to the top of agendas—public and private—throughout the world. The question of income distribution *among* nations has been dramatized by the quintupling of oil prices since late 1973, the effect of which has been a 2 per cent reduction in the GNP of the OECD countries, a 3 per cent GNP reduction on the part of the non-OPEC developing world, and a doubling of the GNP of the OPEC countries. While the aggregate distributional impact of the actions of the OPEC countries could not possibly be duplicated through price changes in any other product, 1974 witnessed many efforts with similar, if less spectacular, redistributional objectives on the part of other developing countries.

Within nations, the issue of income distribution and economic opportunity continued to arouse concern throughout 1974. In its most salient form, the concern focused on the problem of *absolute poverty,* however defined, and on the impact of the 1973-74 food and energy price increases on those living at absolute poverty levels throughout the world.[1] In 1975, as the problems of stagflation and unemployment worsen, concern with and struggles over domestic distribution of income are likely to increase within most developed as well as developing countries. These problems among

---

[1] See Table B-7, p. 228.

others recently led economist Alice Rivlin to suggest that within the United States "income shares and distributional aspects of public actions are going to become a major focus of policy debate in the next few years. I am not predicting how that debate will come out—just that it will take place."[2]

A good deal of the caution inherent in this essay concerns the issue of conceptualization. What can we hope to gain by examining profiles of income distribution for developed countries, developing countries, and for the world as a whole? Egalitarians may be shocked by the present figures, "practical people" may regard them as inevitable, and still others may generally approve of them for a host of reasons—for example, that equality of rewards is not an acceptable norm for society, although equality of opportunity may be. Are we concerned with increasing the equality of rewards, increasing the equality of economic opportunity, eliminating what is generally called *absolute* poverty, or with some combination of these and other possible goals regarding the distribution of income *and* economic opportunity?

The ambivalence inherent in American views on the subject of income inequality within the United States was perhaps best captured by Robert Lampman in the following passage:

> Each program for redistribution, be it public education, unemployment insurance or public housing, has its own philosophy which may have little in common with the philosophy that informs the design of the American standard distribution of income. The latter is, then, a performance indicator to which no social policy is directly keyed. The hiatus is significant. It means that the income distribution is not used in deciding who should help whom; apparently, it is not considered to be a reliable road map for social intervention. It may also mean something else: namely, that Americans don't really seek any particular degree of income equality, but rather seek a system of sharing that recognizes human needs, restrains certain arbitrary or capricious inequalities and serves social purposes.[3]

This view is consonant with that of James Tobin, who, in his essay "On Limiting the Domain of Inequality," suggests that the American ethos regarding income inequality is one which will allow slowly increasing domestic income transfers from rich to poor to meet the latter's wants for a limited but probably expanding number of goods—including food, health

---

[2]Alice Rivlin, "Income Distribution: Can Economists Help?," Richard T. Ely Lecture (Delivered at the Annual Meeting of the American Economic Association, San Francisco, California, December 1974), p. 1.

[3]Robert J. Lampman, "Measured Inequality of Income: What Does it Mean and What Can It Tell Us," *The Annals of the American Academy of Political and Social Science* (September 1973), pp. 90-91.

care, education, and housing.[4] The allocation of these so-called "merit wants" on a subsidized basis will increase real incomes—and more importantly, the future incomes—of the poor. This pattern is a familiar one in many developed countries, and is certainly recognizable in the United States, where more direct forms of income redistribution still appear to be politically unfeasible. As Martin Bronfenbrenner recently noted, "apparently society will trust the poor to a greater extent with that which it thinks the poor ought to want— merit wants—than it will trust the poor with that which they may actually want more—generalized purchasing power."[5] Even in the case of merit wants, recent American history suggests that there are very sharp limitations to this "half-a-loaf" approach to decreasing income concentration.

To the extent that Americans have in the past concerned themselves with the issue of domestic income distribution, it would appear that their vague and for the most part inarticulated objectives have focused on a generalized broadening of equality of opportunity and on eliminating absolute poverty. No matter how skewed, the pattern of income distribution per se has not been, in Lampman's words, "considered to be a reliable road map for social intervention" by U.S. policy makers.

The degree to which American views are shared by other societies, developed and developing, is a matter for further investigation, as is the degree to which American views may be changing at this very point in our own history. The findings would help to suggest the degrees to which conflict or consensus at present characterizes the conceptualization of the income distribution "problem" within domestic societies. But such a survey would do little to delineate the issue as it concerns the *global* distribution of income and wealth. In the latter case, rich and poor within developing countries can unite in pressing their redistribution demands upon the developed countries; domestic conflict within the developing states will arise only if the rhetoric of international egalitarianism begins to suggest to the poorest within the latter states that what is sauce for the international goose is sauce for the domestic gander.

The Growing Focus on Inequality

Existing empirical data for most countries are far too fragmentary to allow many valid generalizations concerning patterns and trends of income distribution. As most of the literature in the field suggests, the data are so limited, and those which we have are of such questionable value, that no convincing explanation of why income gets distributed as it does yet exists.

---

[4]James Tobin, "On Limiting the Domain of Inequality," *Journal of Law and Economics,* Vol. 13 (October 1970), pp. 263-77.

[5]Martin Bronfenbrenner, "Equality and Equity," *The Annals of the American Academy of Political and Social Science* (September 1973), p. 20.

Despite existing conceptual and empirical deficiencies, we have already noted the rapidly increasing degree of thought and action now devoted to aspects of the income distribution issue. The sources of such activity—as well as the means suggested (or used) and the ends sought—have been disparate. A recitation of a few of the leading examples reveals this heterogeneity of objectives, means, and goals. Concerning the issue of *international* distribution, the following examples are worth noting:

Less than two years ago, Zbigniew Brzezinski wrote the following passage:

It is to be expected that in the next two or three decades we will witness an intensified crisis in the developing world brought about by the twin impacts of demographic growth and the spread of education. Both will make global inequality even more intolerable at a time when equality is becoming the most powerful moral imperative of our time, thus paralleling the appeal of the concept of liberty during the nineteenth century.

This quest for equality is already being felt both within societies and on a global scale; it is, therefore, essential that the richer nations develop more comprehensive, more cooperative, and more planned policies toward the poorer parts of the world.[6]

Brzezinski's *objectives* in supporting enhanced efforts at international redistribution appear to be linked primarily to concern about a "peaceful world order"; his preferred *means* seem to be an increase of North-South resource transfers of a more-or-less traditional type; and his *goals*, a decade of the 1980s in which the world's developed countries (in essence, the member countries of the OECD) coordinate their own domestic *and* foreign assistance policies in a manner consonant with their own view of a just world order.

Richard Jolly made the following observation after the OPEC oil embargo and price increases of 1973:

Whatever happens, the world of economic relationships will never be quite the same again. The potential for bargaining in other areas has been dramatically revealed, no doubt to an extent and at a speed which is unlikely to be matched again. But bargaining to much greater degrees is possible in other areas, if only bargaining strength is developed and exploited. Such possibilities include: (i) monopolistic price increases for other primary commodities, (ii) strict

---

[6]Zbigniew Brzezinski, "U.S. Foreign Policy: The Search for Focus," *Foreign Affairs*, Vol. 51, No. 4 (July 1973), p. 726. From the larger context of Brzezinski's article, I assume he is speaking of equality not in the *juridical* but rather in the *socio-economic* sense in the passage quoted above.

embargoes on export of strategic materials, and (iii) restriction of overflying rights or use of military bases.[7]

Noting that growing global economic interdependence makes the need for coordinated actions more necessary, Jolly argues that arms and pollution control, supplies of basic commodities, world monetary management, and control of multinational corporations all offer means "for achieving gains by the poorer countries through the exploitation of mutual advantages, no doubt requiring tougher bargaining, but for mutual gains, not just at the other parties' expense."[8]

Jolly's objectives, means, and goals clearly differ from those of Brzezinski. His *objectives* are primarily redistributive (thus he approves of the OPEC actions and other producer cartel attempts as a starting point in an aggressive North-South bargaining process); his *means* include strategies of conflict as well as compromise—strategies alternatively perceived as "blackmail" and "retribution for past injustices"; and his *goal*, a world of the 1980s in which few if any global or regional institutions or functional "directorates" exclude strong developing-country influence in the making of policy.

Richard Gardner, chairman of the 1974 Rensselaerville meeting devoted to a discussion of the food and energy crises, has presented yet another perspective on the global redistribution question:

> What the world requires now is not more self-serving talk about "sovereignty" but a mutual survival pact between developed and developing countries in which mutually-agreed limitations on the sovereignty of each are undertaken to protect the sovereignty of all. We need to strike a great transcontinental bargain in which access to energy and other raw materials is traded for other kinds of access that developing countries need—access to markets at stable and remunerative prices, access to technology, management skills and investment capital, and access to a fairer share of decision-making in international institutions.
>
> The "world survival bargain" will also have to balance assurances by rich countries to conserve on energy, food and raw materials with commitments by poor countries to change some suicidal demographic, agricultural and environmental practices.[9]

---

[7]Hollis Chenery, Montek S. Ahluwalia, C.L.G. Bell, John H. Duloy, and Richard Jolly, *Redistribution with Growth,* published for the World Bank and the Institute of Development Studies, University of Sussex (Oxford: Oxford University Press, 1974), p. 167.

[8]Ibid.

[9]Richard N. Gardner, "Report of the Seminar," in *The World Food and Energy Crises: The Role of International Organizations* (Rensselaerville, N.Y.: The Institute on Man and Science, 1974), p. 65. The proceedings of an international conference co-sponsored by

The objectives implicit in this statement are both short-term and long-term in nature. The former are to keep the present international economic system free from increasing degrees of North-South conflict by what one would imagine to be a modest "resource transfer" from the rich nations to the poor. Gardner's long-term objectives are informed by a set of problems whose magnitude is still at issue—the problems of the population explosion, the growing restraints on increased food production, the potential for "absolute" resource scarcities, and the ecological implications of economic growth as it has evolved over the past several decades. What are the implications for global energy supplies, food production capacity, and the global ecosystem of present and projected population growth rates? U.N. projections suggest an approximate doubling of the world's population between 1970 and 2000, from 3.6 billion to 7.1 billion. The issue raised by Gardner and by others before him is what the costs, global and regional, of such a population increase are likely to be if Malthusian constraints do not themselves set lower limits. Thus Gardner's *objectives* are to lower the risks implicit in today's rapid population growth rates in developing countries. His *means* embrace a global compact in which the rich countries conserve on consumption of potentially scarce commodities in order to share them with the developing countries; the latter in turn limit their own potential consumption via population control. His *goal* is an orderly world in an "age of scarcity."

These three recent views on the global equity issue are suggestive of the increasing attention the global distribution of wealth and income is receiving and the heterogeneity of the objectives, means, and goals attaching to various views.[10] As the OPEC example and the other raw-material-cartel attempts of the past year suggest, developing-country actions to enforce a redistribution have accompanied as well as provoked the thought process.

The focus of attention on various aspects of domestic income distribution within developing countries is as intense as that on international distribution, though its recent history is somewhat less sudden and dramatic. At least five years ago, as development experts examined the results of the First Development Decade and planned for the Second, a trend toward disillusionment with the distributional aspects of the growth process in most developing countries had already begun. The disillusionment has been shared by developed- and developing-country economists, technicians, and politicians, and by national and international institutions engaged in various aspects of promoting economic growth. The U.N.'s International Development Strategy for the Second United Nations Development Decade, adopted by the General Assembly in 1970, stated that:

The Institute on Man and Science, the Aspen Institute for Humanistic Studies, the Overseas Development Council, and the Charles F. Kettering Foundation. For an allegorical approach to an overlapping set of issues, see McGeorge Bundy, "After the Deluge, the Covenant," *The Saturday Review* (August 24, 1974), pp. 18 ff.

[10]For an even more recent view, see Chapter VI.

As the ultimate purpose of development is to provide increasing opportunities to all people for a better life, it is essential to bring about a more equitable distribution of income and wealth for promoting both social justice and efficiency of production, to raise substantially the level of employment, to achieve a greater degree of income security, to expand and improve facilities for education, health, nutrition, housing and social welfare, and to safeguard the environment. Thus, qualitative and structural changes in the society must go hand in hand with rapid economic growth, and existing disparities—regional, sectoral and social—should be substantially reduced.[11]

The themes sounded in that internationally negotiated document were soon reflected in academic analyses, World Bank rhetoric and programming, and U.S. foreign aid legislation. By 1974, the issue of income distribution within developing countries and the relationship between distribution and economic growth had become the subject of searching examination. If a caricature of the old orthodoxy can be said to have been "concentrate on rapid growth, and the problems of equitable income distribution will be resolved automatically," the newly emerging orthodoxy can with equal accuracy be caricatured as "concentrate on equitable participation in development, and the obstacles to rapid growth will gradually be overcome."[12]

Given the novel degree of interest in both new and old problems of income distribution, greater equality of economic opportunity, and the elimination of absolute poverty, it seems appropriate to review existing empirical evidence concerning a) income distribution per se; b) the relationship of income distribution to economic growth and population growth; and c) the prospects for global efforts to overcome absolute poverty, to begin to restrain population growth, and to promote increased international equality of economic opportunity. The obvious cost of covering so many aspects of the "distribution question" at the same time is superficial treatment; hopefully, the benefit will be in discovering interrelated aspects of several problems which suggest solutions that might be overlooked in a piecemeal approach.

Income Distribution and Poverty: Domestic and International Aspects

The Developing Countries. Most of the world's underdeveloped countries exhibit a markedly greater degree of income inequality than either

[11]*International Development Strategy: Action Programme of the General Assembly for the Second United Nations Development Decade,* U.N. Pub. Sales No. E.71.II.A.2 (New York: United Nations, 1970), p. 4.

[12]See, for example, James P. Grant, *Growth From Below,* Development Paper No. 16 (Washington, D.C.: Overseas Development Council, 1973), pp. 5-6.

the socialist or the developed countries. About half of the underdeveloped countries for which data are available fall in the high inequality range, with another third displaying moderate inequality (see Table A-10, p. 212-13). The average income share of the poorest 40 per cent of the population in all underdeveloped countries as a group amounts to about 12.5 per cent of total national income. In half of those countries, the poorest 40 per cent receive only 9 per cent of total income.

Much of the current academic and technocratic interest in income distribution within less developed countries and developed countries concerns itself as much with the question of *absolute poverty* as with the issue of *relative inequality*. The former problem is measured where possible through such indices as caloric intake, health, sanitation, and access to education.

A recent World Bank estimate, which encompassed approximately 60 per cent of the population of the world's less developed countries, suggested that "about a third of this population falls below the poverty line defined by U.S. $50 per capita and about half falls below U.S. $75 per capita."[13] Much of the poverty-level population (indicated in Table A-12, p. 216-17) is accounted for by low levels of average per capita income in many countries rather than by highly skewed income distribution patterns. India, Pakistan, Bangladesh, and Sri Lanka, with about 55 per cent of the population examined in the Bank study, account for about three quarters of the population living below the poverty line as measured by $50 per annum; yet these countries are all characterized by patterns of low to moderate income inequality (as measured historically).

While these examples suggest that much of the absolute poverty problem within the developing countries is a direct reflection of low levels of average per capita incomes, two caveats should be entered. First, highly skewed patterns of income distribution do contribute to the absolute poverty problem in many developing countries. And second, the IBRD's "low to moderate" income inequality measures are reflections of historical experience, not normative goals. Therefore, they need not be taken as immutable, though they certainly can be demonstrated to represent fundamental constraints on attempts at internal redistribution.

Finally, a word must be said about the label "developing countries." These countries no longer—if they ever did—constitute a single category, even for purposes of the most aggregate analysis. In the post-OPEC price-rise world, they constitute at least three major groupings: the Fourth World (the Indian subcontinent, some of Africa, and the Caribbean), much of which is presently close to economic disaster without some sizeable "bailout" operations; the Third World (much of Latin America and Southeast Asia), which is at a higher level of economic development, more diversified in

---

[13]*Redistribution with Growth,* p. 11.

production and export potential, and established as creditworthy in international capital markets; and the OPEC world, some of which, barring some improbable scenarios, is on its way to reaching the low to moderate inequality category within a decade or two.

The Developed Countries. As a group, the developed countries are characterized by a lesser degree of income inequality than developing countries. They are rather evenly distributed between the IBRD's categories of "low" and "moderate" inequality. The average share of total income of the bottom 40 per cent of their population is approximately 16 per cent, well under the socialist-country average of 25 per cent, but measurably higher than the 12.5 per cent figure for the less developed countries.

Additionally, as the IBRD study notes:

A major problem in comparing income distribution data between developed and underdeveloped countries is that pretax data does not reflect the equalizing impact of progressive taxes combined with welfare-oriented public transfer mechanisms. These fiscal corrections are generally more substantial and more egalitarian in developed countries. If this factor is taken into account, developed countries may be somewhat more egalitarian than appears. . . .[14]

One of the most significant differences in income distribution between an "average" developing country and a developed one is found in the percentage of income flowing to the top 5 per cent of the population in each instance (see Table A-11, p. 214-15). In the developing-country case, the top 5 per cent generally receive about 30 per cent of total income; in the "average" developed country (with a per capita income exceeding $2,000), the figure is about 16 per cent. The data also suggest that the income shifted from the top 5 per cent in the average developed country finds its way into the incomes of the second, third, and fourth quintiles of the population, but not into the pre-tax incomes of the poorest 20 per cent of the population.

Less research has been done on the distribution of wealth within countries than has been undertaken on income. The general approach followed by a group at the U.S. Urban Institute to examine this issue has been to study the concentration of wealth within the top 1 per cent of U.S. wealthholders. Their findings are that while wealth has become less concentrated in the U.S. over the past half century, the diminution has not been great, and "it all occurred during periods when the market system was functioning under duress or was in administrative abeyance, specifically, the great depression and World War II."[15] In 1929, the richest 0.5 per cent owned 32.4 per cent of

[14]Ibid., p. 7.
[15]James D. Smith and Stephen Franklin, "The Concentration of Personal Wealth, 1922-69," (Paper delivered at the Annual Meeting of the American Economic Association, New York, N.Y., December 1973), p. 3.

the net wealth of all individuals. By the late 1940s, that figure had dropped by about a third, to approximately 20 per cent. According to the Urban Institute's latest calculations, the 20 per cent figure has remained relatively stable since the late 1940s. For five selected years, the shares of the richest 0.5 per cent and 1.0 per cent of the net wealth of all individuals (measured by net worth) are as follows:

	1953	1958	1962	1965	1969
Top 0.5%	22.0%	21.7%	21.6%	23.7%	19.9%
Top 1.0%	27.5%	26.9%	27.4%	29.2%	24.9%

In presenting these estimates, the authors stress that the biases which entered their calculations tend to *understate* the shares of wealth held by these two groups.

While little if any work of equal sophistication has been undertaken within developing countries, it is generally held by those making rough estimates that, on the average, the concentration of wealth is *significantly greater* in developing countries than it is in developed countries.

Global Income Distribution. The "gap" between the rich and the poor nations has been the subject of intense analysis and debate for at least a decade. Differing judgments with regard to methodologies of measurement and empirical evidence result in a somewhat bewildering array of estimates. Therefore, even the most carefully constructed findings should be treated as at best representing orders of magnitude.

An oft-quoted estimate by Rosenstein-Rodan is that "differences in income per head between the poor and rich countries were around 1:2 at the beginning of the 19th century; they are around 1:40 today in nominal or around 1:20 in real terms."[16] The 1:20 estimate seems to be accepted as representative by Simon Kuznets and others who have worked most closely with the problems of "gap" measurement.

Attempts to project this gap over the next several decades are subject to even more margin for error than the above figures. There is general agreement that the *absolute* gap between per capita incomes in the rich and the poor states will continue to widen rather rapidly. Whether the *relative* gap will also increase is somewhat more questionable. Perhaps the most one can say from examining projections made by Rosenstein-Rodan, Jagdish Bhagwati, and others is that even the relative gap between the per capita incomes of the rich and the poor nations will narrow little if at all in the standard "surprise-free" scenario upon which such calculations are generally based.

Table A-13 (p. 213) presents Bhagwati's estimates on the "gap" projected

---

[16]P. N. Rosenstein-Rodan, "The Haves and Have-Nots Around the Year 2000," in Jagdish N. Bhagwati, ed., *Economics and World Order from the 1970s to the 1990s* (London: The Macmillan Company, 1972), p. 29.

to the year 2000. For the developing countries, it indicates a real per capita GNP growth from $145 in 1965 to $388 in 2000. The corresponding increase for developed-country per capita incomes will be from $1,729 to $6,126. This calculation, as good as—if not better than—most others, suggests that, by the year 2000, the average per capita income of the developing countries will be approximately 6 per cent of that of the world's developed countries.

The Impact of Economic Development on Income Distribution

Most recent empirical investigation has to a greater or lesser degree substantiated the early Kuznets view that, during the process of economic development within countries, inequality in the distribution of income tends to increase for a considerable period of time before the pattern is reversed and a trend toward greater equality appears. Some evidence for this pattern is illustrated in the data presented in Table A-11 (p. 214).

At the lowest levels of development (where gross domestic product is $100 or less per capita), approximately 7 per cent of total personal income is directed toward the poorest quintile of the population. Simply stated, countries at this level of economic development (and per capita GDP) cannot afford much greater income inequality without pushing the lowest 10-20 per cent of their population into starvation. Moving one level upward, to countries with a per capita GDP of $101-$200, the percentage of income going to the poorest 20 per cent reveals growing income inequality. This trend reaches its apex in the next two groupings, the countries in the $201-$300 range and the $301-$500 range. Here the income of the poorest 20 per cent falls to less than 5 per cent of total personal income.

In countries above the $500 per capita range, a trend toward greater equality in income distribution sets in. The reversal is particularly noticeable in the so-called "Gini ratios" in Table A-11 (p. 214).[17] Also worthy of note is the falling percentage of income concentrated in the highest income brackets—for example, the drop in the income of the top 5 per cent of the population from 32 per cent of the total in the $201-$300 range to 16 per cent of the total in the over $2,000 range.

While these figures generally support the Kuznets hypothesis that inequality first rises, then later falls, as an economy progresses from very low to more advanced levels of development, recent empirical work has also supported the view that many countries have deviated substantially from the Kuznets norm. It has been noted that levels of inequality vary substantially among poor countries (as well as rich), that many factors appear to operate on

---

[17]These ratios are a commonly used measurement of inequality in which 0.0 equals absolute equality and 1.0 equals absolute inequality. As noted in the table, these ratios fall steadily from an average of 0.499 at the $201-$300 range to 0.365 for those countries whose per capita incomes exceed $2,000.

the distribution of income during the process of economic growth, and that there is considerable scope for governmental policies to *alter* the "Kuznets normal" patterns of income distribution in the process. Several major research projects are at the present time attempting to develop an adequate theory of income distribution and to assess the impact of alternative governmental strategies on that distribution.

With regard to *global* income distribution, the development process over the past 150 years has, as noted above, increased the real per capita income gap between rich and poor nations from about 2:1 to approximately 20:1. As the growth rates of the developing countries increased markedly over the past two decades, to the point where they equalled and often exceeded those of many developed countries, their higher population growth rates alone prevented the 20:1 ratio from beginning to close. Looking to the future, the capacity to narrow that ratio will continue to depend in large degree upon the willingness and ability of developing-country governments to adopt a set of policies which will significantly diminish present crude birth rates in the developing regions of the world.

To conclude, both *absolute* and *relative* gaps in per capita income between rich and poor countries, especially between the *very poorest* countries and most other groups of countries, have been growing steadily over many decades, including those decades of rapid aggregate growth in the less developed countries. The present levels of inequality in average per capita incomes *between* rich and poor countries is greater than that *within* the vast majority of countries, developed or developing. And the *very poor* countries of the world are falling farther and farther behind, as noted in Table A-9 (p. 211). In these countries, little growth momentum has been achieved; the vast majority of their populations live below the $75 per annum poverty line, and they will suffer most severely from the impact of the 1974-75 food and fuel crises.

Emerging Development Strategies: Growth for What and for Whom?

To an increasing number of governments, economists, World Bank officials, aid administrators, and concerned citizens of the rich as well as the poor countries, the data presented in the two preceding sections describe an acute problem rather than an acceptable state of affairs in the present international setting. To the non-economists among them, the problem is one of overcoming unacceptable magnitudes of absolute poverty within the developing world—magnitudes now approximating 750 million persons. To the economists, the problem is that close to two decades of rapid economic growth have done little to improve living conditions for the poorest 40 per cent of most developing-countries' populations, and that new strategies of economic development must be created which will have as their primary goal a much more equitable balance in the distribution of the benefits of economic growth.

The general development strategies of the 1950s and 1960s placed their bets—and therefore their incentives—on limiting consumption, raising savings and investment rates as rapidly as possible, investing heavily in the protected "modern" sector of the economy, and concentrating government expenditures on "economic" as opposed to "social" overhead projects such as education, health, housing, and sanitation. The costs to the poorest 40 per cent of the population in many countries that followed this "trickle-down" strategy have now become clear. Not only have their *relative* incomes and standards of living decreased, sometimes markedly; there is considerable evidence to suggest that the *absolute* incomes of the bottom 10-20 per cent also may have fallen.

The reason that the "trickle-down" strategy has produced such distributional results even in cases where it has also achieved commendable aggregate growth rates—for example, Mexico, where the average annual growth rate has exceeded 6 per cent in real terms for over thirty years—can be understood when one identifies the constituents of the "forgotten 40 per cent." The overwhelming majority of the poverty group is rural in origin, composed of landless rural labor or subsistence farm families. For the developing world in general, these rural groups constitute over 70 per cent of the poverty population. Obviously, a strategy of economic development which concentrates tax structures, commercial policies, and public expenditures on the development of a modern, capital-intensive industrial sector does nothing of a direct nature to increase the development prospects for the rural poor. "Trickle-down" policies will affect such groups only as increased employment in the modern sector absorbs surplus labor (thus creating a situation in which rural wages may be expected to increase) and increases the urban demand for agricultural production (which may also increase rural wages *unless* capital-intensive modes of agricultural production limit the use of rural labor and increase the concentration of landholding to the detriment of the country's smallest agricultural producers). Much evidence suggests that agricultural production in developing countries following the "trickle-down" strategy has become more extensive *and* capital-intensive, contributing directly to the falling relative incomes of the rural poverty groups.

The impact of the standard "trickle-down" strategy has produced similarly equivocal, if not detrimental, results for urban poverty groups—the unemployed, the underemployed, and the self-employed in the service sector and in the traditional manufacturing sector. The concentrated rewards to both capital and labor in the protected modern sector—resulting from limited competition, skewed factor prices favoring capital-intensive modes of production (despite average unemployment rates of 20-25 per cent), and the development of a "labor aristocracy" within modern industries—have severely limited the capacity of the modern sector to perform the function required for "trickle-down" to benefit an entire population, i.e., to rapidly absorb the urban unemployed and to draw down the excess labor reserves from the rural areas.

To summarize, the "standard" development strategy of the past two decades emphasized rapidly increased marginal savings, investment, and employment in the *modern* sector of industry. It generally limited its agricultural concerns to the production of commercial crops to feed urban populations and earn foreign exchange. Its explicit or implicit premise was that it would produce significantly higher marginal rates of savings and investment than alternative strategies, and that the growth of the modern manufacturing sector would eventually ease whatever unemployment problems were developing in rural areas and traditional urban sectors as a result of the concentration of incentives in the modern sector.

Even in countries where this policy approach has succeeded in *aggregate growth terms*, it has generally failed by all equity measures for several reasons. First, and in many ways foremost, rates of increased employment in the modern sector have with a few exceptions been very disappointing. In some countries, like Mexico, they have exceeded population growth rates, but not by enough to limit rising rates of urban and rural unemployment. In many other countries, labor absorption in the modern sector has hardly done more than keep pace with population growth.

A second reason, intimately related to the first, is that living conditions in rural areas have often deteriorated for landless laborers and subsistence farmers.[18] Without producing high rates of labor absorption in the modern sector, a policy which concentrated rewards almost exclusively in that sector (and, to a degree, in *commercial* agriculture) necessarily contributed to a steady deterioration of living standards for these two rural groups. Only a comprehensive strategy of rural development, including family planning, could have produced alternative results. Without such a strategy, conditions for the poorest segments in rural areas were bound to deteriorate, if only because rural population growth rates in the developing countries have averaged close to 2.5 per cent annually.

Third, the urban poor—the unemployed and major segments of the service and traditional manufacturing sectors—have benefited little from the "trickle-down" approach. In simplified terms, the major reason has been that while output per worker has grown faster in the modern than in the traditional sector, the modern sector has not grown significantly as a proportion of the total labor force. Contributing to this phenomenon have been the emerging political power of unionized labor in the modern sector, the use within it of capital-intensive technology, and inappropriate governmental policies which encouraged such development (e.g., subsidized credit, overvalued exchange

---

[18]For but one country example, see Roger D. Hansen, *The Politics of Mexican Development* (Baltimore: The Johns Hopkins University Press, 1971), Chapter IV.

rates for capital goods imports, and high degrees of protection). Thus the traditional manufacturing and service sectors have also paid a price in terms of relative deprivation for the standard "trickle-down" strategy.

The aggregate results of that strategy have, as noted, led a growing number of governments, economists, and aid practitioners to examine alternative approaches to the problems of economic development in the past several years. While it would certainly be an exaggeration to suggest that anything approaching unanimity exists concerning all the major ingredients of a new approach, it would not be misleading to suggest that a general consensus does seem to be emerging on several conceptual issues which could well provide the major impetus for significant changes in development strategies.

Perhaps the first and foremost conceptual issue on which rethinking has centered concerns the supposed trade-off between a strategy aimed at *output* maximization and one aimed at *employment* maximization. Gustav Ranis captures the breakdown of the old consensus and the potential emergence of a new one in the following passage:

What I am, in fact, suggesting is that the general experience of the 50s and 60s which indicates the existence of a severe conflict in terms of rising output and unemployment levels is entirely misleading because the very strategy which was followed in the pursuit of output maximization was erroneous while a different set of policies might well have given us more growth *and* more employment. As economists and perpetrators of the dismal science, we seem to have difficulty in accepting the notion that it is possible to have more of both, i.e., more output and more employment. It is an incontrovertible fact that a substantial part of the profession and an even larger majority of policy makers implicitly or explicitly assume the existence of a conflict and are proceeding to talk about employment strategies as a way to ameliorate or amend the "output only" policies of the past. They talk about dethroning the GNP on behalf of employment and distribution. My point is that it may well come to that, but it may also be true that we have not even begun to explore a set of policies and development strategies which would give us increased output as a direct consequence of utilizing our unemployed or underemployed labor more effectively.[19]

Work done since Ranis wrote this passage leaves a good deal of room for hope that in many parts of the world, there may be little if any conflict between these two objectives. Much analysis also suggests that even if a conflict does

---

[19]Gustav Ranis, "Output and Employment in the 1970's: Conflict or Complements," in Ronald G. Ridker and Harold Lubell, eds., *Employment and Unemployment Problems of Southeast and South Asia* (New Delhi: Vikas Publications, 1971), Vol. I, p. 61.

exist, the proper set of policies can a) minimize whatever cost there may be in terms of foregone growth, and b) return economies accepting the trade-off to equally high or higher growth rates within a period of a decade or two at much more equitable levels of income distribution.

Two examples should suffice to elucidate the variety of empirical analyses underlying this changing consensus. The first concerns savings rates in developing countries. It had generally been accepted in recent decades that any policies which had the effect of redistributing income from the rich to the poor would reduce total savings and investment, and thereby reduce the rate of growth. As Charles Frank and Richard Webb have recently noted, however, the validity of this argument depends on fairly large differences in *marginal*—not average—savings rates between the rich and the poor. Much new empirical work indicates that such large differences do *not* seem to exist, and that the trade-off between policies promoting increased employment and more equitable income distribution on the one hand and savings rates on the other is very small if it exists at all.

A second example concerns the general effect of land reform measures on agricultural production. A recent study by William Cline using Brazilian farm survey data suggests that the breakup of large estates into small family farms would incur no loss in potential efficiency since per acre yields do *not* increase as the size of farms increases. Furthermore, Cline's findings suggest that increased labor inputs on small holdings would be likely to induce per acre production gains in the neighborhood of 25 per cent. Cline's findings are representative of much recent work attempting to measure the production impact of changing structures of land tenure, particularly in Latin America.

It has, of course, been argued that policies of land redistribution to increase rural employment and to begin to limit income inequality have far less room for application on the Indian subcontinent, where the land-to-man ratios are extremely low in comparison to those in most of Latin America and Africa. But the argument remains unsubstantiated. As Cline has noted, the idea of an optimal farm size, while extremely popular, is simply inconsistent with almost all empirical evidence, which shows constant per acre returns (considering inputs actually used) as well as *greater utilization* of available land as farm size *diminishes*.[20]

The two examples—presented without any attempt to capture the nuances of the analysis put forward by supporters or critics—are suggestive, at a minimum, of a considerably widened scope for policies which attempt to lower present levels of poverty and to move toward a greater degree of equality in income distribution within developing countries. With some simplification, one can conceptualize the newly emerging general approach—which attempts to maximize *employment* as well as growth—as having four

---

[20]William R. Cline, "Policy Instruments for Rural Income Redistribution" (Paper delivered at the Conference on Income Distribution in the Developing Countries, Princeton University, Princeton, N.J., September 1974).

major ingredients: 1) a strategy for rural development; 2) a strategy for urban development; 3) a strategy for human resource development; and 4) a strategy for population control.[21] These ingredients are closely related and are not exhaustive of other ingredients; they are analyzed separately simply to facilitate an examination of an alternative approach to a more equitable form of economic development. It should be noted that a degree of asset redistribution—introduced to facilitate the trend toward a more equitable pattern of income distribution and a much lower level of "absolute" poverty— is integral to each of the first three components of the approach.

A Strategy for Rural Development. A strategy for rural development designed to meet the goals of increased employment, fewer cases of "absolute" poverty, and greater equity in income distribution would ideally entail significant changes in: a) land tenure; b) access to agricultural production inputs in addition to land; c) increased expenditures on rural public works projects; and d) increasing rural access to health and educational facilities.

The fundamental ingredient of the rural strategy will in most cases be change in the structure of land tenure to put ownership or control of more arable land in the hands of increased numbers of landless laborers and subsistence farmers. Without this crucial asset transfer, other programs designed to raise rural standards of living will disproportionately benefit large landowners—and may even induce a net loss for the poorest strata—as they have in the past. To cite but one example, the overwhelming percentage of long-term benefits of rural public works projects (roads, irrigation, etc.) will flow to landowners; if the structure of land tenure is not altered, the rest of the strategy's efforts may simply compound the problems of poverty and inequality.

Land reform is both the key to the success of the rural strategy and its most formidable political obstacle. Clearly, reforms which adequately and promptly compensate former owners for expropriated holdings will be easier to achieve than most others. While land reform will be politically difficult, thinking on the subject has advanced to the point where any number of repayment schemes are worth serious investigation. It is quite possible that in many Latin American countries, for example, repayment could be financed out of the earnings of those who become landholders as a result of land reform measures. In more densely populated countries, land-man ratios and the subsequent size of arable landholdings probably will not allow for this particular form of financing; alternative sources of payment might have to be found.[22]

---

[21]For some of the major elements of this emerging approach, see, for example, *Redistribution with Growth*, op. cit.; Edgar Owens and Robert Shaw, *Development Reconsidered* (Lexington, Mass.: Lexington Books, D.C. Heath and Company, 1972); and James P. Grant, *Growth from Below*, op. cit.

[22]In Taiwan in the early 1950s, landholders receiving one- and two-acre parcels via land reform paid for most of their new holdings out of the profits from their agricultural production.

The second ingredient of the strategy involves access to agricultural production inputs other than land. An approach which combined credit, agricultural extension services, crop insurance, and a complete package of inputs (improved seeds, fertilizer, pesticides, etc.) would enable small farmers to shift from traditional agriculture to the cropping of the new high-yield varieties. The potential for significantly increased output from small-scale, labor-intensive use of new varieties is well established; the package approach would permit the transition to take place on a large scale, minimizing the lag one would otherwise predict and increasing the aggregate agricultural output in a relatively short period of time. Almost all empirical evidence supports this conclusion and underlines the crucial nature of a system of credit and agricultural inputs in a successful strategy of rural development.[23]

Certain rural public works programs can add directly to permanent employment as well as alleviate short-term unemployment problems. Some pertinent examples are forestry and fishing infrastructure activities; construction activities related to school, health, and other "social infrastructure" programs; and irrigation projects (which, by increasing intensity of cropping, also provide increased employment opportunities for rural labor).

A third major ingredient in an effective strategy to overcome rural poverty involves increased rural access to health and educational facilities. Since the contribution of these facilities is intimately linked to the problems of human resources and population, discussion of the issue is postponed briefly.

A Strategy for Urban Development. Like its rural counterpart, the new strategy for urban development attempts to achieve two related goals: to overcome some of the past deficiencies of overrewarding growth in the modern sector; and to undertake a new set of policies which will increase employment in the traditional urban sectors and gradually transfer some assets to the poor which will improve their longer-term life chances. It now seems generally agreed that in all but the most exceptional developing countries, continued reliance on a capital-intensive expansion of the modern sector to solve the urban poverty problem will produce disappointing results. Skepticism concerning the capacity of the modern sector to absorb the already excessive urban labor force is based on the present rates of urbanization (often in excess of 4 per cent per annum), the small share of the modern sector in total urban employment, and the generally low opportunities for job creation through modern-sector growth.

A first step to be taken is to remove those factor-price distortions which appear to have contributed to the capital-intensive nature of production within the modern sector. While the degree of substitution between capital and labor in present modern-sector technologies is uncertain, there is by now

---

[23]For an excellent review of recent empirical evidence, see William R. Cline, "Policy Instruments for Rural Income Distribution," op. cit.

enough empirical evidence to make the effort seem worthwhile in many instances.

A second step is to deliberately encourage the growth of small and traditional-sector producers. This can be accomplished by: a) elimination of special incentives (subsidized credit, overvalued exchange rates, licensing systems, etc.) that aid the large modern producers; b) the establishment of agencies to advise small firms on technical matters; and c) the reform of interest-rate structures and credit-allocation mechanisms to make a greater volume of credit available to the small producer.

Properly devised and administered, such policies could contribute significantly to increased employment and asset diversification. First, there is much evidence that smaller firms have lower capital-output ratios than larger firms; they may also be more efficient producers, though this point has not been unambiguously established.[24] Second, if these strengthened small firms can become suppliers to the modern sector—as they were in Europe and the United States a century ago and have been more recently in such countries as Japan, Korea, Hong Kong, Taiwan, and Singapore—they can indirectly increase the labor-absorbing nature of the modern sector as well.[25]

Finally, a major effort should be made to restructure urban health, education, and housing facilities and to make them all more accessible to the urban poor. The need for restructuring is obvious. In developing countries, public-health budgets still favor *curative* care over *preventive* care by a margin of 4 to 1, despite the obvious need for a reversal of priorities. In the case of education, public funds spent on secondary-school and college training consume a large and growing proportion of total educational outlays, while large numbers of rural and urban poor often are unable to take advantage of the underfinanced primary school system. Thus present patterns of educational expenditures are highly discriminatory against the poor. To the extent that the lack of adequate levels of health and education is a barrier to adequate employment, the poverty syndrome becomes self-reinforcing and hence increasingly difficult to overcome.

A Strategy for Human Resource Development. It is for this very reason, as well as for humanitarian reasons, that a good deal of thinking is now being devoted to the general question of human resource development. The emphasis is on the provision of adequate levels of education (formal, informal, on-the-job training, etc.), nutrition, and health to enable entire populations to contribute to economic development within a policy framework that is geared to provide increasing job opportunities. The rural and urban strategies noted previously are essentially designed to expand

---

[24]See Edgar Owens and Robert Shaw, *Development Reconsidered,* op. cit., pp. 64-66 and 115.

[25]For a detailed description of the subcontracting process in Hong Kong and Singapore, see Theodore Geiger with Frances Geiger, *Tales of Two City-States: Hong Kong and Singapore* (Washington, D.C.: National Planning Association, 1973), pp. 75-78.

employment opportunities; both imply increased access by the poor in all areas of the country to primary-education and health facilities, with greater emphasis on preventive medicine, post-natal care, and nutrition. The provision of such facilities not only creates jobs in the initial construction phase; the completed facilities themselves are part of the asset-transfer process whereby the poor develop an enhanced capacity to increase their standard of living by their own efforts and rise above "absolute" poverty levels. It is worth underscoring this point by noting the conclusion of the World Bank's recent study:

> The design of a poverty-oriented strategy requires the selection of a mix of policy instruments that can reach the target groups that have been identified. While we advocate maximum use of instruments that operate through factor and product markets, often they will not be sufficient for this purpose. We have therefore given particular attention to a range of direct measures, such as land reform, the distribution of education, and other public services, and measures to redistribute assets toward the poverty groups. Without such a redistribution of at least the increments of capital formation, other distributive measures are not likely to have a lasting impact on the poverty problem.[26]

A Strategy for Population Control. Population in the world's developing countries is presently growing at close to 2.5 per cent per year, a little more than twice as fast as that of the developed countries. The developing countries accounted for 78 per cent of the world's population growth between 1930 and 1950, 80 per cent of the growth between 1950 and 1970, and are expected to account for 88 per cent of the projected increase between 1970 and 1990. At present rates of growth, the aggregate developing-country population would double every 32 years, while a doubling of the developed-country population would take 83 years.

The decade of the 1960s witnessed a rapid growth of anti-natalist movements throughout the world. At the present time, over 70 per cent of the world's population lives in countries which offer family planning in their existing public health services; over 80 per cent of the developing world's population is located in countries which sponsor official family planning programs; and over 90 per cent of the people in Asia live in countries whose deliberate policy objectives are to reduce fertility.

Despite the growing sentiment—national and international—in favor of slowing rapid population growth rates, policies currently being implemented in behalf of this objective are inadequately conceptualized, seriously underfinanced, and far short of meeting the demonstrated demand for them.

---

[26]*Redistribution with Growth,* p. xvii.

As a recent World Bank study noted, "induced abortion is universal and not all unwanted conceptions are aborted. The number of children whose births are not desired by their parents must be very large indeed."[27]

The reasons for including a strategy for population control in the new development perspective goes well beyond the demonstrated demand for birth control facilities. Some proponents are concerned for the most part with the ecological capacity of the globe to absorb population increases, which at present rates double the world's population every thirty-five years (or, more dramatically, lead to a sevenfold increase over a century). Others are more specifically concerned with the effect of high population-growth rates on the poorest strata of the population in the developing world. They reason that a labor force growing faster than employment opportunities in most developing countries leads to lower wages, increasing unemployment, greater fragmentation of miniscule agricultural landholdings and increasing numbers of landless rural laborers, and fewer social infrastructure expenditures to give the poor access to basic health and educational facilities.

Finally, there are those proponents of population control policies who choose to emphasize a more subtle argument—that high birth rates in developing countries are a *reflection* of poverty and exaggerated income inequality, and that birth rates will fall as a consequence of the successful implementation of the other development strategies sketched above.

The evidence on this point is still too limited to be considered conclusive. Past experience suggests that a demographic transition from high to low fertility rates accompanies economic development. The crucial question at issue regarding today's developing countries is what can be done, if anything, to induce fertility decline *before* levels of economic development are reached which correlate such fertility declines in the presently industrialized world. A cautious conclusion based on demographic transition patterns in a variety of developing countries over the past decade or two suggests that policies which begin to alleviate "absolute" poverty, thus changing the socio-economic and psychological frames of reference for the poorest strata of developing societies, *can* lower birth rates. The World Bank's recent examination of the available evidence produced the following judgment:

> With economic development, developing countries are ... experiencing slow but significant improvements in educational levels. The effective costs and benefits of children change as employment possibilities for children fall and those for women increase. The desired number of children will also fall as individual couples perceive the benefits of development, and raise their aspirations for their children.

---

[27]Timothy King, ed., *Population Policies and Economic Development,* published for the World Bank (Baltimore: Johns Hopkins University Press, 1974), p. 137.

It is not possible to identify precisely the threshold levels of infant mortality, literacy, and industrialization or urbanization beyond which fertility would spontaneously decline. There are signs, however, that the speed of transition in those developing countries where fertility began to decline in the 1950s has been faster than it was in Europe. *In most of these developing countries, economic development has meant perceptible improvements in living standards among the poor. In all developing countries, policies which succeed in improving the conditions of life for the poor, and in providing education and employment opportunities for women, are likely to help reduce fertility. An improvement in the welfare of the poor appears to be essential before fertility can fall to developed country levels.*[28]

Thus the major elements in a modified approach to economic development close the circle. One starts with the hypothesis that a new mix of policy priorities can achieve much greater productive employment and a much more equitable pattern of income distribution than was achieved in the 1950s and 1960s—but with little sacrifice in rates of economic growth. From this base flow logical policy prescriptions for coping with the problems of rural and urban poverty and unemployment. Inherent in such prescriptions are efforts to slowly redistribute assets to the poorest strata of society, thus providing them with access to long-term benefits from continued economic growth. Among the asset transfers are health and educational infrastructure expenditures which bring to the poor those forms of health and nutritional care, family planning advice and implements, and education most relevant to their needs. Almost always these are the least expensive forms—for example, preventive medicine via paramedics, and primary rather than secondary and college education. Finally, the creation of more jobs, rising levels of literacy, and health standards which lower infant mortality rates lead to changing views on optimal family size and to gradually lowering fertility rates within the target groups of the new strategy.

Of course this summary presents the best case for a new development strategy and, in doing so, avoids many complex issues of empirical evidence and political feasibility. This is particularly true of the discussion of a strategy for rural development, which fails to deal with the crucial ingredients of political will and organizational capacity. If economic development with full employment and more equity were politically, economically, and administratively as easy to accomplish as the previous paragraph suggests, the

---

[28]Ibid., p. 54. Emphasis added. Also see the earlier presentation of a similar point of view by William Rich in *Smaller Families Through Social and Economic Progress,* Monograph No. 7 (Washington, D.C.: Overseas Development Council, 1973).

world would have witnessed a good deal more of it over the past twenty years.[29]

But this essay is concerned with the *next* twenty years. Thus there is time for the changing perceptions noted in this section to influence events in a manner heretofore not possible.

Perceptions and Options:
Northern and Southern Perspectives

Where are these changing perceptions on present and projected levels of global inequalities, the "absolute" poverty problem within developing countries, and the growing concern over rapid population growth likely to lead us over the coming decade? Will approaches to these problems remain marginal, as one might easily predict in view of past history? Or has the world reached a turning point in the sense that people and governments of developed and developing countries are rather rapidly being conditioned by events to consider and undertake some actions—both unilateral and multilateral— unthinkable until the mid-1970s? One can begin to outline the perceptions and the options now coming into play in both the North and South, even if it is far too early to predict which perceptions will predominate and which options eventually may be chosen.

A View from the North. The perceptions of the problems of gross inequality in global income distribution and life chances, of absolute poverty in the developing countries, and of rapid population growth rates in the world's developing countries are presently viewed from four major perspectives in the North. One perception is captured by the phrase, "it's their problem, not ours." This view emphasizes the degree to which many developing countries have overcome most of these problems by their own efforts and is generally skeptical about the degree to which outside assistance and influence can (or should) affect the outcome of the development process. Its proponents range from the new left to the old right.

Two other Northern perceptions view the problems of poverty and income distribution as "ours" as well as "theirs." The difference between the holders of these two perceptions is that some would share in an international effort to overcome the problems out of moral and humanitarian concerns, while others would act out of what might best be termed an "enlightened" self-interest. This latter group, concerned about such problems as environment, nuclear proliferation, a viable monetary system, and a host of other issues that can only be successfully managed with at least a minimum degree of global

---

[29]On the other hand, it should be remembered that most economists and economic advisors to developing-country governments were not advocating the strategies discussed above, further limiting the prospects for their implementation during the 1950s and 1960s.

cooperation, is willing to consider schemes of North-South cooperation in raising employment levels, working toward the elimination of "absolute" poverty, and lowering birth rates in exchange for Southern cooperation in "the management of interdependence."

Intimately related to this "interdependence" self-interest view is a fourth perception with a more specific stake in North-South cooperation. It is one generally associated with multinational corporations and some other transnational actors in present-day international politics that have some very concrete interests at stake. These groups see their interests as generally best protected through patterns of North-South accommodation and carry that message to their home governments with increasing frequency.

From these four perceptions flow at least four distinct Northern policy options. The first might be characterized as an across-the-board Northern Project Independence. If the problems discussed in this essay are to be viewed as "theirs" and not "ours," and if, as is already clear, the Southern countries do not see the problems of development as theirs alone but as systemic problems which can only be overcome by a more responsive international system restructured to meet these needs, then a North-South clash of increasing dimensions is inevitable. In anticipation of growing conflict, those who hold this view begin to perceive a need for a North-South "decoupling" in which the OECD countries take positive and comprehensive steps to limit all potentially costly forms of dependence upon the South.

The second option might, without a great deal of inaccuracy, be characterized as a giant Red Cross effort. In order to avoid the worst potential repercussions of the first option, to satisfy the North's humanitarian instincts, and to attempt to garner the fruits of self-interest at a rather modest price, the North might cooperate in the development of various international and national systems of emergency relief. The obvious targets of such efforts would be the victims of floods, famines, widespread disease, and other disasters. In a sense, this option would amount to the international institutionalization of efforts already carried on for the past two or three decades, often at the bilateral level.

A third option might best be characterized as the incrementalist option, although an ambitious version of it might belie the title. It would encompass reinvigorated Northern efforts to manage growing international economic problems in a manner most likely to contribute to development progress within the South. The beginnings of such an approach in the food area can be seen already in various proposals submitted to the World Food Conference in Rome last November and in the nascent institutions resulting from the Conference.[30] Northern efforts to propose, negotiate, and implement programs which are global in scope and designed with particular attention to the needs of the developing world as well as the developed in other sectors

---

[30]See Chapter III.

(energy provides the best current example), would constitute the essential ingredients in this incrementalist option. This third option is incrementalist in its "one-step-at-a-time" approach, which clearly contrasts it with the far more ambitious "global compact" notions that, as noted in the introduction, have appeared with some frequency in recent months.

The fourth and final option would entail a much more ambitious package of *explicit* and mutual commitments from the North and the South to attack the problem of absolute poverty, and through this strategy, to attack all the problems noted in the section on emerging development strategies: food production, population growth, increasing global and national inequities in the distribution of income and economic opportunities, etc.

In such a package, Northern commitments would include a broad range of policies whose ultimate purpose would be to underwrite, *to a degree to be negotiated*, a Southern attack on major development problems and, undoubtedly, to assure Northern access to raw materials within the South which might not be so forthcoming under other circumstances. The package would include increased aid flows, increased access to Northern markets for the South's growing production of manufactured goods, assured access to Northern capital markets, new international monetary arrangements which in effect guarantee the South an increased call upon international resources, programs of "controlled growth" to constrain Northern consumption of potentially scarce global resources, or some combination thereof.

All such Northern commitments would to differing degrees—and given proper internal policy choices in developing countries—enhance developing-country claims on the world's resources and speed the growth process within the South. Thus one could expect an end to widening levels of relative global income inequalities and an undramatic but noticeable trend toward a more equitable global distribution of economic opportunity. The degree to which such a package also would directly aid the poorest strata of society in Southern countries would depend to a considerable extent upon the intent of Southern governments and the fine print in the "global compact" of which such Northern commitments would presumably constitute but one half. This point will be elaborated below.

A View from the South. Southern perceptions are not as easily categorized as those of the North. However, one or two generalizations can be suggested. On the issue of global income distribution, the developing countries are united in their opposition to present degrees of inequality. This unity has been witnessed for years in international organizations and conferences of all sorts—and most recently in the U.N. General Assembly's Special Session on raw materials in May 1974 and its regular session in the fall of 1974.

The South, quite naturally, would prefer to achieve a redistribution of income and economic opportunities without paying any price whatsoever. But the developing countries as a whole are certain to discover quite soon—if they do not realize it already—that unilateral actions to achieve this goal may not carry them very far. The OPEC example of achieving significant redistribution unilaterally is likely to prove unique; a few other Southern cartel actions may be modestly successful. In general, however, this approach seems destined to produce limited results, and each success with an individual commodity is likely to prove counter-productive to development efforts of other Southern states to the extent that it increases the cost of their imports. Therefore, while unilateral and cartel-type actions to alter present distributional patterns are undoubtedly with the world economy to stay, a Southern disenchantment with their aggregate results is bound to set in, especially if the international economy is in for several years of slow growth.

On the question of domestic income distribution and the emerging development strategy examined above, Southern perceptions vary widely. Many countries have already begun to implement such strategies (China, Cuba, Singapore, Sri Lanka, Taiwan, etc.); others appear to be seriously considering changes consonant with such a strategy; many others as yet show little serious interest in the subject.

What are the existing Southern options? At least three seem worth noting as ideal types. The first is a minimum-cooperation, maximum-confrontation strategy in which developing states use every opportunity to restructure commodity prices, international rules and organizations, and bilateral and regional economic arrangements in their favor. Their weapons in this strategy are control of "scarce" raw materials and sites for Northern military bases, veto power in some international institutions such as the IMF, "hostage" multinational corporations, and the potential of OPEC money to finance such a strategy in countries threatened by Northern economic retaliation. It is worth noting that the OPEC countries have already pledged over $10 billion in grants and loans to developing countries during the past year. While many Northerners are skeptical of these figures, even they should recognize that "calling OPEC's bluff" might produce some unanticipated results.

The second Southern option involves a strategy which falls somewhere between using what bargaining power it now has (based mostly upon a perceived natural resource scarcity problem and a growing Northern concern about population growth) to speed the pace of reform of the present international economic system on the one hand, and a "mini" global compact on the other. The strategy would *not* involve any Southern commitments regarding domestic efforts on behalf of the "forgotten 40 per cent." What the developing countries might offer would be "access to raw materials" and perhaps some vague promises to "do something" about the population problem. In exchange, the developed countries would offer a rather standard package of several of the following: a) more aid, b) greater market access for developing-country manufactures, c) a link between monetary reform and increased developing-country shares of the new international currency, d) greater voting power in the International Monetary Fund and the World

Bank, and e) some form of agreement aiming to raise and stabilize international commodity prices.

The third Southern option would involve a commitment to restructure developing-country internal growth policies along the lines explored earlier in this essay in the section on development strategies. This option would involve a targeted attack on domestic poverty conditions which embraced many of the reforms needed to increase employment, health, education, and general living standards among the poorest strata of the developing world.

Is it reasonable to expect that developing countries not already committed to this approach would accept the third option? Consider the potential economic and political costs to their governing elites. Concerning economic costs, some very hazy orders of magnitude can be suggested. Using the World Bank estimate of $50 per capita income as a poverty floor, and assuming 700 million persons at an average of $15 per person below that level, the present yearly cost of raising them all to a $50 minimum floor would approximate $11 billion (assuming no price rises in wage goods). If a GNP deflator is applied to the Bank's 1969 figure, the volume required is obviously much higher.

An entirely different—and more relevant—type of calculation is suggested in the World Bank's study, *Redistribution with Growth*. The authors assume that an annual domestic transfer of 2 per cent of GNP to the bottom 40 per cent of the population in developing countries over a 25-year period will very significantly raise the percentage of GNP accruing to that target group thereafter, due to the asset buildup which the 2 per cent transfer over 25 years implies. The Bank views this strategy as entirely feasible, and suggests it as an essential ingredient in any "attack on poverty" strategy.

Two per cent of annual developing-country GNP today approximates $10 billion. Stated this way, the annual transfer sounds manageable. It sounds less manageable when one considers that 2 per cent of GNP is equal to 10-20 per cent of total government revenues in most developing countries. In order to transfer that 2 per cent to the poor via new investment programs, either taxes (or other forms of government revenue) will have to be significantly raised, or major cutbacks will have to be made in present governmental programs. The adoption of either option would guarantee dissent of varying proportions from those domestic groups currently favored by tax profiles and government expenditure programs.

Thus one inevitably arrives at the political constraint on any ambitious "attack on poverty" program. In this context, it is worth quoting the reaction of Pranab K. Bardhan to the World Bank's proposed strategy mix:

The problems of poverty in India remain intractable, not because redistribution objectives were inadequately considered in the planning models, nor because the general policies of the kind prescribed in this volume were not attempted . . . the major constraint is rooted in the power realities of a political system dominated by a complex constellation of forces representing rich farmers, big business, and the so-called petite bourgeoisie, including the unionized workers of the organized sector. In such a context, it is touchingly naive not to anticipate the failures of asset distribution policies or the appropriation by the rich of a disproportionate share of the benefits of public investment.[31]

One rather obvious conclusion following from the above considerations is that the likelihood of a major movement within a large number of developing countries toward the comprehensive development strategy outlined earlier may depend *very significantly* upon the degree to which the world's developed countries share the costs, thereby easing the political constraints on such an approach. Is it realistic to expect such cost-sharing to be forthcoming in the foreseeable future?

The "Global Compact": Empty Phrase or Feasible Target?

The record to date does not induce euphoria regarding the prospects for a global compact in which developed and developing countries design and cooperate in the administration of an international development program whose primary objective is to raise living standards of the poorest strata in the developing countries and whose secondary objective is to reverse the continuing trend toward greater North-South income inequalities. An examination of developed-country performance in both the trade and the aid fields over the past decade suggests the extremely limited degree of Northern commitment to the development process at the present moment.[32] And within most of the South, growing levels of domestic income inequality, "absolute" poverty, and unemployment suggest a similar indifference (at best, a low priority) regarding the primary objective of raising the living standards of the poorest.

But is past history all that relevant? It all depends upon the speed with which past perceptions of these problems are changing. Within the North, one cannot read a newspaper or listen to a news program without being alerted to altering perceptions on such issues as "interdependence," the population explosion, present food scarcities, potential natural resource shortages, and environmental decay. And generally the message is the same: each of these problems calls for *global* management or cooperation if it is to be successfully resolved.

Within the South, changing perceptions regarding domestic develop-

[31]*Redistribution with Growth,* p. 261.
[32]See Table D-4, p. 258.

ment strategies are also evident—sometimes dramatically so. The rapid acceptance within recent years of the need for family planning, the attempts to move from capital-intensive forms of import substitution to labor-intensive forms of export expansion, and an incipient renewal of interest in strategies of rural development all reflect the spreading disenchantment with the "trickle-down" approach to economic development of past decades. To be sure, the political quicksands between a disenchantment with old policies and the implementation of new ones may swallow many a government and not a few regimes; nevertheless, a general concern within Southern elite groups may create the opportunity for change, provided incentives are properly structured.

Thus a global compact which targets benefits primarily to the poorest strata in the developing world may some day in the not-too-distant future come to be viewed as beneficial to a large majority of governments in both the North and the South. The reasons it is viewed as beneficial will vary greatly. The concerns at play will range from the purely humanitarian to the most calculatingly self-interested in both North and South. Examples of the self-interested type include Northern concern (in governments and in the private sector) about access to resources, and Southern concern (on the part of socio-political elites) about holding on to the reins of power and hierarchical positions in domestic society. What may bring these divergent governments and interest groups together is the shared recognition that a successful and *jointly financed* attack on poverty can ease the problems of a) population growth (by speeding the pace of the "demographic transition" in developing countries); b) food shortages (by increasing the labor-intensiveness of food production as part of rural development strategies); c) environmental damage (to the degree that it is related to sheer size of population); and d) growing unemployment in developing countries. Those Northern and Southern governments unconvinced of the merits of this package might well be persuaded if the issue of rules of access to resources (for the North) and to markets (for the South) were directly tied to the "attack on poverty" compact.

The discussion thus far suggests only that the idea of a global compact involves a significant *mutuality of interests*. It does not examine the issue of *feasibility*—an issue which raises major problems. Even at this very preliminary stage of thought, four of those problems deserve some mention. The first concerns the degree of participation that can be expected. Put simply, how many players will join the game? In talking about the North and the South, one constantly runs the risk of reifying entities which do not exist. The "South" is at least three worlds—the oil rich, the Third World (Brazil, Mexico, etc.), and the Fourth World (India, Sri Lanka, etc.). It is constituted by countries facing different national situations, regional settings, and development potential. Are there not, for example, many Southern states which might opt out of such a compact on the assumption that they could successfully follow their own development paths without accepting the

185

constraints implicit in the global package? Why should a generally resource-rich and "population-poor" country like Brazil enlist—as long as its appeal to foreign direct investors, to resource-poor developed and developing countries, and to players in the international diplomatic-strategic game continue to guarantee any of its "international" needs? The same general reasoning applies to the OPEC oil states and to several other individual countries of the South.

And why should all Northern states be eager to enter into the compact? Will not many of them fear that the South will constantly up the ante, continually demanding more by way of Northern redistributive flows to the South? Once the "egalitarian" genie escapes the bottle, can it be controlled?

Finally, how much *can* Northern states contribute to such a package? With so many of them presently in the grips of "the dilemma of rising demands and insufficient resources" first noted by Harald and Margaret Sprout, how much can they allocate to resource-transfer programs? Obviously, the problem is not one of potential funds, but of the capacity of Northern governments to raise taxes still further or to restructure expenditure programs to free additional sums for development purposes (aid, development-related trade adjustment-assistance programs, etc.).

Hopefully the proper question here is not *whether*, but *how soon* and in *what degree* Northern governments could begin to restructure expenditures to finance their share of a compact. After all, if the developed countries were simply able and willing to meet the 0.7 per cent of GNP aid target generally accepted over the past decade, the volume of aid funds available for North-South transfers would presently approximate $14-$15 billion—almost 50 per cent more than present levels. A $15 billion figure surpasses that amount that would be required to raise the entire global population above the World Bank's poverty line, and is 40 per cent larger than the amount implicit in the Bank's "asset-transfer" model of development, whereby developing countries themselves transfer 2 per cent of their own annual GNP to their poverty populations. Thus, assuming the policies necessary to make the transfers with an absolute minimum of leakage, the North could—if it chose to do so—cover the expenses of the asset transfer approach entirely by meeting the goal of a 0.7 per cent North-South transfer. (This does assume, however, that the additional $4-$5 billion transferred would be in *grants*. However, a part of the package deal might be to make such transfers on concessional lending terms, holding Southern participants accountable for partial repayments.)

The second obvious problem concerns the treatment to be accorded to those Southern states that choose not to participate in the program. Can and should one expect Northern states to restrict their contributions to those developing countries willing to follow the reformist development strategy constituting the compact's central core? Following this course—and thereby cutting off aid and other potential benefits to non-members—would appear highly interventionary in an indirect sense. On the other hand, if such a policy were not followed, the discipline needed to make the program effective could be dissipated from the very outset. Additionally, increased assistance to governments uncommitted to an internationally negotiated "reformist" approach to development would highlight some moral issues concerning the use of "aid" which heretofore have been rather easy to evade.

This line of argument leads directly to a third major problem. Can such a compact work under today's decentralized and heterogeneous aid and trade relationships? It is clear that much of today's foreign aid is channeled on the basis of the donor's view of the political exigencies of any particular year; sometimes, as in 1974, the political time span is even shorter. A priori, it would seem impossible to implement the type of compact discussed above under present bureaucratic and institutional mechanisms. The price of success will undoubtedly be a significant loss of national decision-making power in the aid, trade, and international investment fields. When, if ever, will states be willing to pay that price?

The final major problem concerns the difficulties of assuring implementation of such a program within developing countries. The easiest way to conceptualize this problem is to consider the potential "leakage" effects. Every Northern dollar that flows into a program to finance a reformist development strategy potentially frees an equivalent amount of developing-country funds for expenditures elsewhere. Northern support for such an effort could very well prove sustainable *only if* it were demonstrated that developing-country commitments of an agreed magnitude were being faithfully met. Political constraints on many developing-country governments will encourage them to limit their own contributions and to maximize Northern assistance. How long, and by what means, could mutual confidence be sustained? Is there any way to avoid a good deal of "intervention" in the form of program oversight, even if the oversight institution is some "depoliticized" international body? And where do we find, or how are we able to constitute, a "depoliticized" international institution?

Conclusion

Even this very brief examination of a few of the basic problems inherent in a global effort directed at raising living standards of the poorest strata in developing countries suggests that the objective will initially be dismissed as unfeasible by many persons. The magnitude of change required in perceptions, governmental behavior, and the structure of the international system all seem to support this negative judgment.

If this is the case, one can easily see the North-South debate turning to "more manageable" goals such as "increasing the general global equality of opportunity," leaving each country free to interpret the phrase according to national exigencies. Such an approach would minimize the problems of centralization, intervention, and all the other implicit limitations on state sovereignty which might well have to accompany a global attack on poverty. Furthermore, there are two very positive sides to this less ambitious program.

The first is that it could still incorporate new rules concerning access to raw materials and access to industrial markets, new commitments to "an equitable international division of labor," new aid-oriented approaches to monetary reform, and new rules on foreign investment and technology transfer—in short, it could include commitments on many standard items of legitimate concern to developing countries. The net result of this lesser "compact" might well set tolerable limits on North-South economic conflicts and contribute somewhat more than the present international economic system and norms do to the process of economic development.

Its second positive feature is that it might circumvent exhaustive and acrimonious debate over the details of a global compact and permit a series of initiatives to be undertaken much more quickly on such sectoral issues as agriculture and energy as part of the third, or "incremental," Northern option discussed above. As long as Northern and Southern views on international "equity" issues remain as incongruent as they are at the present time, the strength of the incremental option lies in its pragmatic potential for progress in overcoming some major international economic and political obstacles to development progress on a step-by-step (or sector-by-sector) basis. Furthermore, it is always possible for optimists to believe that the incremental option may eventually produce an unwritten and unheralded "global compact" by stealth, avoiding the pitfalls—and perhaps the guaranteed failure—of the more difficult and direct approach.

All this said, the less ambitious approach to a global bargain contains an inherent danger which can ill afford to be overlooked. Unless it is carried out with a commitment and generousness of spirit uncharacteristic of the North and South in recent decades, it may simply produce a repeat of the 1950s and 1960s in much of the South. That is to say, even with decent aggregate growth rates, there would be growing inequalities in income distribution and life chances, rapidly increasing population, steadily rising unemployment, food production which is increasingly unable to keep pace with developing-country food demands, and all the other problems which the more ambitious "global compact" approach would attempt to redress.

This brings us back to the crucial question of timing. Whether the more ambitious global compact is viewed as being unfeasible or not may ultimately depend on one's time frame. Certainly it is unfeasible if one thinks of negotiating it within two or three years and beginning to implement it shortly thereafter. Nevertheless, the time does seem propitious to begin to give the subject some serious thought. If the *premises* upon which the need for the broader compact rests are flawed, then the concept should be dismissed. But if the problems are inherent not in the concept itself but rather in the present constraints which constitute "feasibility," then we should begin to examine what can be done to alter those constraints while there is time to do so.

STATISTICAL ANNEXES

Mildred Weiss

Contents

Note to the Annexes

The Organisation for Economic Co-operation and Development (OECD) was created in December 1960 to promote economic growth and employment together with financial stability within its member countries; to encourage economic expansion in all countries; and to further non-discriminatory world trade. Its members are Australia, Austria, Belgium, Canada, Denmark, Finland, France, the Federal Republic of Germany, Greece, Iceland, Ireland, Italy, Japan, Luxembourg, the Netherlands, New Zealand, Norway, Portugal, Spain, Sweden, Switzerland, Turkey, the United Kingdom, and the United States.

The Development Assistance Committee (DAC) is a specialized committee of the OECD whose members periodically review the amounts and natures of their aid programs and consult each other on their development assistance policies. Australia, Austria, Belgium, Canada, Denmark, France, the Federal Republic of Germany, Italy, Japan, the Netherlands, New Zealand, Norway, Sweden, Switzerland, the United Kingdom, the United States, and the European Community comprise its membership. Portugal withdrew from DAC in October 1974. The European Community (EC) is composed of Belgium, France, the Federal Republic of Germany, Italy, Luxembourg, the Netherlands, Denmark, Ireland, and the United Kingdom. The latter three joined on January 1, 1973.

The twelve members of the Organization of Petroleum Exporting Countries (OPEC) are Saudi Arabia, Kuwait, Qatar, United Arab Emirates, Libya, Iran, Venezuela, Iraq, Algeria, Ecuador, Indonesia, and Nigeria. Gabon is an Associate Member.

The various agencies that are the sources of the data provided in the annexes that follow differ in their classifications of countries. The United Nations, the General Agreement on Tariffs and Trade (GATT), the U.S. Agency for International Development (AID), and DAC (of the OECD) do not agree in all instances on whether to call particular countries "developed" or "developing." In part, such discrepancies can be attributed to reasons of convenience and to the internal organizational politics that are part of the decision-making process within each organization. Examples of such variation are provided by the cases of Greece, Spain, Turkey, Yugoslavia, Malta, and Israel. The United Nations consider the first four to be "developed" and the latter two "developing." The GATT considers only Israel a developing country. In contrast, the World Bank, AID, and DAC call all of them developing. Differences among the sources also arise from the fact that some organizations provide data for more nations than do others, e.g., territories and small islands are not always included in the totals.

Official Development Assistance (ODA) is defined by DAC as "those flows to developing countries and multilateral institutions provided by official agencies, including state and local governments, or by their executive agencies, each transaction of which meets the following tests: a) it is administered with the promotion of the economic development and welfare of developing countries as its main objective and, b) it is concessional in character and contains a grant element of at least 25 per cent." ODA is made up of 1) soft bilateral loans, 2) bilateral grants, and 3) multilateral flows in the form of grants, capital subscriptions, and concessional loans to multilateral agencies.

Public Law 480 (P.L. 480 or Food for Peace), Title I, provides for U.S. agricultural sales for foreign currency or U.S. dollars on credit terms, both at export market value. Title II is concerned with donations of U.S. agricultural commodities either to help politically friendly nations that are suffering famine or are otherwise in need of relief or to help promote economic development. This includes transfers of agricultural goods to the World Food Programme and to voluntary relief agencies.

Aid commitments are obligations or pledges; disbursements are actual payments. Gross disbursements minus amortization (i.e., repayment of principal) paid on past loans are equal to "net disbursements" or "net flow." Net disbursements minus interest payments on past loans result in "net transfers." Net commitments are equal to gross commitments minus amortization.

As a result of rounding, the "totals" shown may not always be equal to the sum of the other figures. An entry of "n.a." signifies that the information was not available.

The Development Gap

A-1. Infant Mortality in Selected Countries (per 1,000 Live Births)

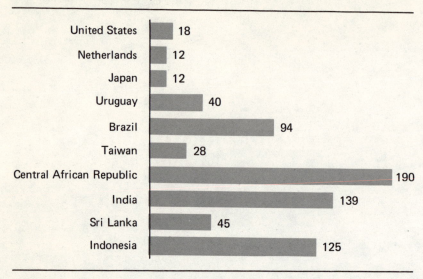

United States	18
Netherlands	12
Japan	12
Uruguay	40
Brazil	94
Taiwan	28
Central African Republic	190
India	139
Sri Lanka	45
Indonesia	125

SOURCE: Population Reference Bureau, "1975 World Population Data Sheet."

A-2. Literacy, for Selected Countries (percentages)

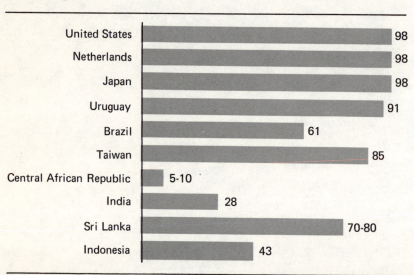

United States	98
Netherlands	98
Japan	98
Uruguay	91
Brazil	61
Taiwan	85
Central African Republic	5-10
India	28
Sri Lanka	70-80
Indonesia	43

SOURCES: Report by the Chairman of the Development Assistance Committee, *Development Co-operation, 1974 Review* (Paris: OECD, 1974), pp. 280-283; U.S. Agency for International Development, Bureau for Population and Humanitarian Assistance, *Population Program Assistance: Annual Report, Fiscal Year 1973* (Washington, D.C.: U.S. Government Printing Office, 1974), pp. 162-167.

A-3. Birth Rate per 1,000, for Selected Countries, 1970-1975 Average

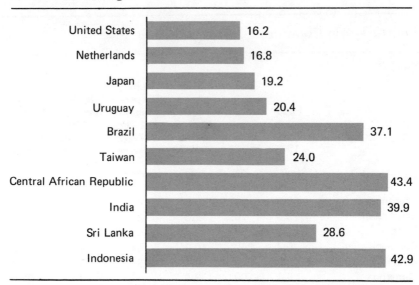

United States	16.2
Netherlands	16.8
Japan	19.2
Uruguay	20.4
Brazil	37.1
Taiwan	24.0
Central African Republic	43.4
India	39.9
Sri Lanka	28.6
Indonesia	42.9

SOURCE: Population Reference Bureau, "1975 World Population Data Sheet."

A-4. Per Capita GNP, for Selected Countries, 1972 ($)

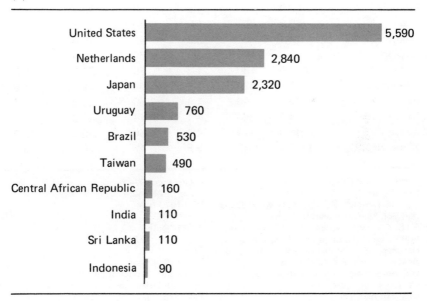

United States	5,590
Netherlands	2,840
Japan	2,320
Uruguay	760
Brazil	530
Taiwan	490
Central African Republic	160
India	110
Sri Lanka	110
Indonesia	90

SOURCE: *World Bank Atlas, 1974: Population, Per Capita Product, and Growth Rates* (Washington, D.C.: World Bank Group, 1974).

A-5. Selected Social and Economic Indicators of Development, by Groups of Countries

Fourth World Countries

	Population, mid-1975	Per Capita GNP, 1972	Per Capita GNP Growth Rate, 1965-72	Life Expectancy at Birth, 1970-75 Average	Birth Rate per 1,000, 1970-75 Average	Death Rate per 1,000, 1970-75 Average
	(mil.)	($)	(%)	(yrs.)		
Afghanistan	19.3	80[a]	0.8[a]	40	49.2	23.8
Bangladesh	73.7	70	-1.6	36	49.5	28.1
Bhutan	1.2	80[a]	0.4[a]	44	43.6	20.5
Botswana	0.7	240[a]	10.0[a]	44	45.6	23.0
Burundi	3.8	70[a]	1.1[a]	39	48.0	24.7
Cameroon	6.4	200	3.8	41	40.4	22.0
Central African Rep.	1.8	160	2.3	41	43.4	22.5
Chad	4.0	80	1.6	38	44.0	24.0
Dahomey	3.1	110	1.7	41	49.9	23.0
El Salvador	4.1	340	1.2	58	42.2	11.1
Ethiopia	28.0	80	1.2	38	49.4	25.8
Ghana	9.9	300	1.0	44	48.8	21.9
Guinea	4.4	90	-0.3	41	46.6	22.9
Guyana	0.8	400	1.3	68	32.4	5.9
Haiti	4.6	130	1.3	50	35.8	16.5
Honduras	3.0	320	1.7	54	49.3	14.6
India	613.2	110	1.4	50	39.9	15.7
Ivory Coast	4.9	340	4.1	44	45.6	20.6
Kenya	13.3	170	4.1	50	48.7	16.0
Khmer Rep. (Cambodia)	8.1	120[a]	-3.8[a]	45	46.7	19.0

[a]Tentative estimate.
[b]1972 figure.
[c]United Nations, *Monthly Bulletin of Statistics*, Vol. 29, No. 1, January 1975.
[d]U.S. Agency for International Development, Bureau for Population and Humanitarian Assistance, *Population Program Assistance: Annual Report, FY 1973* (Washington, D.C.: U.S. Government Printing Office, 1973).
[e]August 1974 figure.
[f]October 1974 figure.
[g]March 1974 figure.
[h]November 1974 figure.
[i]December 1974 figure.

[j]September 1974 figure.
[k]June 1971 figure.
[l]Mid-1973 figure.
[m]1966 figure.
[n]1971 figure.
[o]December 1973 figure.
[p]f.o.b.
[q]June 1974 figure.
[r]Associate Member of OPEC.
[s]Belgium-Luxembourg.
[t]See Belgium.
[u]Includes Botswana, Lesotho, Namibia, and Swaziland.

Infant Mortality per 1,000 Live Births	Literacy	Per Capita Energy Consumption, 1971	Total Exports, f.o.b., 1973	Total Imports, c.i.f., 1973	Net Bilat. ODA from DAC Countries and Multilat. Concessional Flows, 1973	International Reserves, January 1975
	(%)	(kg. coal equiv.)	($ mil.)	($ mil.)	($ mil.)	($ mil.)
182	8	27	90[bc]	181[bc]	57.4	74
132	22[d]	n.a.	357	874	425.4	n.a.
n.a.	n.a.	n.a.	n.a.	n.a.	0.5	n.a.
97	20	n.a.	n.a.	n.a.	35.0	n.a.
150	10	11	30[c]	31[c]	26.1	162
137	10-15	97	353	334	61.5	98[e]
190	5-10	60	39[bc]	34[bc]	25.6	2[e]
160	5-10	27	38[c]	82[c]	40.9	8[e]
185	20	38	47[bc]	94[bc]	26.2	32[f]
58	49	223	352	373	12.8	92
181	5	32	240	215	64.3	278
156	25	192	619	450	40.7	104
216	5-10	108	n.a.	n.a.	20.5	n.a.
40	76	996	135	164	7.6	24[g]
150	10	29	52	74	7.2	15[h]
115	45	234	237	262	13.9	44[i]
139	28	186	2,958	3,236	771.4	1,508[h]
164	20	265	858	710	62.1	77[f]
135	20-25	171	461	615	95.9	205
127	41	24	7[b]	80[b]	144.8	n.a.

SOURCES: Unless otherwise indicated, figures for population, life expectancy, birth rate, death rate, and infant mortality are from Population Reference Bureau, "1975 World Population Data Sheet;" per capita GNP and per capita GNP growth rates are from *World Bank Atlas, 1974: Population, Per Capita Product, and Growth Rates* (Washington, D.C.: World Bank Group, 1974); figures for literacy and per capita energy consumption are from United Nations, *Handbook of International Trade and Development Statistics: Supplement 1973*, Publication Sales No. E/F.74.II.D.7, pp. 102-115; exports, imports, and international reserves are from International Monetary Fund, *International Financial Statistics*, Vol. 28, No. 3, March 1975; and figures for net flow of bilateral ODA and multilateral concessional flows are from Report by the Chairman of the Development Assistance Committee, *Development Co-operation, 1974 Review* (Paris: OECD, 1974), pp. 266-267.

	Popu-lation, mid-1975	Per Capita GNP, 1972	Per Capita GNP Growth Rate, 1965-72	Life Expec-tancy at Birth, 1970-75 Average	Birth Rate per 1,000, 1970-75 Average	Death Rate per 1,000, 1970-75 Average
	(mil.)	($)	(%)	(yrs.)		
Laos	3.3	130[a]	3.1[a]	40	44.6	22.8
Lesotho	1.1	90[a]	1.1[a]	46	39.0	19.7
Malagasy Republic	8.0	140	1.4	44	50.2	21.1
Malawi	4.9	100	2.9	41	47.7	23.7
Maldives	0.1	100[a]	0.6[a]	n.a.	46.0	23.0
Mali	5.7	80	1.3	38	50.1	25.9
Mauritania	1.3	180	2.0	38	44.8	24.9
Nepal	12.6	80	0.1	44	42.9	20.3
Niger	4.6	90	-5.1	38	52.2	25.5
Pakistan	70.6	130	1.7	50	47.4	16.5
Rwanda	4.2	60[a]	2.1[a]	41	50.0	23.6
Senegal	4.4	260	-0.7	40	47.6	23.9
Sierra Leone	3.0	190	1.8	44	44.7	20.7
Somalia	3.2	80[a]	1.1[a]	41	47.2	21.7
Sri Lanka	14.0	110	2.0	68	28.6	6.4
Sudan	18.3	120[a]	-1.1[a]	49	47.8	17.5
Tanzania	15.4	120	2.9	44	50.2	20.1
Uganda	11.4	150	2.0	50	45.2	15.9
Upper Volta	6.0	70	0.6	38	48.5	25.8
Western Samoa	0.2[acl]	150[a]	0.4[a]	63[bd]	42.0[bd]	8.0[bd]
Yemen, Arab Rep.	6.7	90[a]	2.4[a]	45	49.6	20.6
Yemen, People's Rep.	1.7	100[a]	-7.2[a]	45	49.6	20.6

Third World Countries

Angola	6.4	390	5.5	38	47.3	24.5
Argentina	25.4	1,290	2.8	68	21.8	8.8
Bahamas	0.2	2,240[a]	0.6[a]	n.a.	23.8	5.7
Bahrain	0.3	670	6.0	47	49.6	18.7
Barbados	0.2	800	6.2	69	21.6	8.9
Bolivia	5.4	200	1.4	47	43.7	18.0
Brazil	109.7	530	5.6	61	37.1	8.8
Burma	31.2	90	1.0	50	39.5	15.8
Chile	10.3	800	2.2	63	27.9	9.2
China, People's Rep.	822.8	170[a]	2.6[a]	62	26.9	10.3

Infant Mortality per 1,000 Live Births	Literacy	Per Capita Energy Consumption, 1971	Total Exports, f.o.b., 1973	Total Imports, c.i.f., 1973	Net Bilat. ODA from DAC Countries and Multilat. Concessional Flows, 1973	International Reserves, January 1975
	(%)	(kg. coal equiv.)	($ mil.)	($ mil.)	($ mil.)	($ mil.)
123	15	91	3[b]	44[b]	73.5	n.a.
181	59	n.a.	n.a.	n.a.	11.7	n.a.
170	39	71	203	203	52.4	48
148	15	49	99	142	28.6	79
n.a.	n.a.	n.a.	n.a.	n.a.	0.5	n.a.
188	5	25	54[c]	115[c]	67.9	5[e]
187	1-5	133	100[b]	69[b]	22.5	96[h]
169	9	9	n.a.	n.a.	31.2	138[f]
200	5	22	56[c]	68[c]	69.6	47[f]
132	16[d]	n.a.	961	981	270.9	380
133	10	10	31[c]	28[c]	37.8	13[i]
159	5-10	129	195	361	76.8	12[j]
136	10	109	132	158	14.1	48
177	5	31	57	112	35.1	51
45	70-80	163	388	421	52.9	74
141	10-15	119	434	436	46.3	67
162	15-20	70	368	488	94.8	50
160	20	72	326	163	13.4	44[k]
182	5-10	13	24[c]	63[c]	57.3	74[j]
57[dm]	97	112	6	19	1.8	n.a.
152	10	14	8[c]	125[c]	20.9	n.a.
152	10	639	121	170	6.9	68[e]
203	10-15	157	728	529	8.9	n.a.
60	91	1,773	3,269	2,241	13.4	1,323[h]
33	85	5,600	531	757	0.4	n.a.
138	29	7,186	246[n]	280[b]	0.7	n.a.
31	91	1,238	54	170	4.8	n.a.
108	32	224	280	256	22.5	191
94	61	500	6,199	6,999	63.3	5,531[f]
126	60	68	128	102	70.9	162
71	84	1,516	1,231	941[b]	39.7	221[n]
55	25[d]	561	n.a.	n.a.	—	n.a.

	Population, mid-1975	Per Capita GNP, 1972	Per Capita GNP Growth Rate, 1965-72	Life Expectancy at Birth, 1970-75 Average	Birth Rate per 1,000, 1970-75 Average	Death Rate per 1,000, 1970-75 Average
	(*mil.*)	(*$*)	(%)	(*yrs.*)		
Colombia	25.9	400	2.4	61	40.6	8.8
Congo, People's Rep.	1.3	300	1.4	44	45.1	20.8
Costa Rica	2.0	630	4.1	68	33.4	5.9
Cuba	9.5	450[a]	-1.0[a]	70	29.1	6.6
Cyprus	0.7	1,180	6.4	71	22.2	6.8
Dominican Rep.	5.1	480	5.0	58	45.8	11.0
Egypt	37.5	240	0.6	52	37.8	14.0
Equatorial Guinea	0.3	240	-1.5	44	36.8	19.7
Gambia, The	0.5	140	1.4	40	43.3	24.1
Grenada	0.1	420[a]	5.0[a]	69	27.9	7.8
Guadeloupe	0.4	910[a]	5.0[a]	69	29.3	6.4
Guatemala	6.1	420	2.2	53	42.8	13.7
Guinea-Bissau	0.5	230	3.4	38	40.1	25.1
Hong Kong	4.2	980	5.7	70	19.4	5.5
Jamaica	2.0	810	3.9	70	33.2	7.1
Jordan	2.7	270	-2.8	53	47.6	14.7
Korea, Dem. Rep.	15.9	320[a]	4.0[a]	61	35.7	9.4
Korea, Republic of	33.9	310	8.5	61	28.7	8.8
Lebanon	2.9	700	1.4	63	39.8	9.9
Liberia	1.7	250	4.0	44	43.6	20.7
Malaysia	12.1	430	2.9	59	38.7	9.9
Martinique	0.4	1,050[a]	4.6[a]	69	29.7	6.7
Mauritius	0.9	300	0.0	66	24.4	6.8
Mexico	59.2	750	2.8	63	42.0	8.6
Mongolia	1.4	380[a]	0.6[a]	61	38.8	9.4
Morocco	17.5	270	3.0	53	46.2	15.7
Mozambique	9.2	300	5.6	44	43.1	20.1
Netherlands Antilles	0.2	1,500[a]	0.6[a]	74	19.7	4.7
Nicaragua	2.3	470	1.5	53	48.3	13.9
Oman	0.8	530	22.5	47	49.6	18.7
Panama	1.7	880	4.5	66	36.2	7.2
Papua-New Guinea	2.7	290	7.5	48	40.6	17.1
Paraguay	2.6	320	2.1	62	39.8	8.9
Peru	15.3	520	1.1	56	41.0	11.9
Philippines	44.4	220	2.4	58	43.8	10.5
Réunion	0.5	1,010[a]	4.6[a]	63	31.2	8.5

Infant Mortality per 1,000 Live Births	Literacy	Per Capita Energy Consumption, 1971	Total Exports, f.o.b., 1973	Total Imports, c.i.f., 1973	Net Bilat. ODA from DAC Countries and Multilat. Concessional Flows, 1973	International Reserves, January 1975
	(%)	(kg. coal equiv.)	($ mil.)	($ mil.)	($ mil.)	($ mil.)
76	73	638	1,084	876	133.3	412
180	20	250	125[c]	134[c]	27.2	22[e]
54	84	446	339	451	15.7	14[n]
25	78	1,152	803[bc]	1,292[bc]	4.9	n.a.
33	76	1,451	179	447	6.0	273
98	65	264	442	486	19.5	100
103	30	282	1,119	905	73.0	603[j]
165	20[d]	183	n.a.	n.a.	—	n.a.
165	10	68	25[c]	31[c]	6.2	35[f]
34	76[d]	n.a.	n.a.	n.a.	—	n.a.
46	83	452	64	201	83.5	n.a.
79	38	250	442	431	18.3	218
208	n.a.	103	n.a.	n.a.	8.6	n.a.
17	71	1,040	5,051	5,637	0.9	n.a.
26	82	1,338	392	668	15.6	174
99	35-40	318	58	335	88.8	472
n.a.	n.a.	2,294	n.a.	n.a.	—	n.a.
60	71	860	3,220	4,219	279.0	1,056[i]
54	86	841	573	1,184	11.7	1,672
159	9	368	324	193	10.0	n.a.
75	43[d]	n.a.	2,950	2,402	42.7	1,618[i]
32	85	660	55[c]	244[c]	101.8	n.a.
65	61	183	132	171	11.9	139
61	78	1,270	2,631	4,146	12.6	1,280[f]
n.a.	95[d]	945	n.a.	n.a.	—	n.a.
149	14	205	872	1,099	91.2	417[i]
165	7	178	304[c]	478[c]	3.9	n.a.
25	n.a.	n.a.	950	1,250	22.0	n.a.
123	50	389	277	327	26.2	166[i]
138	n.a.	62	260[b]	134[b]	0.1	n.a.
47	78	2,121	133	489	22.2	2,303[o]
159	29	133	511[c]	316[cp]	195.0	n.a.
84	74	142	127	122	14.7	89
110	61	621	1,047	863	73.8	551[o]
78	72	298	1,788	1,773	220.4	1,607
43[adn]	52	334	50[b]	196[b]	176.3	n.a.

Third World Countries (Continued)

	Population, mid-1975	Per Capita GNP, 1972	Per Capita GNP Growth Rate, 1965-72	Life Expectancy at Birth, 1970-75 Average	Birth Rate per 1,000, 1970-75 Average	Death Rate per 1,000, 1970-75 Average
	(mil.)	($)	(%)	(yrs.)		
Rhodesia	6.3	340	2.9	52	47.9	14.4
Singapore	2.2	1,300	10.3	70	21.2	5.2
Surinam	0.4	810	4.7	66	41.6	7.5
Swaziland	0.5	260[a]	5.3[a]	44	49.0	21.8
Syrian Arab Rep.	7.3	320	3.8	54	45.4	15.4
Taiwan	16.0	490	6.9	69	24.0	5.0
Thailand	42.1	220	4.2	58	43.4	10.8
Togo	2.2	160	3.3	41	50.6	23.5
Tonga	0.1[acl]	320[a]	2.0[a]	56[bd]	39.0[bd]	10.0[bd]
Trinidad and Tobago	1.0	970	3.6	70	25.3	5.9
Tunisia	5.7	380	3.7	54	40.0	13.8
Turkey	39.9	370	4.3	57	39.4	12.5
Uruguay	3.1	760	0.4	70	20.4	9.3
Vietnam, Dem. Rep.	23.8	110[a]	-0.1[a]	48	41.4	17.9
Vietnam, Republic of	19.7	170	-0.7	40	41.7	23.6
Zaire	24.5	100[a]	3.9[a]	44	45.2	20.5
Zambia	5.0	380	-0.1	44	51.5	20.5

OPEC Countries

	Population, mid-1975	Per Capita GNP, 1972	Per Capita GNP Growth Rate, 1965-72	Life Expectancy at Birth, 1970-75 Average	Birth Rate per 1,000, 1970-75 Average	Death Rate per 1,000, 1970-75 Average
Algeria	16.8	430	3.5	53	48.7	15.4
Ecuador	7.1	360	3.8	60	41.8	9.5
Gabon[r]	0.5	880	10.0	41	32.2	22.2
Indonesia	136.0	90	4.3	48	42.9	16.9
Iran	32.9	490	7.2	51	45.3	15.6
Iraq	11.1	370	1.8	53	48.1	14.6
Kuwait	1.1	4,090	-1.3	67	47.1	5.3
Libyan Arab Rep.	2.3	1,830	8.1	53	45.0	14.8
Nigeria	62.9	130	5.4	41	49.3	22.7
Qatar	0.1	2,530	6.1	47	49.6	18.7
Saudi Arabia	9.0	550[a]	6.8[a]	45	49.5	20.2
United Arab Emirates	0.2	3,220	16.2	47	49.6	18.7
Venezuela	12.2	1,240	1.1	65	36.1	7.1

Infant Mortality per 1,000 Live Births	Literacy	Per Capita Energy Consumption, 1971	Total Exports, f.o.b., 1973	Total Imports, c.i.f., 1973	Net Bilat. ODA from DAC Countries and Multilat. Concessional Flows, 1973	International Reserves, January 1975
	(%)	(kg. coal equiv.)	($ mil.)	($ mil.)	($ mil.)	($ mil.)
122	25-30	618	499[bc]	417[bcp]	0.9	n.a.
20	75	851	3,605	5,063	25.7	1,392[q]
30	84	2,229	172[b]	144[b]	29.4	n.a.
149	36	n.a.	n.a.	n.a.	10.3	n.a.
93	35	485	339	595	10.4	773[f]
28	85	n.a.	4,378	3,797	-20.5	1,191[i]
65	68	296	1,584	2,057	60.5	1,905
179	5-10	73	61[c]	101[c]	25.8	47[j]
107[dm]	90-95[d]	n.a.	n.a.	n.a.	0.9	n.a.
35	89	3,962	658	776	1.3	394
128	30	255	386	608	129.7	418[i]
119	46	516	1,318	2,091	82.4	1,861[i]
40	91	958	322	285	15.8	216[h]
n.a.	65	165	n.a.	n.a.	—	n.a.
n.a.	60	290	59	620	447.2	240[i]
160	35-40	77	691[b]	787[b]	139.2	140[i]
157	15-20	458	1,142	604	45.2	221[h]
128	25-30	492	1,802	2,338	108.3	1,497
78	68	315	561	532	29.1	336
229	12	1,028	287	160	34.1	47[e]
125	43	123	3,211	2,347	589.2	1,624
139	23	895	6,914	3,370	-3.3	8,513
99	20	650	2,292	899	12.4	3,273[i]
44	47	7,888	3,789	1,042	-3.2	1,654
130	27	571	4,085	1,723	12.9	3,523
180	25	59	3,358	1,874	72.8	5,981
138	10-15[d]	2,025	332[b]	128[b]	0.4	n.a.
152	5-15	988	8,638	1,993	3.3	14,285[i]
138	20[d]	802	1,510	800	0.1	n.a.
50	76	2,518	4,727	2,813	8.3	6,191

Developed Countries

	Population, mid-1975	Per Capita GNP, 1972	Per Capita GNP Growth Rate, 1965-72	Life Expectancy at Birth, 1970-75 Average	Birth Rate per 1,000, 1970-75 Average	Death Rate per 1,000, 1970-75 Average
	(mil.)	($)	(%)	(yrs.)		
Albania	2.5	530	5.7	69	33.4	6.5
Australia	13.8	2,980	3.1	72	21.0	8.1
Austria	7.5	2,410	5.0	71	14.7	12.2
Belgium	9.8	3,210	4.6	73	14.8	11.2
Bulgaria	8.8	1,420	5.9	72	16.2	9.2
Canada	22.8	4,440	3.2	72	18.6	7.7
Czechoslovakia	14.8	2,180	4.5	69	17.0	11.2
Denmark	5.0	3,670	3.7	74	14.0	10.1
Finland	4.7	2,810	4.9	70	13.2	9.3
France	52.9	3,620	4.8	73	17.0	10.6
Germany, Dem. Rep.	17.2	2,100	3.5	73	13.9	12.4
Germany, Fed. Rep.	61.9	3,390	4.1	71	12.0	12.1
Greece	8.9	1,460	7.3	72	15.4	9.4
Hungary	10.5	1,520	4.2	70	15.3	11.5
Iceland	0.2	2,800	1.8	74	19.3	7.7
Ireland	3.1	1,580	3.7	72	22.1	10.4
Israel	3.4	2,610	7.1	71	26.5	6.7
Italy	55.0	1,960	4.3	72	16.0	9.8
Japan	111.1	2,320	9.7	73	19.2	6.6
Luxembourg	0.3	3,190	3.0	71	13.5	11.7
Malta	0.3	950	7.4	71	17.5	9.0
Netherlands	13.6	2,840	4.3	74	16.8	8.7
New Zealand	3.0	2,560	1.8	72	22.3	8.3
Norway	4.0	3,340	3.8	74	16.7	10.1
Poland	33.8	1,500	4.0	70	16.8	8.6
Portugal	8.8	780	5.3	68	18.4	10.1
Romania	21.2	810	6.7	67	19.3	10.3
South Africa	24.7	850	2.1	52	42.9	15.5
Spain	35.4	1,210	5.0	72	19.5	8.3
Sweden	8.3	4,480	2.5	73	14.2	10.5
Switzerland	6.5	3,940	2.9	72	14.7	10.0
U.S.S.R.	255.0	1,530	5.9	70	17.8	7.9
United Kingdom	56.4	2,600	2.0	72	16.1	11.7
United States	213.9	5,590	2.0	71	16.2	9.4
Yugoslavia	21.3	810	5.5	68	18.2	9.2

Infant Mortality per 1,000 Live Births	Literacy	Per Capita Energy Consumption, 1971	Total Exports, f.o.b., 1973	Total Imports, c.i.f., 1973	Net Bilat. ODA from DAC Countries and Multilat. Concessional Flows, 1973	International Reserves, January 1975
	(%)	(kg. coal equiv.)	($ mil.)	($ mil.)	($ mil.)	($ mil.)
87	70[d]	631	n.a.	n.a.	—	n.a.
17	98[d]	5,359	9,517	7,658	—	4,194
24	98[d]	3,231	5,287	7,119	—	3,608
17	97[d]	6,116[s]	22,488[s]	21,988[s]	—	5,529
26	95[d]	4,029	3,301[c]	3,266[cp]	—	n.a.
17	98	9,326	26,309	24,918	—	5,802
21	100[d]	6,615	6,288[c]	6,137[cp]	—	n.a.
14	99[d]	5,327	6,248	7,802	—	918
10	99[d]	4,334	3,828	4,333	—	594
16	97[d]	3,928	36,659	37,727	—	9,007
18	99[d]	6,308	7,521[c]	7,854[cp]	—	n.a.
20	99[d]	5,223	67,502	54,552	—	33,075
27	80[d]	1,470	1,440	3,456	-12.3	936[i]
34	97[d]	3,291	4,433[c]	3,919[c]	—	n.a.
12	99[d]	4,311	291	359	—	39
18	98[d]	3,285	2,135	2,794 ·	—	1,242
21	84[d]	2,710	1,449	4,240	186.1	1,202[i]
26	93-95[d]	2,682	22,224	27,796	—	6,630
12	98[d]	3,267	36,982	38,347	—	13,509
16	98[d]	t	t	t	—	n.a.
24	83	981	98	240	26.9	407
12	98[d]	5,069	24,071	24,735	—	7,284
16	98[d]	2,934	2,599	2,179	—	658
13	99[d]	5,189	4,692	6,245	—	1,827
28	98[d]	4,374	6,374[c]	7,814[cp]	—	n.a.
44	65[d]	805	1,836	3,007	—	2,352[i]
40	98-99[d]	2,975	3,698[c]	3,468[cp]	—	n.a.
117	35[d]	2,895[u]	3,435[c]	5,020[c]	—	1,188
15	86[d]	1,614	5,164	9,522	-8.8	6,277[h]
10	99[d]	6,089	12,201	10,628	—	1,786
13	98[d]	3,575	9,477	11,613	—	8,200
26	99[d]	4,535	21,463[c]	21,108[cp]	—	n.a.
18	98-99[d]	5,507	30,535	38,847	—	7,021
18	98[d]	11,244	71,339	73,575	—	16,262
43	80[d]	1,608	3,024	4,776	120.4	1,201

A-6. Average Annual Per Capita Consumption of Selected Major Commodities, 1970 (kilograms)

	Developed Market Economies	Developing Countries
Grains[a]	96.8	129.3
Starchy roots	71.0	63.9
Pulses and nuts	5.5	15.4
Meats[b]	66.5	11.4
Fish	21.5	6.9
Dairy products[c]	168.2	38.8
Fruits and vegetables	178.3	71.9
Vegetable oils	11.1	4.1
Animal fats	4.5	0.4
Sugar	37.7	19.4
Fibers[d]	13.7	2.6
Fossil fuels (petroleum equivalent)	4,420.0	246.0
Steel	480.3	44.0
Selected other metals[e]	25.1	2.0

[a]Wheat, rice, maize, millet, sorghum, and other cereals.
[b]Beef, veal, pig meat, poultry, mutton, lamb, and other meats.
[c]Milk, eggs, cheese, and butter.
[d]Cotton, wool, cellulosic, and non-cellulosic.
[e]Aluminum, lead, copper, zinc, tin, and nickel.

SOURCE: United Nations, Dept. of Economic and Social Affairs, *World Economic Survey, 1973. Part One: Population and Development,* Publication Sales No. E.74.II.C.1, pp. 160-61.

A-7. Average Annual Per Capita Cereal Consumption (Direct and Indirect), 1964-1966 and 1972-1974 (pounds)

	1964-66 Average	1972-74 Average
United States	1,600	1,850
U.S.S.R.	1,105	1,435
European Community	900[a]	1,000[a]
Japan	530[a]	620[a]
China	420	430
Developing Countries (excluding China)	370[b]	395

[a]Widespread use of non-cereal livestock feed somewhat reduces the figures for European Community cereal consumption. Large imports of meat reduce Japan's figures.
[b]Depressed by two bad crop years in India.

SOURCE: Report by the Chairman of the Development Assistance Committee, *Development Co-operation, 1974 Review* (Paris: OECD, 1974), p. 98.

209

A-8. Gross National Product and Population, 1972 (percentages)

	GNP	Population
North America	34.6	6.2
Europe, excluding U.S.S.R.	30.2	13.4
U.S.S.R.	10.4	6.6
Asia, including Middle East and excluding Japan	8.9	52.4
Japan	6.8	2.9
Central and South America[a]	5.3	7.9
Africa	2.4	10.1
Oceania	1.3	0.6
Total	100.0	100.0
Developed Market Economies[b]	67.0	17.9
Centrally Planned Economies[c]	18.9	32.1
Developing Countries	14.1	49.9
Total	100.0	100.0

[a]Includes Mexico.
[b]Australia, Austria, Belgium, Canada, Denmark, Finland, France, Federal Republic of Germany, Iceland, Ireland, Italy, Japan, Luxembourg, Netherlands, New Zealand, Norway, Portugal, Puerto Rico, South Africa, Sweden, Switzerland, United Kingdom, United States.
[c]Albania, Bulgaria, China, Cuba, Czechoslovakia, German Democratic Republic, Hungary, Democratic Republic of Korea, Mongolia, Poland, Romania, U.S.S.R., Democratic Republic of Vietnam.

NOTE: In 1972, world GNP was $3.7 trillion; population was 3.7 billion.

SOURCE: Based on *World Bank Atlas, 1974: Population, Per Capita Product, and Growth Rates* (Washington, D.C.: World Bank Group, 1974), pp. 8, 10.

A-9. GNP, Per Capita GNP, and Population: 1970 Levels and 1960-1970 Annual Growth Rates

	Per Capita GNP, 1970 ($)	Total GNP, 1970 ($ billions)	Per Capita GNP Annual Growth Rate, 1960-1970 (percentages)	GNP Annual Growth Rate, 1960-1970 (percentages)	Population, 1970 (millions)	Population Annual Growth Rate, 1960-1970 (percentages)
Rich Countries	2,790	2,570	4.4	5.5	920	1.1
Middle-Income Countries	870	270	4.5	6.5	310	2.0
Poor Countries	300	155	3.2	6.0	520	2.8
Very Poor Countries	120	230	1.8	4.0	1,930	2.2
World	880	3,225	4.1	6.1	3,680	2.0

SOURCE: Richard Jolly, "International Dimensions," in Hollis Chenery et al., *Redistribution with Growth* (Oxford: Oxford University Press for World Bank and Institute of Development Studies, University of Sussex, 1974), p. 160.

A-10. Cross-Classification of Selected Countries by Per Capita Income Level and Inequality

Per Capita GNP up to $300

High Inequality[a]

	Per Capita GNP ($)	Lowest 40%	Middle 40%	Top 20%
		(percentages)		
Kenya (1969)	136	10.0	22.0	68.0
Sierra Leone (1968)	159	9.6	22.4	68.0
Iraq (1956)	200	6.8	25.2	68.0
Philippines (1971)	239	11.6	34.6	53.8
Senegal (1960)	245	10.0	26.0	64.0
Ivory Coast (1970)	247	10.8	32.1	57.1
Rhodesia (1968)	252	8.2	22.8	69.0
Tunisia (1970)	255	11.4	53.6	55.0
Honduras (1968)	265	6.5	28.5	65.0
Ecuador (1970)	277	6.5	20.0	73.5

Moderate Inequality[b]

	Per Capita GNP ($)	Lowest 40%	Middle 40%	Top 20%
		(percentages)		
Burma (1958)	82	16.5	38.7	44.8
Dahomey (1959)	87	15.5	34.5	50.0
Tanzania (1967)	89	13.0	26.0	61.0
India (1964)	99	16.0	32.0	52.0
Malagasy Republic (1960)	120	13.5	25.5	61.0
Zambia (1959)	230	14.5	28.5	57.0
Turkey (1968)	282	9.3	29.9	60.8
El Salvador (1969)	295	11.2	36.4	52.4

Low Inequality[c]

	Per Capita GNP ($)	Lowest 40%	Middle 40%	Top 20%
		(percentages)		
Chad (1958)	78	18.0	39.0	43.0
Sri Lanka (1969)	95	17.0	37.0	46.0
Niger (1960)	97	18.0	40.0	42.0
Pakistan (1964)	100	17.5	37.5	30.0
Uganda (1970)	126	17.1	35.8	47.1
Thailand (1970)	180	17.0	37.5	45.5
Korea (1970)	235	18.0	37.0	45.0
Taiwan (1964)	241	20.4	39.5	40.1

Per Capita GNP $300-$750[a]

Country	GNP per capita			
Malaysia (1970)	330	11.6	32.4	56.0
Colombia (1970)	358	9.0	30.0	61.0
Brazil (1970)	390	10.0	28.4	61.5
Peru (1971)	480	6.5	33.5	60.0
Gabon (1968)	497	8.8	23.7	67.5
Jamaica (1958)	510	8.2	30.3	61.5
Costa Rica (1971)	521	11.5	30.0	58.5
Mexico (1969)	645	10.5	25.5	64.0
South Africa (1965)	669	6.2	35.8	58.0
Panama (1969)	692	9.4	31.2	59.4

Per Capita GNP above $750[a]

Country	GNP per capita			
Venezuela (1970)	1,004	7.9	27.1	65.0
Finland (1962)	1,599	11.1	39.6	49.3
France (1962)	1,913	9.5	36.8	53.7

Per Capita GNP $300-$750[b]

Country	GNP per capita			
Dominican Republic (1969)	323	12.2	30.3	57.5
Iran (1968)	332	12.5	33.0	54.5
Lebanon (1960)	508	13.0	26.0	61.0
Guyana (1956)	550	14.0	40.3	45.7
Uruguay (1968)	618	16.5	35.5	48.0
Chile (1968)	744	13.0	30.2	56.8

Per Capita GNP above $750[b]

Country	GNP per capita			
Argentina (1970)	1,079	16.5	36.1	47.4
Puerto Rico (1968)	1,100	13.7	35.7	50.6
Netherlands (1967)	1,990	13.6	37.9	48.5
Norway (1968)	2,010	16.6	42.9	40.5
Germany, Fed. Rep. (1964)	2,144	15.4	31.7	52.9
Denmark (1968)	2,563	13.6	38.8	47.6
New Zealand (1969)	2,859	15.5	42.5	42.0
Sweden (1963)	2,949	14.0	42.0	44.0

Per Capita GNP $300-$750[c]

Country	GNP per capita			
Surinam (1962)	394	21.7	35.7	42.6
Greece (1957)	500	21.0	29.5	49.5
Yugoslavia (1968)	529	18.5	40.0	41.5
Bulgaria (1962)	530	26.8	40.0	33.2
Spain (1965)	750	17.6	36.7	45.7

Per Capita GNP above $750[c]

Country	GNP per capita			
Poland (1964)	850	23.4	40.6	36.0
Japan (1963)	950	20.7	39.3	40.0
Hungary (1969)	1,140	24.0	42.5	33.5
Czechoslovakia (1964)	1,150	27.6	41.4	31.0
United Kingdom (1968)	2,015	18.8	42.2	39.0
Australia (1968)	2,509	20.0	41.2	38.8
Canada (1965)	2,920	20.0	39.8	40.2
United States (1970)	4,850	19.7	41.5	38.8

[a]The share of the lowest 40 per cent is less than 12%.

[b]The share of the lowest 40 per cent is between 12% and 17%.

[c]The share of the lowest 40 per cent is 17% and above.

NOTE: The income shares of each percentile group were read off a free-hand Lorenz curve fitted to observed points in the cumulative distribution of pre-tax income. This table uses GNP figures at factor cost for the year indicated in constant 1971 U.S. dollars.

SOURCE:: Hollis Chenery et al., *Redistribution with Growth* (Oxford: Oxford University Press for the World Bank and the Institute of Development Studies, University of Sussex, 1974) pp. 8-9.

A–11. Distribution of Pre-Tax Personal Income in 56 Countries

	Income Share by Percentile of Recipients[a]						Gini Ratio	Per Capita GDP, 1965
	Below 20%	21%-40%	41%-60%	61%-80%	81%-95%	96%-100%		
			(percentages)					($)
Per Capita GDP up to $100[b]	7.0	10.0	13.1	19.4	21.4	29.1	0.419	78.3
Chad (1958)	8.0	11.6	15.4	22.0	20.0	23.0	0.35	68
Dahomey (1959)	8.0	10.0	12.0	20.0	18.0	32.0	0.42	73
Niger (1969)	7.8	11.6	15.6	23.0	19.0	23.0	0.34	81
Nigeria (1959)	7.0	7.0	9.0	16.1	22.5	38.4	0.51	74
Sudan (1969)	5.6	9.4	14.3	22.6	31.0	17.1	0.40	97
Tanzania (1964)	4.8	7.8	11.0	15.4	18.1	42.9	0.54	61
Burma (1958)	10.0	13.0	13.0	15.5	20.3	28.2	0.35	64
India (1956-57)	8.0	12.0	16.0	22.0	22.0	20.0	0.33	95
Malagasy Rep. (1960)	3.9	7.8	11.3	18.0	22.0	37.0	0.53	92
Per Capita GDP $101-$200[b]	5.3	8.6	12.0	17.5	31.6	24.9	0.468	147.6
Morocco (1965)	7.1	7.4	7.7	12.4	44.5	20.6	0.50	180
Senegal (1960)	3.0	7.0	10.0	16.0	28.0	36.0	0.56	192
Sierra Leone (1968)	3.8	6.3	9.1	16.7	30.3	33.8	0.56	142
Tunisia (1971)	5.0	5.7	10.0	14.4	42.6	22.4	0.53	187
Bolivia (1968)	3.5	8.0	12.0	15.5	25.3	35.7	0.53	132
Sri Lanka (1963)	4.5	9.2	13.8	20.2	33.9	18.4	0.44	140
Pakistan (1963-64)	6.5	11.0	15.5	22.0	25.0	20.0	0.37	101
Korea, Rep. of (1966)	9.0	14.0	18.0	23.0	23.5	12.5	0.26	107
Per Capita GDP $201-$300[b]	4.8	8.0	11.3	18.1	25.7	32.0	0.499	244.4
Malaya (1957-58)	6.5	11.2	15.7	22.6	26.2	17.8	0.36	278
Fiji (1968)	4.0	8.0	13.3	22.4	30.9	21.4	0.46	295
Ivory Coast (1959)	8.0	10.0	12.0	15.0	26.0	29.0	0.43	213
Zambia (1959)	6.3	9.6	11.1	15.9	19.6	37.5	0.48	207
Brazil (1960)	3.5	9.0	10.2	15.8	23.1	38.4	0.54	207
Ecuador (1968)	6.3	10.1	16.1	23.2	19.6	24.6	0.38	202
El Salvador (1965)	5.5	6.5	8.8	17.8	28.4	33.0	0.53	249
Peru (1961)	4.0	4.3	8.3	15.2	19.3	48.3	0.61	237
Iraq (1956)	2.0	6.0	8.0	16.0	34.0	34.0	0.60	285
Philippines (1961)	4.3	8.4	12.0	19.5	28.3	27.5	0.48	240
Colombia (1964)	2.2	4.7	9.0	16.1	27.7	40.4	0.62	275

[a]For year indicated.
[b]Group average.

	Income Share by Percentile of Recipients[a]						Gini Ratio	Per Capita GDP, 1965
	Below 20%	21%- 40%	41%- 60%	61%- 80%	81%- 95%	96%- 100%		
	(*percentages*)							(*$*)
Per Capita GDP								
$301-$500[b]	4.5	7.9	12.3	18.0	27.4	30.0	0.494	426.9
Gabon (1960)	2.0	6.0	7.0	14.0	24.0	47.0	0.64	368
Costa Rica (1969)	5.5	8.1	11.2	15.2	25.0	35.0	0.50	360
Jamaica (1958)	2.2	6.0	10.8	19.5	31.3	30.2	0.56	465
Surinam (1962)	10.7	11.6	14.7	20.6	27.0	15.4	0.30	424
Lebanon (1955-60)	3.0	4.2	15.8	16.0	27.0	34.0	0.55	440
Barbados (1951-52)	3.6	9.3	14.2	21.3	29.3	22.3	0.45	368
Chile (1968)	5.4	9.6	12.0	20.7	29.7	22.6	0.44	486
Mexico (1963)	3.5	6.6	11.1	19.3	30.7	28.8	0.53	441
Panama (1969)	4.9	9.4	13.8	15.2	22.2	34.5	0.48	490
Per Capita GDP								
$501-$1,000[b]	5.1	8.9	13.9	22.1	24.7	25.4	0.438	723.3
South Africa (1965)	1.9	4.2	10.2	26.4	18.0	39.4	0.58	521
Argentina (1961)	7.0	10.4	13.2	17.9	22.2	29.3	0.42	782
Trinidad and Tobago (1957-58)	3.4	9.1	14.6	24.3	26.1	22.5	0.44	704
Venezuela (1962)	4.4	9.0	16.0	22.9	23.9	23.2	0.42	904
Greece (1957)	9.0	10.3	13.3	17.9	26.5	23.0	0.38	591
Japan (1962)	4.7	10.6	15.8	22.9	31.2	14.8	0.39	838
Per Capita GDP								
$1,001-$2,000[b]	4.7	10.5	15.9	22.2	25.7	20.9	0.401	1,485.2
Israel (1957)	6.8	13.4	18.6	21.8	28.2	11.2	0.30	1,243
United Kingdom (1964)	5.1	10.2	16.6	23.9	25.0	19.0	0.38	1,590
Netherlands (1962)	4.0	10.0	16.0	21.6	24.8	23.6	0.42	1,400
Germany,Fed.Rep.(1964)	5.3	10.1	13.7	18.0	19.2	33.7	0.45	1,667
France (1962)	1.9	7.6	14.0	22.8	28.7	25.0	0.50	1,732
Finland (1962)	2.4	8.7	15.4	24.2	28.3	21.0	0.46	1,568
Italy (1948)	6.1	10.5	14.6	20.4	24.3	21.1	0.40	1,011
Puerto Rico (1963)	4.5	9.2	14.2	21.5	28.6	22.0	0.44	1,101
Norway (1963)	4.5	12.1	18.5	24.4	25.1	15.4	0.35	1,717
Australia (1966-67)	6.6	13.4	17.8	23.4	24.4	14.4	0.30	1,823
Per Capita GDP								
$2,001 and above[b]	5.0	10.9	17.9	24.1	26.3	16.4	0.365	2,572.3
Denmark (1963)	5.0	10.8	16.8	24.2	26.3	16.9	0.37	2,078
Sweden (1963)	4.4	9.6	17.4	24.6	26.4	17.6	0.39	2,406
United States (1969)	5.6	12.3	17.6	23.4	26.3	14.8	0.34	3,233

SOURCE: Felix Paukert, "Income Distribution at Different Levels of Development: A Survey of Evidence," *International Labor Review*, Vol. 108, No. 2-3, August-September 1973, pp. 114-15.

A-12. Population Below the Poverty Line, 1969

	Per Capita GNP, 1969 ($)	Population, 1969 (millions)	Population Below $50 Per Capita (millions)	Population Below $50 Per Capita (percentage of population)	Population Below $75 Per Capita (millions)	Population Below $75 Per Capita (percentage of population)
Latin America[a]	**545**	**244.5**	**26.6**	**10.8**	**42.5**	**17.4**
Ecuador	264	5.9	2.2	37.0	3.5	58.5
Honduras	265	2.5	0.7	28.0	1.0	38.0
El Salvador	295	3.4	0.5	13.5	0.6	18.4
Dominican Republic	323	4.2	0.5	11.0	0.7	15.9
Colombia	347	20.6	3.2	15.4	5.6	27.0
Brazil	347	90.8	12.7	14.0	18.2	20.0
Guyana	390	0.7	0.1	9.0	0.1	15.1
Peru	480	13.1	2.5	18.9	3.3	25.5
Costa Rica	512	1.7	b	2.3	0.1	8.5
Jamaica	640	2.0	0.2	10.0	0.3	15.4
Mexico	645	48.9	3.8	7.8	8.7	17.8
Uruguay	649	2.9	0.1	2.5	0.2	5.5
Panama	692	1.4	0.1	3.5	0.2	11.0
Chile	751	9.6	b	b	b	b
Venezuela	974	10.0	b	b	b	b
Argentina	1,054	24.0	b	b	b	b
Puerto Rico	1,600	2.8	b	b	b	b
Asia[a]	**132**	**872.0**	**320.0**	**36.7**	**499.1**	**57.2**
Burma	72	27.0	14.5	53.6	19.2	71.0
Sri Lanka	95	12.2	4.0	33.0	7.8	63.5
India	100	537.0	239.0	44.5	359.3	66.9

216

Pakistan[c]	100	111.8	36.3	32.5	64.7	57.9
Thailand	173	34.7	9.3	26.8	15.4	44.3
Korea, Republic of	224	13.3	0.7	5.5	2.3	17.0
Philippines	233	37.2	4.8	13.0	11.2	30.0
Turkey	290	34.5	4.1	12.0	8.2	23.7
Iraq	316	9.4	2.3	24.0	3.1	33.3
Taiwan	317	13.8	1.5	10.7	2.0	14.3
Malaysia	323	10.6	1.2	11.0	1.6	15.5
Iran	350	27.9	2.3	8.5	4.2	15.0
Lebanon	570	2.6	b	1.0	0.1	5.0
Africa[a]	**303**	**83.8**	**23.8**	**28.4**	**36.6**	**43.6**
Chad	75	3.5	1.5	43.1	2.7	77.5
Dahomey	90	2.6	1.1	41.6	2.3	90.1
Tanzania	92	12.8	7.4	57.9	9.3	72.9
Niger	94	3.9	1.3	33.0	2.3	59.9
Malagasy Republic	119	6.7	3.6	53.8	4.7	69.6
Uganda	128	8.3	1.8	21.3	4.1	49.8
Sierra Leone	165	2.5	1.1	43.5	1.5	61.5
Senegal	229	3.8	0.9	22.3	1.3	35.3
Ivory Coast	237	4.8	0.3	7.0	1.4	28.5
Tunisia	241	4.9	1.1	22.5	1.6	32.1
Rhodesia	274	5.1	0.9	17.4	1.9	37.4
Zambia	340	4.2	0.3	6.3	0.3	7.5
Gabon	547	0.5	0.1	15.7	0.1	23.0
South Africa	729	20.2	2.4	12.0	3.1	15.5
Total[a]	**228**	**1,200.3**	**370.4**	**30.9**	**578.2**	**48.2**

[a]Covers only listed countries.
[b]Negligible.
[c]Includes Bangladesh.

SOURCE: Hollis Chenery et al., *Redistribution with Growth* (Oxford: Oxford University Press for World Bank and Institute of Development Studies, University of Sussex, 1974), p. 12.

A-13. Estimates of Per Capita GNP for 1965 and 2000 (1965 dollars)

	Bhagwati Estimates			Kahn-Weiner Estimates	
	1965	2000	Annual Growth Rate, 1965-2000	1965	2000
Developing Countries	145	388	2.85	135	325
Africa	144	281	1.95	141	277
Asia	118	324	2.95	114	302
South America	379	928	2.60	357	695
Developed Countries	1,729	6,126	3.67	1,675	5,775
Europe	1,377	5,087	3.80	1,364	5,055
Japan	866	8,656	6.80	857	8,590
North America	3,023	7,921	2.80	2,632	6,255
Oceania	1,641	3,344	2.05	2,000	4,310
World	646	1,769	2.90	631	1,696

NOTE: The two sets of estimates differ in both their definitions of North America and their population estimates.

SOURCE: Jagdish N. Bhagwati, "Economic and World Order from the 1970s to the 1990s: The Key Issues," in Bhagwati, ed., *Economics and World Order from the 1970s to the 1990s* (London: The MacMillan Company, 1972), p. 28.

Trade

B–1. Exports, by Country Groupings, 1960, 1965, 1970, 1972, 1973 ($ billions, f.o.b., and percentages)

	Industrial Areas[a]		Developing Areas		Eastern Trading Area[b]		Total World[c]	
	($ billions)	(percentage of total world exports)	($ billions)	(percentage of total world exports)	($ billions)	(percentage of total world exports)	($ billions)	(percentage of total world exports)
Industrial Areas[a]								
1960	54.4	42.5	20.9	16.3	2.9	2.3	81.8	63.8
1965	87.6	46.9	25.5	13.7	4.7	2.5	123.1	65.9
1970	160.6	51.5	39.9	12.8	8.2	2.6	215.8	69.2
1972	217.9	52.5	50.1	12.1	11.7	2.8	287.0	69.2
1973	293.0	51.7	69.7	12.3	17.8	3.2	391.1	69.0
Developing Areas								
1960	19.2	15.0	6.3	4.9	1.2	1.0	27.5	21.4
1965	25.4	13.6	7.7	4.1	2.4	1.3	36.4	19.5
1970	40.0	12.8	11.1	3.6	3.2	1.0	55.5	17.8
1972	55.4	13.4	14.5	3.5	3.5	0.8	74.7	18.0
1973	75.4	13.3	19.9	3.5	5.4	1.0	102.5	18.1

Eastern Trading Area [b]

Year							
1960	2.8	2.2	1.3	1.0	10.9	8.5	15.0	11.7
1965	4.7	2.5	3.2	1.7	13.8	7.4	21.7	11.6
1970	7.7	2.5	5.1	1.6	20.0	6.4	32.9	10.5
1972	10.3	2.5	6.0	1.4	26.2	6.3	42.6	10.3
1973	15.7	2.8	8.7	1.5	32.9	5.8	57.4	10.1

Total World [c]

Year							
1960	79.3	61.9	29.2	22.8	15.2	11.8	128.2	100.0
1965	121.6	65.2	37.3	20.0	21.3	11.4	186.7	100.0
1970	213.9	68.5	57.6	18.5	31.6	10.1	312.0	100.0
1972	291.1	70.2	72.7	17.5	41.8	10.1	414.7	100.0
1973	395.2	69.7	101.3	17.9	56.7	10.0	566.7	100.0

[a] Austria, Belgium-Luxembourg, Canada, Denmark, Fed. Rep. of Germany, Finland, France, Gibraltar, Greece, Iceland, Ireland, Italy, Japan, Mr'ta, Netherlands, Norway, Portugal, Spain, Sweden, Switzerland, Turkey, United Kingdom, United States, Yugoslavia.
[b] Albania, Bulgaria, China, Czechoslovakia, Dem. Rep. of Korea, Dem. Rep. of Vietnam, German Dem. Rep., Hungary, Mongolia, Poland, Romania, U.S.S.R.
[c] Includes Australia, New Zealand, and South Africa. They are excluded elsewhere.

SOURCE: *International Trade, 1973-74* (Geneva: General Agreement on Tariffs and Trade, 1974), Publication Sales No. GATT/1974-4, Table 2, p. 3.

B-2. U.S. Trade, 1971-1974
($ millions)

	1971	1972	1973	1974
U.S. Trade with All Countries				
Exports	44,130	49,778	71,339	98,506
Imports	45,562	55,583	69,475	100,973
Trade Balance	-1,432	-5,805	1,864	-2,466
U.S. Trade with Developing Countries				
Exports	12,701	14,015	19,994	31,485
Imports	11,370	14,114	20,007	39,163
Trade Balance	1,331	-99	-13	-7,678
U.S. Trade with Fourth World Countries				
Exports	1,406	1,302	1,806	2,727
Imports	1,172	1,271	1,572	1,914
Trade Balance	234	32	234	813
U.S. Trade with Third World Countries				
Exports	9,014	9,947	14,568	22,036
Imports	8,192	10,156	13,845	21,606
Trade Balance	823	-209	723	430
U.S. Trade with OPEC Countries[a]				
Exports	2,281	2,766	3,620	6,723
Imports	2,007	2,687	4,590	15,644
Trade Balance	274	78	-970	-8,921
U.S. Trade Balance with Developing Countries, by Region				
Africa	122	-286	-621	-3,490
Africa less OPEC[b]	2	-94	30	277
East and South Asia	106	-891	-443	-1,067
East and South Asia less OPEC[c]	51	-921	-380	91
Near East	645	808	752	-487
Near East less OPEC[d]	163	202	-759	485
Latin America	449	275	327	-2,608
Latin America less OPEC[e]	833	641	1,093	450
Oceania	8	-6	-27	-26

[a]Includes Gabon.
[b]Africa OPEC: Algeria, Libya, Nigeria, Gabon.
[c]South and East Asia OPEC: Indonesia.
[d]Near East OPEC: Iran, Iraq, Kuwait, Saudi Arabia, Qatar, United Arab Emirates.
[e]Latin America OPEC: Venezuela, Ecuador.

NOTE: Exports are f.a.s.; imports, customs value.

SOURCES: Based on U.S. Department of Commerce, *U.S. Foreign Trade: Highlights of Exports and Imports,* December 1972 and December 1973, and U.S. Department of Commerce, *Highlights of U.S. Export and Import Trade,* December 1974.

B–3. Major Import Sources for Sixteen of the Poorest Developing Countries, 1966-1973 ($ millions and percentages)

	Total Imports	Imports from the United States		Imports from Industrialized Europe[a]		Imports from Japan		Imports from Developing Countries	
	($ millions)	($ millions)	(percentage of total imports)	($ millions)	(percentage of total imports)	($ millions)	(percentage of total imports)	($ millions)	(percentage of total imports)
1966	6,123.3	1,580.0	25.8	2,232.5	36.5	389.1	6.4	993.0	16.2
1967	6,103.1	1,672.8	27.4	2,195.4	36.0	378.9	6.2	880.9	14.4
1968	6,261.5	1,452.5	23.2	2,194.5	35.0	475.9	7.6	1,114.8	17.8
1969	6,084.8	1,144.1	18.8	2,250.1	37.0	451.2	7.4	1,191.1	19.6
1970	6,464.1	1,228.0	19.0	2,322.1.	35.9	499.9	7.7	1,329.1	20.6
1971	7,119.3	1,115.0	15.7	2,718.3	38.2	645.3	9.1	1,553.0	21.8
1972	6,831.8	912.6	13.4	2,647.5	38.8	629.9	9.2	1,738.0	25.4
1973	9,284.3	1,411.0	15.2	3,425.1	36.9	892.5	9.6	2,200.6	23.7

[a]Austria, Belgium-Luxembourg, Denmark, France, Fed. Rep. of Germany, Italy, Netherlands, Norway, Sweden, Switzerland, United Kingdom.

NOTE: The sixteen countries are Bangladesh, Bolivia, Burma, Cameroon, Ethiopia, Haiti, India, Kenya, Malagasy Republic, Pakistan, Sierra Leone, Sri Lanka, Sudan, Tanzania, Uganda, and Zaire. They were the largest importers among those countries with a per capita GNP of less than $200, together accounting for 80 percent of that group's imports in 1973. Nigeria and Indonesia, being oil exporters, were excluded. China and Dem. Rep. of Vietnam were also excluded, for lack of data.

SOURCES: Based on International Monetary Fund, *Direction of Trade Annual, 1966-1970* and *Direction of Trade Annual, 1969-1973.*

B-4. U.S. Financing of Its Exports, FY 1974

	Developed Market Economies	Importing Countries[a] — Countries with Per Capita GNP Under $200, 1972	All Other Countries
U.S. Exports, CY 1974	$63.9 billion	$ 3.1 billion	$34.8 billion
U.S. Share of Country's Imports, CY 1973	13.2%	16.9%	22.5%
U.S. Financing Commitments, FY 1974			
A.I.D., including technical assistance[b]	$ 0.06 billion	$ 0.7 billion[c]	$ 0.4 billion
Export-Import Bank[d]	$ 1.5 billion	$ 0.3 billion	$ 2.9 billion
P.L. 480[b]	$ 0.007 billion	$ 0.7 billion[e]	$ 0.1 billion

[a] Excludes centrally planned economies.
[b] Preliminary.
[c] Republic of Vietnam and Khmer Republic accounted for 68 per cent of this figure.
[d] Loans, guarantees, and medium term insurance.
[e] Republic of Vietnam and Khmer Republic accounted for 61 per cent of this figure.

NOTE: In 1972, the populations of the three groups of importing countries were: developed market economies, 548 million; countries with a per capita GNP under $200, 980 million; and all other countries, 798 million. That same year, the gross national products for the same groupings were, respectively, $1,343 billion, $107 billion, and $323 billion.

SOURCE: Figures for U.S. exports are from U.S. Department of Commerce, *U.S. Foreign Trade: Highlights of Exports and Imports*, December 1973, and *Highlights of U.S. Export and Import Trade*, December 1974; those for U.S. imports are from IMF and IBRD, *Direction of Trade Annual, 1969-1973*. AID and P.L. 480 figures are from U.S. Agency for International Development, Office of Financial Management, Statistics and Reports Division, *U.S. Overseas Loans and Grants and Assistance from International Organizations: Obligations and Loan Authorizations, July 1, 1945-June 30, 1973*, and *U.S. Overseas Loans and Grants, Preliminary FY 1974 Data, Obligations and Loan Authorizations, July 1, 1973-June 30, 1974*. Figures for the Export-Import Bank are from *Export-Import Bank of the United States: Cumulative Records*; and those for population and GNP are from *World Bank Atlas, 1974: Population, Per Capita Product, and Growth Rates* (Washington, D.C.: World Bank Group, 1974).

B–5. Export Credits from DAC Countries to Developing Countries, 1970-1973 ($ millions)

	Net Export Credits Extended				Stock of Export Credits Outstanding
	1970	1971	1972	1973	1973 (end)
Australia	44	182	38	-65	202
Austria	72	72	15	44	374
Belgium	115	77	81	160	867
Canada	150	144	101	48	775
Denmark	18	48	6	48	300
France	304	222	271	354	5,831
Germany	232	508	-31	-223	4,108
Italy	335	447	134	72	3,267
Japan	736	766	457	694	5,977[a]
Netherlands	2	5	68	44	535
New Zealand	n.a.	n.a.	3	2	n.a.
Norway	3	6	-24	-13	32
Portugal	n.a.	n.a.	-5	11	n.a.
Sweden	40	19	-4	3	196
Switzerland	22	88	-20	115	606
United Kingdom	436	583	535	282	6,869
United States	211	238	529	745	7,288
DAC Total	**2,720**	**3,405**	**2,153**	**2,320**	**37,227[a]**

[a]Estimate.

NOTE: The figures include official export credits. Negative figures result from repayments on old credits exceeding new credit extensions.

SOURCE: Report by the Chairman of the Development Assistance Committee, *Development Co-operation, 1974 Review* (Paris: OECD, 1974), p. 147.

B-6. Developing Country Exports of Selected Commodities, 1973 and 1970-1972 Average ($ millions and percentages)

	Developing Country Exports, 1973	Developing Country Exports, 1970-1972 Average		Major Developing Country Suppliers, 1970-1972, with Percentage of Total Exports Supplied by Each
	($ millions)	($ millions)	(as percentage of world exports of commodity)	
Cocoa	955	759	100	Ghana, 32% · Ivory Coast. 12% Nigeria, 24% · Brazil, 9%
Coffee	3,892	2,855	97	Brazil, 30% · Colombia, 14%
Tea	560	590	83	India, 29% · Sri Lanka, 27%
Wheat	245	118	3	—
Rice	516	431	39	Thailand, 15%
Maize	585	459	23	Argentina, 13%
Cotton	2,029	1,502	57	Egypt, 14% · Sudan, 8%
Jute	209	171	95	Bangladesh, 65% · Thailand, 24%
Sisal	148	69	97	Tanzania, 31% · Mexico, 13% Brazil, 25% · Angola, 11%
Copra	185	173	100	Philippines, 60% · Papua-New Guinea, 9% Indonesia, 9%

Commodity				Leading producers
Coconut oil	145	149	83	Philippines, 53%; Sri Lanka, 12%
Palm oil	215	199	92	Malaysia, 53%; Indonesia, 19%; Zaire, 11%
Groundnuts	145	153	72	Nigeria, 19%; Sudan, 11%
Groundnut oil	155	120	77	Senegal, 31%; Nigeria, 15%; Brazil, 13%; Argentina, 8%
Fish meal	n.a.	318	65	Peru, 55%
Sugar	2,845	2,055	71	Cuba, 27%; Philippines, 7%
Bananas	n.a.	519	92	Ecuador, 19%; Honduras, 16%; Costa Rica, 12%; Panama, 12%
Natural rubber	1,698	983	98	Malaysia, 50%; Indonesia, 22%; Thailand, 10%
Copper	3,259	2,431	54	Zambia, 17%; Chile, 16%; Zaire, 10%
Tin	739	638	85	Malaysia, 43%; Bolivia, 14%; Thailand, 10%; Indonesia, 9%
Iron ore	1,219	998	38	Brazil, 9%
Petroleum	36,810	19,906	73	Venezuela, 11%; Saudi Arabia, 10%; Iran, 9%; Libya, 9%

SOURCE: World Bank/International Development Association, *Commodity Trade and Price Trends (1974 Edition)*, Report No. EC-166/74, August 1974; 1973 figures are from World Bank, Economic Analysis and Projections Dept.

227

B-7. Prices of Selected Commodities, 1970-1974 (Annual and Quarterly)

	1970	1971	1972	1973	1974	1973 (iv)	1974 (i)	(ii)	(iii)	(iv)
Cocoa[a] (cents/lb.)	34	27	32	65	98	75	76	109	107	101
Coffee[b] (cents/lb.)	56	49	57	73	78	71	78	82	75	77
	52	46	50	62	66	63	71	71	63	59
	55	45	51	67	68	71	72	73	63	64
	42	43	45	50	59	53	60	64	57	56
Tea[c] (cents/kg.)	112	102	107	111	140	111	132	145	135	149
	117	115	109	110	152					
	96	96	94	96	131					
Wheat[d] ($/metric ton)	63	64	71	147	209	206	217	202	194	223
Rice[e] ($/metric ton)	144	129	147	350	542	473	566	617	519	466
	100	85	84	124	328	124	328	328	328	328
Maize[f] ($/metric ton)	69	67	72	119	159	137	156	145	160	175
	71	68	67	118	155	127	142	131	151	162
Cotton[g] (cents/lb.)	27	33	34	56	59	73	69	59	58	50
	63	62	65	102	154	156	158	159	161	137
Jute[h] ($/metric ton)	333	346	359	354	416	345	339	381	439	524
Sisal[i] ($/metric ton)	152	170	240	527	1,056[j]	702	1,023	1,059	1,070	1,070
Copra[k] ($/metric ton)	225	189	141	353	662	524	780	726	629	513
Coconut oil[l] ($/metric ton)	397	371	234	513	998	801	1,206	1,062	962	763
Palm oil[m] ($/metric ton)	260	261	217	378	669	454	626	603	681	766
Groundnuts[n] ($/metric ton)	230	249	261	393	595	423	584	611	n.a.	n.a.
Groundnut oil[n] ($/metric ton)	379	441	426	546	1,077	656	1,058	1,095	1,051	1,102

Fish meal° ($/metric ton)	197	167	239	542	372[j]	586	523	374	289	301[j]
Sugar^p (cents/lb.)	3.7	4.5	7.3	9.5	29.7	10.6	19.3	23.0	30.4	47.1
Bananas^p (cents/lb.)	7.5	6.4	7.3	7.5	8.3	7.3	7.2	8.5	9.6	8.1
Natural rubber^q (cents/kg.)	45	37	37	78	77[j]	100	104	80	66	59
	46	40	40	79	87	94	113	93	75	65
Copper^r ($/metric ton)	1,413	1,081	1,071	1,784	2,059	2,189	2,357	2,784	1,728	1,369
	1,272	1,134	1,116	1,298	1,690	1,358	1,499	1,723	1,874	1,664
Tin^r ($/metric ton)	3,674	3,500	3,765	4,826	8,199	5,825	7,443	9,184	8,832	7,339
	3,841	3,689	3,913	5,016	8,736	5,944	7,635	9,998	9,299	8,012
Iron ore^s ($/metric ton)	9.3	10.5	10.8	10.1	12.8[j]	10.2	11.4	13.4	13.1	13.4[j]
Petroleum^t ($/barrel)	1.3	1.7	1.9	2.7	9.8	3.5	9.2	9.7	9.9	10.4

^aGhana.
^bColombia, Guatemala, Brazil, Angola.
^cNorthern India, Kenya, Malawi. Quarterly figures are average prices.
^dCanada.
^eThailand, Burma.
^fArgentina, United States.
^gUnited States.
^hBangladesh.
^iEast Africa.
^jEstimate.

^kPhilippines.
^lPhilippines and Indonesia.
^mMalaysia.
^nNigeria.
^oPeru and other.
^pWorld.
^qLondon Market, New York Market.
^rLondon Metal Exchange, New York Market.
^sSweden.
^tSaudi Arabia.

SOURCES: Figures for average annual prices are from World Bank/International Development Association, *Commodity Trade and Price Trends (1974 Edition)*, Report No. EC-166/74, August 1974; figures for quarterly prices are from World Bank, Economic Analysis and Projections Dept., "Commodity Price Data," January 15, 1975, and from World Bank, Economic Analysis and Projections Dept.

B-8. Fertilizer Prices, 1970-1974
($/ton)

	1970	1971	1972	1973	1974[a]
Urea[b]	48	46	59	125	300
Potash[c]	32	33	34	43	45
Triple Super Phosphate[d]	43	43	68	100	200
Phosphate Rock[e]	11	11	12	14	63

[a]Estimate.
[b]Europe.
[c]Canada.
[d]United States.
[e]Morocco.

SOURCE: Lester R. Brown with Erik P. Eckholm, *By Bread Alone* (New York: Praeger Publishers, 1974), p. 120.

B-9. Composition of Exports and Imports, 1972 (percentages)

	Developed Market Economies	Developing Market Economies	Centrally Planned Economies	World
EXPORTS				
Primary products	22.5	75.4	30.2	32.6
Food, beverages, and tobacco	11.4	21.7	10.8	13.2
Crude materials excluding fuels; oils and fats	7.7	16.2	10.0	9.4
Mineral fuels and related materials	3.4	37.5	9.4	10.0
Manufactured products	75.9	23.8	63.1	65.6
Chemicals	8.6	1.9	5.1	7.1
Machinery and transport equipment	36.5	3.8	31.5	30.3
Other manufactured goods	30.8	18.1	26.5	28.2
Miscellaneous transactions and commodities, and residual	1.6	0.8	6.7	1.8
Total	100.0	100.0	100.0	100.0
IMPORTS				
Primary products	34.5	26.7	28.4	32.6
Food, beverages, and tobacco	13.4	12.5	12.8	13.2
Crude materials excluding fuels; oils and fats	10.2	6.2	9.7	9.4
Mineral fuels and related materials	10.9	8.0	5.9	10.0
Manufactured products	64.1	69.5	68.9	65.6
Chemicals	6.5	9.2	6.8	7.1
Machinery and transport equipment	28.3	35.7	34.6	30.3
Other manufactured goods	29.3	24.6	27.5	28.2
Miscellaneous transactions and commodities, and residual	1.4	3.8	2.7	1.8
Total	100.0	100.0	100.0	100.0

SOURCE: Based on *U.N. Monthly Bulletin of Statistics*, Vol. 28, No. 9, September 1974, Special Table D, pp. xviii-xxxv.

Energy, Minerals, Food, and Fertilizer

C-1. World Energy Consumption, by Groups of Countries and Types of Energy, 1961, 1965, 1970, 1972 (percentages)

		Developed Market Economies					Centrally Planned Economies	Developing Countries		
		North America	Western Europe	Japan	Southern Hemisphere	Total		OPEC	Non-OPEC	Total
Solid Fuels	1961	23.4	62.3	52.9	73.5	39.0	74.7	3.1	32.2	27.1
	1965	23.2	49.2	37.0	69.2	33.8	67.3	2.4	30.7	26.0
	1970	20.1	32.7	26.9	63.2	25.9	59.7	1.4	24.2	20.2
	1972	18.9	26.2	22.2	60.9	22.8	57.7	1.7	22.0	18.3
Liquid Fuels	1961	41.9	32.0	39.2	24.9	38.1	16.7	71.9	57.3	59.9
	1965	41.2	44.3	56.4	28.9	42.6	19.0	66.5	57.3	58.8
	1970	41.5	55.8	68.4	33.2	47.9	23.0	54.2	61.6	60.3
	1972	43.2	57.9	72.6	33.9	49.8	24.4	51.5	63.7	61.4
Natural and Imported Gas	1961	32.7	2.2	1.1	—	20.3	7.1	24.6	7.6	10.6
	1965	33.6	2.7	1.5	—	20.8	12.7	30.6	8.8	12.4
	1970	36.3	8.0	1.6	1.6	23.6	16.2	43.3	10.4	16.2
	1972	35.5	12.3	1.6	3.0	24.6	16.8	45.4	10.4	17.0
Hydro, Nuclear, and Imported Electricity	1961	2.1	3.5	6.7	1.6	2.7	0.9	0.3	2.9	2.5
	1965	2.1	3.8	5.1	1.9	2.8	1.1	0.6	3.3	2.8
	1970	2.2	3.5	3.2	2.1	2.7	1.2	1.1	3.8	3.3
	1972	2.4	3.7	3.6	2.2	2.9	1.1	1.4	3.8	3.4

SOURCE: United Nations, Dept. of Economic and Social Affairs, *World Economic Survey, 1973. Part Two: Current Economic Developments*, Publication Sales No. E.74.II.C.2, p. I-41.

C-2. Energy and Oil Dependence, 1973
(percentages)

	Net Imports as Percentage of Total Primary Energy Needs		Net Oil Imports as Percentage of Total Oil Needs
	Energy	*Oil*	
Canada	−21.2[a]	−8.0[a]	−15.2[a]
United States	16.4	16.9	36.6
Japan	92.4	81.0	100.0
France	82.0	72.1	100.0
Germany	56.0	49.6	96.8
Italy	83.3	76.4	96.3
United Kingdom	46.8	46.9	98.3
Belgium	85.5	60.2	96.6
Netherlands	19.2	52.3	92.0
Denmark	100.0	90.4	100.0
Norway	47.4	44.7	89.6
Sweden	81.1	76.7	98.4
Spain	79.0	73.3	100.0
European Community	61.6	59.4	98.2
OECD Europe	64.0	61.0	97.8
OECD Total[b]	36.9	36.2	66.0

[a]Negative figures indicate net exports.
[b]Excluding New Zealand.

SOURCE: Organisation for Economic Co-operation and Development, *OECD Economic Outlook*, December 1974, Table 44, p. 110.

C-3. World Oil Trade and Consumption, 1973 (thousand barrels/day and percentages)

	World	United States	Western Europe	Japan	Canada	Centrally Planned Economies[a]	Others
				(thousand barrels/day)			
Total Oil Consumption	58,000	17,300	15,400	5,400	1,800	9,100	9,000
Total Oil Imports	33,000	6,200	15,200	5,400	1,000	500	4,700
from Arab countries	17,850	1,590	10,600	2,390	220	400	2,650
			(percentage of total oil consumption)				
Total Oil Imports	56.9	35.8	98.7	100.0	55.6	5.5	52.2
from Arab countries	30.8	9.2	68.8	4.3	12.2	4.4	29.4
Saudi Arabia	12.9	3.4	26.0	23.0	4.4	–	17.7
Kuwait	5.2	0.9	11.4	10.0	b	–	6.1
Libya	3.6	3.0	10.3	0.4	2.2	1.1	b
Iraq	3.1	0.3	7.9	b	1.1	2.2	3.4
Abu Dhabi	2.2	0.9	3.9	8.0	3.3	b	0.6
Algeria	1.7	0.8	4.4	–	–	0.5	1.6
Other Arab	2.0	0.8	5.0	3.0	1.1	0.5	0.1

from non-Arab countries	26.1	26.6	29.9	55.7	43.4	1.1	22.8
Iran	9.7	2.4	12.3	32.0	10.0	1.1	14.1
Venezuela	5.3	10.6	2.9	0.2	26.1	–	3.8
Nigeria	3.3	3.2	7.3	1.9	4.4	–	0.4
Indonesia	2.1	1.4	b	15.6	b	–	1.2
Canada	1.9	6.4	–	–	–	–	–
Other non-Arab	3.9	2.6	7.3	6.1	2.8	–	3.2

[a]Albania, Bulgaria, China, Cuba, Czechoslovakia, German Democratic Republic, Hungary, Poland, Romania, U.S.S.R.
[b]Negligible.

NOTE: This table allocates imports on a direct and indirect basis, i.e., refined products from export refineries are traced to the source of the crude oil.

SOURCE: *International Economic Report of the President, Transmitted to the Congress March 1975* (Washington, D.C.: U.S. Government Printing Office, 1975), Table 67.

C-4. Total Exports, Total Imports, and Fertilizer, Petroleum, and Food Grain Imports, by Selected Developing Countries, 1973 and 1974 ($ millions)

	Total Exports, f.o.b.		Total Imports, c.i.f.		Of which: (Fertilizer)		(Petroleum)		(Food Grain)	
	1973	1974	1973	1974	1973	1974	1973	1974	1973	1974
Afghanistan	160	192	190	226	8	8	8	9	8	n.a.
Bangladesh	413	431	775	1,080	21	44	78	124	313	379
Brazil	6,198	7,700	6,016	12,400	136	440	615	2,500	334	450
Burundi	31	32	32	45	—	—	2	3	2	2
Cameroon	348	332	331	373	4	7	21	43	16	18
Central African Republic	61	65	66	83	1	1	6	10	n.a.	n.a.
Chad	47	66	98	130	n.a.	n.a.	13	17	26	43
Chile	1,325	1,944	1,608	2,243	33	88	80	355	116	230
Costa Rica	344	425	444	695	13	15	15	37	17	40
El Salvador	359	453	373	557	20	49	21	54	20	22
Ghana	571	693	408	702	6	3	35	161	29	30
Guatemala	442	588	391	621	13	16	35	106	12	26
Guinea	53	80	159	136	n.a.	n.a.	5	17	n.a.	n.a.
Haiti	55	80	74	110	—	1	6	15	10	17
Honduras	259	263	268	379	4	5	22	54	10	10
India	2,958	3,850	3,146	5,000	205	450	447	1,300	455	1,000
Ivory Coast	795	1,070	656	966	3	9	30	113	24	36
Jamaica	393	631	570	811	n.a.	n.a.	72	198	121	178
Kenya	390	460	543	810	12	35	5	90	14	25

Country										
Khmer Republic	15	14	214	270	n.a.	n.a.	13	19	125	162
Korea, Republic of	3,271	4,494	4,240	6,844	28	77	277	1,172	444	613
Laos	5	10	53	57	—	—	6	10	9	9
Liberia	324	371	194	310	1	3	15	55	12	10
Malagasy Republic	187	219	213	290	2	2	5	26	12	52
Malawi	96	121	123	161	4	8	13	17	4	4
Mali	57	59	117	180	n.a.	n.a.	9	19	38	73
Mauritania	140	200	138	187	n.a.	n.a.	7	20	30	24
Mauritius	140	276	145	273	n.a.	n.a.	7	29	n.a.	n.a.
Nicaragua	278	377	327	539	n.a.	n.a.	17	51	10	7
Pakistan	934	1,100	1,037	1,740	64	94	91	362	96	210
Paraguay	128	160	136	185	3	3	14	36	5	8
Peru	1,137	1,550	1,235	2,400	25	95	49	178	140	194
Philippines	1,871	2,625	1,751	3,443	n.a.	n.a.	187	700	n.a.	n.a.
Senegal	205	390	400	529	9	2	12	48	62	96
Sierra Leone	128	135	153	204	n.a.	1	8	25	11	25
Somalia	58	54	114	130	n.a.	n.a.	4	5	12	15
Sri Lanka	382	552	428	819	17	51	22	85	187	290
Sudan	440	390	325	520	n.a.	n.a.	24	84	n.a.	n.a.
Tanzania	353	418	494	718	n.a.	n.a.	29	89	60	150
Turkey	1,317	1,500	2,086	3,550	132	100	222	666	27	215
Upper Volta	35	38	95	132	n.a.	n.a.	2	6	n.a.	n.a.
Uruguay	324	367	287	480	54	175	n.a.	n.a.	n.a.	n.a.
Vietnam, Republic of	61	75	775	947	50	75	76	135	120	185
Yemen, Democratic Republic	27	26	132	174	9	33	n.a.	n.a.	n.a.	n.a.
Zaire	1,047	1,376	753	1,004	2	3	48	32	28	32

SOURCE: Informal government estimates.

C–5. OPEC Countries: Oil Revenues, Trade, Per Capita GNP, Population, International Reserves, Crude Production, and Petroleum Reserves

	Estimated Oil Revenues ($ millions)		Non-Oil Exports, 1973 ($ millions)	Imports, 1973[c] ($ millions)	Estimated Per Capita GNP[a] ($)		Population, mid-1975 (millions)	International Reserves, January 1975 ($ millions)	Crude Production, 1973 (million barrels/day)	Petroleum Reserves at 1973 Production Rate (years)	Estimated Petroleum Reserves (billion barrels)
	1973	1974[b]			1973	1974					
High-Income											
Saudi Arabia	5,100	20,000		1,993	980	2,900	9.0	14,285[e]	7.7	51	140.8
Kuwait	1,900	7,000		1,042	4,100	8,500	1.1	1,654	3.1	66	72.7
United Arab Emirates	900[f]	4,100[f]	577[d]	800	9,000	21,000	0.2	n.a.	1.5	45	25.5
Qatar	400	1,600		170	3,300	12,000	0.1	n.a.	0.5	31	6.5
Libya	2,300	7,600	106	1,723	3,000	5,800	2.3	3,523	2.2	32	25.6
Middle-Income											
Iran	4,100	17,400	864	3,370	520	940	32.9	8,513	5.9	28	60.2
Venezuela	2,800	10,600	1,232	2,813	1,150	1,850	12.2	6,191	3.5	11	14.2
Iraq	1,500	6,800	22	899	430	930	11.1	3,273[e]	2.0	44	31.2
Algeria	900	3,700	270	2,338	350	530	16.8	1,497	1.0	20	7.4
Ecuador	100	800	n.a.	532	320	420	7.1	336	0.2	78	5.7
Gabon[g]	100	400	n.a.	160	900	1,540	0.5	47[h]	0.2	n.a.	1.0

Low-Income

Nigeria	2,000	7,000	287	1,874	150	230	62.9	5,981	2.0	27	19.9
Indonesia	900	3,000	1,923	2,347	80	100	136.0	1,624	1.3	22	10.8
Total OPEC	**23,000**	**90,000**	**5,281**	**20,061**		**292.2**		**46,924**	**30.9**		**420.5**

[a]The estimates for per capita GNP of some OPEC countries vary widely among sources, sometimes by 50 per cent or more. The World Bank's estimates for 1974 are not yet available; its estimates for 1973 are the following: Saudi Arabia, 690; Kuwait, 4,354; United Arab Emirates, n.a.; Qatar, 3,447; Libya, 2,007; Iran, 585; Venezuela, 1,303; Iraq, 443; Algeria, 432; Ecuador, 392; Gabon, 988; Nigeria, 152; Indonesia, 102.

[b]These are highly tentative estimates. The most recent guess is that OPEC revenues, when calculated on an accrual basis rather than on payment actually received, reached some $100 billion in 1974.

[c]The International Monetary Fund estimates the 1974 import bill for the 12 OPEC members plus Gabon, Bahrain, Brunei, Oman, and Trinidad and Tobago at $36 billion, a sharp rise from their $21.3 billion import bill for 1973.

[d]Figure is the total figure for Saudi Arabia, Kuwait, Abu Dhabi (a member of the United Arab Emirates), and Qatar.

[e]December 1974 figure.

[f]Figure is for Abu Dhabi, a member of the U.A.E.

[g]An Associate Member of OPEC.

[h]August 1974 figure.

SOURCES: Estimates for oil revenues and non-oil exports, and most figures for per capita GNP, are from the Report by the Chairman of the Development Assistance Committee, *Development Co-operation, 1974 Review* (Paris: OECD, 1974), p. 44. Per capita GNP figures for U.A.E. and Libya are from *The Economist*, February 15, 1975, p. 72. Figures for imports and international reserves are taken from International Monetary Fund, *International Financial Statistics*, Vol. 28, No. 3, March 1975. Population figures are from Population Reference Bureau, "1975 World Population Data Sheet." Figures for crude production, years of petroleum reserves, and petroleum reserves are from *Business Week*, January 13, 1975, p. 80, with the exception of Gabon, whose figures for crude production and petroleum reserves are from The Royal Dutch Shell Group of Companies, *Information Handbook 1974-5* (London: Shell International Petroleum Company Limited, 1974), pp. 65 and 67.

C–6. U.S. Imports of Selected Minerals from Major Suppliers (percentages)

	Imports as Percentage of U.S. Consumption			Major Developed-Country Suppliers, with Imports Supplied by Each, 1970-1973	Major Developing-Country Suppliers, with Imports Supplied by Each, 1970-1973
	1972	1973	1974[a]		
Alumina	n.a.	n.a.	n.a.	Australia, 49%	Jamaica, 27% Surinam, 16%
Aluminum	13.8[b]	9.0[b]	8.7[b]	Canada, 77%	—
Bauxite	86.1	84.9	87.9	—	Jamaica, 54% Surinam, 20% Dominican Rep., 8% Guyana, 7%
Chromite	93.1	67.1	88.0	U.S.S.R., 31% South Africa, 29%	Turkey, 18% Philippines, 15%
Cobalt	98.5	102.4	76.6	Belgium-Luxembourg, 28% Finland, 7% Norway, 6% Canada, 5%	Zaire, 49%
Copper	18.6	17.1	26.6	Canada, 34% South Africa, 6%	Peru, 26% Chile, 18%
Iron Ore	28.2	29.5	34.2	Canada, 51%	Venezuela, 30% Liberia, 6% Brazil, 5%

Lead	23.4	18.4	14.1	Canada, 30% Australia, 21%	Peru, 22% Mexico, 10%
Manganese Ore	69.5[c]	70.6[c]	66.7[c]	South Africa, 9%	Brazil, 35% Gabon, 33% Zaire, 7%
Mercury	55.2	84.9	86.2	Canada, 53% Spain, 11%	Algeria, 12% Mexico, 11%
Nickel	109.2[d]	96.6[d]	102.4[d]	Canada, 76% Norway, 8%	—
Sulfur	12.1[b]	11.9[b]	19.6[b]	Canada, 71%	Mexico, 28%
Tin (Metal and Ore)	81.9	67.4	61.0	—	Malaysia, 62% Thailand, 25%
Titanium	31.2[e]	28.0[e]	36.6[e]	Japan, 68% U.S.S.R., 24% United Kingdom, 8%	—
Tungsten	41.8[f]	70.1[f]	70.9[f]	Canada, 35%	Bolivia, 16% Peru, 11% Thailand, 11%
Vanadium	26.8[f]	40.7[f]	41.5[f]	South Africa, 58% U.S.S.R., 5%	Chile, 35%
Zinc Ore	n.a.	n.a.	n.a.	Canada, 60%	Mexico, 23% Peru, 7%

[a]Estimates.
[b]Apparent consumption.
[c]Industrial consumption.
[d]Reported consumption. Excludes most secondary consumption.
[e]Primary consumption.
[f]Reported industrial consumption.

SOURCE: U.S. Department of the Interior, Bureau of Mines, *Commodity Data Summaries, 1975.*

C-7. Indicators of World Food Security, 1961-1974
(million metric tons and days)

	Reserve Stocks of Grain	Grain Equivalent of Idled U.S. Cropland	Total Reserves	Reserves as Days of Annual Grain Consumption
	(million metric tons)			
1961	154	68	222	95
1962	131	81	212	88
1963	125	70	195	77
1964	128	70	198	77
1965	113	71	184	69
1966	99	79	178	66
1967	100	51	151	55
1968	116	61	177	62
1969	136	73	209	69
1970	146	71	217	69
1971	120	41	161	51
1972	131	78	209	66
1973	106	24	130	40
1974[a]	90	–	90	26

[a]Preliminary.

SOURCE: Lester R. Brown with Erik P. Eckholm, *By Bread Alone* (New York: Praeger Publishers, 1974), p. 60.

C-8. World Net Grain Trade, FYs 1970-1974 (million metric tons)

	FY 1970-FY 1972 Average	FY 1972	FY 1973	FY 1974
Developed Market Economies	31.9	41.9	62.4	58.4
United States	39.8	42.8	73.1	72.5
Canada	14.8	18.3	18.8	13.1
Australia and New Zealand	10.6	10.8	5.8	9.9
South Africa	2.5	3.7	0.4	4.0
European Community (9 members)	-16.6	-14.0	-13.4	-13.0
Other Western Europe	-4.8	-4.5	-5.3	-8.9
Japan	-14.4	-15.0	-17.0	-19.2
Centrally Planned Economies	-6.8	-13.0	-32.2	-15.9
Eastern Europe	-7.6	-9.2	-8.0	-4.8
U.S.S.R.	3.9	-4.3	-19.6	-4.4
China	-3.1	-15.4	-4.6	-6.7
Developing Countries	-19.1	-26.9	-23.2	-30.3
North Africa and Middle East	-9.2	-11.9	-8.1	-14.9
South Asia	-5.7	-5.4	-4.5	-7.0
Southeast Asia	3.2	3.3	1.2	2.5
East Asia	-8.4	-9.2	-10.4	-10.2
Latin America	3.2	-2.0	—	0.7
Central Africa	-1.9	-2.0	-2.0	-2.1
East Africa	-0.3	0.3	0.6	0.7
Other	-0.2	-0.2	-0.3	-0.3
Total World Exports	107.6	111.2	141.8	151.0

NOTE: Negative figures indicate net imports.

SOURCE: U.S. Department of Agriculture, Economic Research Service, *The World Food Situation and Prospects to 1985*, Foreign Agricultural Economic Report No. 98, December 1974, p. 4.

C-9. U.S. Agricultural Exports, 1960-1974 ($ millions)

| | Public Law 480 | | | | | Other Agricultural Exports | | Total Agricultural Exports | Public Law 480 as Percentage of Total |
| | Title I | | | | | | | | |
	Sales for foreign Currency	Long-term dollar credit sales	Title II	Title III[a]	Total	Mutual Security (AID) Programs[b]	Commercial Sales[c]		
1960	1,014	–	173	117	1,304	157	3,371	4,832	27
1961	878	1	244	181	1,304	179	3,541	5,024	26
1962	1,006	42	259	137	1,444	35	3,555	5,034	29
1963	1,161	52	259	37	1,509	11	4,064	5,834	27
1964	1,233	97	248	43	1,621	23	4,704	6,348	26
1965	899	152	253	19	1,323	26	4,880	6,229	21
1966	815	239	211	41	1,306	47	5,528	6,881	19
1967	736	194	287	13	1,230	33	5,117	6,380	19
1968	540	384	251	3	1,178	11	5,039	6,228	19
1969	337	428	256	–	1,021	n.a.	4,915	5,936	17
1970	276	490	255	–	1,021	12[d]	6,226	7,693	13
1971	174	518	290	–	982	87	6,624	7,693	13
1972	70	660	377	–	1,107	45	8,249	9,401	12

1973	4	537	209	—	750	113	16,814	17,677	4
1974[e]	—	488	272	—	760	10	21,224	21,994	3
Total[e]	9,143	4,283	3,844	591	17,861	789	103,860	122,500	

[a]Barter. Annual exports have been adjusted for 1963 and subsequent years by deducting exports under barter contracts which improve the balance of payments and rely primarily on authority other than Public Law 480. These exports are included in the column headed "Commercial Sales."

[b]Sales for foreign currency, economic aid, and expenditures under development loans.

[c]Commercial sales for dollars include, in addition to unassisted commercial transactions, shipments of some commodities with government assistance in the form of short- and medium-term credit, export payments, sales of government-owned commodities at less than domestic market prices, and, for 1963 and subsequent years, exports under barter contracts which benefit the balance of payments and rely primarily on authority other than Public Law 480.

[d]Covers shipments for only July through December.

[e]Preliminary.

SOURCES: Figures for 1960-1973 are from *1973 Annual Report on Public Law 480*, 93rd Congress, 2nd Session, House Document No. 93-362, p. 64; 1974 figures are informal estimates from U.S. Department of Agriculture, Economic Research Service.

C-10. Ten Major Recipients of P.L. 480, Title I, FYs 1970-1974 ($ millions)

FY 1970		FY 1971		FY 1972		FY 1973		FY 1974[a]	
India	181	Rep. of Vietnam	165	Rep. of Korea	196	Rep. of Vietnam	179	Rep. of Vietnam	269
Indonesia	122	India	156	Indonesia	115	Rep. of Korea	146	Khmer Rep.	183
Pakistan[b]	81	Rep. of Korea	88	Pakistan	93	Indonesia	110	Bangladesh	48
Rep. of Korea	76	Indonesia	88	Rep. of Vietnam	63	Pakistan	75	Pakistan	32
Rep. of Vietnam	76	Pakistan[b]	77	Israel	54	Israel	59	Egypt	10
Israel	41	Israel	56	Philippines	34	Khmer Rep.	26	Jordan	8
Turkey	34	Brazil	23	Morocco	28	Philippines	21	Bolivia	6
Brazil	20	Turkey	22	Khmer Rep.	21	Thailand	16	Sri Lanka	6
Tunisia	15	Philippines	20	Tunisia	17	Sri Lanka	10	Guinea	5
Colombia	12	Morocco	18	Sri Lanka	15	Dominican Rep.	10	Philippines	3
Total, 10 Major Recipients	657		712		635		651		570
Total, All Recipients	711		790		716		723		577
5 Major Recipients, as Percentage of Total	75.2%		72.6%		72.6%		78.7%		93.9%
10 Major Recipients, as Percentage of Total	92.3%		90.0%		88.6%		90.0%		98.8%

[a]Preliminary.
[b]Includes Bangladesh.

SOURCE: Figures for FYs 1970-1973 are based on U.S. Agency for International Development, Office of Financial Management, Statistics and Reports Division, *U.S. Overseas Loans and Grants and Assistance from International Organizations: Obligations and Loan Authorizations, July 1, 1945-June 30, 1973*; those for FY 1974 are based on *U.S. Overseas Loans and Grants, Preliminary FY 1974 Data: Obligations and Loan Authorizations, July 1, 1973-June 30, 1974*.

C-11. Ten Major Recipients of P.L. 480, Title II, FYs 1970-1974 ($ millions)

	FY 1970		FY 1971		FY 1972		FY 1973		FY 1974[a]
Brazil	43	India	79	India	105	India	64	India	71
India	42	Pakistan[b]	24	Bangladesh	87	Bangladesh	59	Niger	20
Colombia	41	Rep. of Vietnam	23	Afghanistan	19	Philippines	16	Morocco	17
Rep. of Vietnam	35	Morocco	22	Rep. of Korea	16	Rep. of Korea	13	Mali	16
Rep. of Korea	28	Rep. of Korea	20	Peru	11	Brazil	10	Ethiopia	14
Indonesia	25	Taiwan	19	Colombia	10	Rep. of Vietnam	9	Philippines	13
Morocco	17	Tunisia	19	Pakistan	10	Colombia	9	Indonesia	11
Tunisia	13	Brazil	12	Lebanon	10	Morocco	9	Pakistan	10
Turkey	12	Indonesia	10	Botswana	10	Indonesia	9	Mauritania	9
Nigeria	8	Jordan	10	Indonesia	10	Pakistan	7	Upper Volta	8
Total, 10 Major Recipients	264		237		287		205		189
Total, All Recipients	426		433		477		394		396
5 Major Recipients, as Percentage of Total	44.1%		38.7%		49.7%		41.1%		34.8%
10 Major Recipients, as Percentage of Total	62.0%		54.8%		60.1%		51.9%		47.7%

[a] Preliminary.
[b] Includes Bangladesh.

SOURCE: Figures for FYs 1970-1973 are based on U.S. Agency for International Development, Office of Financial Management, Statistics and Reports Division, *U.S. Overseas Loans and Grants and Assistance from International Organizations: Obligations and Loan Authorizations, July 1, 1945-June 30, 1973;* those for FY 1974 are based on *U.S. Overseas Loans and Grants, Preliminary FY 1974 Data: Obligations and Loan Authorizations, July 1, 1973-June 30, 1974.*

C–12. U.S. Food Shipments under P.L. 480, Title I, Selected Years, 1960-1974 (thousand metric tons)

	1960[a]	1965[a]	1970	1972	1973	1974[b]
Wheat and products	8,199	13,705	5,765	4,615	2,517	1,005
Milk (dried)	8	42	18	19	2	–
Rice	453	561	884	813	987	620
Corn, oats, sorghum and products	787	728	1,078	1,217	1,289	454
Vegetable oils	339	364	240	193	107	148

[a]Includes aid under Titles I and IV in previous legislation.
[b]Estimate.

NOTE: Table covers sales for dollars and foreign currencies. All years but 1970 are on a fiscal-year basis.

SOURCE: Lester R. Brown with Erik P. Eckholm, *By Bread Alone* (New York: Praeger Publishers, 1974), p. 65.

C–13. U.S. Food Shipments under P.L. 480, Title II, Selected Years, 1960-1974 (thousand metric tons)

	1960	1965	1970	1972	1973	1974[a]
Wheat and products	979	1,473	1,464	1,614	1,649	718
Milk (dried)	147	199	133	115	26	–
Rice	89	–	7	248	33	–
Corn, oats, sorghum and products	359	498	330	257	246	379
Blended food products	–	–	149	266	195	182
Vegetable oils	–	106	81	187	111	53

[a]Estimate.

NOTE: Table covers voluntary agency grants, World Food Programme, and government-to-government grants for disaster relief and economic development. All years but 1970 are on a fiscal-year basis.

SOURCE: Lester R. Brown with Erik P. Eckholm, *By Bread Alone* (New York: Praeger Publishers, 1974), p. 66.

C-14. Developing Country Imports of Manufactured Fertilizers, 1971-1974
(million metric tons and $ millions)

	1971	1972[a]	1973[a]	1974[b]
	(million metric tons)			
Nitrogenous	2.3	2.5	2.6	2.0
Phosphate	1.0	1.2	1.4	1.1
Potash	1.3	1.5	1.8	1.8
Total	4.6	5.2	5.8	4.9
	($ millions)			
Nitrogenous	311	341	462	900
Phosphate	126	183	275	380
Potash	96	101	138	170
Total	533	625	875	1,450

[a]Estimate.
[b]Projection.

NOTE: This table does not include oil-exporting developing countries or China.

SOURCE: Report by the Chairman of the Development Assistance Committee, *Development Co-operation, 1974 Review* (Paris: OECD, 1974), p. 71.

Resource Flows

D-1. Foreign Exchange Receipts and Uses by Developing Countries, 1970-1973 ($ billions)

	All Developing Countries[a]				Major Oil-Exporting Developing Countries[b]				Other Developing Countries			
	1970	1971	1972	1973[c]	1970	1971	1972	1973[c]	1970	1971	1972	1973[c]
RECEIPTS												
Exports of goods and services	64.0	70.2	83.2	116.3	17.0	21.1	24.0	37.4	47.0	49.1	59.2	78.9
Exports of goods, f.o.b.[d]	54.0	59.5	71.1	102.0	15.9	19.7	22.3	35.1	38.1	39.8	48.8	66.9
Receipts for non-factor services (gross)[e]	10.0	10.7	12.1	14.3	1.1	1.4	1.7	2.3	8.9	9.3	10.4	12.0
Private transfer receipts (gross)	2.2	2.3	2.9	3.5	0.3	0.3	0.3	0.4	1.9	2.0	2.6	3.1
Official flows (gross)[f]	10.2	11.8	13.0	15.2	1.4	1.8	1.7	1.6	8.8	10.0	11.3	13.6
Direct investment and other private long-term flows (net)[g]	3.9	4.4	5.8	9.1	0.6	0.3	0.5	0.3	3.3	4.1	5.3	8.8
Private export credits (gross)[h]	4.3	5.3	5.2	6.0	0.9	1.5	1.5	2.0	3.4	3.8	3.7	4.0
Allocation of SDRs	0.8	0.7	0.7	—	0.1	0.1	0.1	—	0.7	0.6	0.6	—
Total Receipts	85.4	94.7	110.8	150.1	20.3	25.1	28.1	41.7	65.1	69.6	82.7	108.4

USES

Debt service on public and publicly guaranteed debt[l]	5.4	6.2	7.5	10.0	0.8	1.1	1.5	2.0	4.6	5.1	6.0	8.0
Amortization	3.7	4.3	5.3	7.2	0.6	0.8	1.0	1.5	3.1	3.5	4.3	5.7
Interest	1.7	1.9	2.2	2.8	0.2	0.3	0.5	0.5	1.5	1.6	1.7	2.3
Other investment income payments (net)[j]	7.7	8.8	10.7	14.0	4.5	6.1	7.7	10.6	3.2	2.7	3.0	3.4
Other uses (net)[k]	2.4	-0.3	0.3	2.4	1.5	-0.1	-1.4	0.3	0.9	-0.2	1.7	2.1
Changes in reserves[l]	+3.0	+4.9	+7.9	+12.4	+0.8	+3.4	+2.5	+3.8	+2.2	+1.5	+5.4	+8.6
Private transfer payments (gross)	1.2	1.3	1.4	1.8	0.4	0.5	0.6	0.9	0.8	0.8	0.8	0.9
Imports of goods and services	65.7	73.8	83.0	109.5	12.3	14.1	17.2	24.1	53.4	59.7	65.8	85.4
Imports of goods, c.i.f.	55.8	62.9	70.8	94.4	9.9	11.5	14.0	19.5	45.9	51.4	56.8	74.9
Payments for non-factor services (gross)[m]	9.9	10.9	12.2	15.1	2.4	2.6	3.2	4.6	7.5	8.3	9.0	10.5
Total Uses	**85.4**	**94.7**	**110.8**	**150.1**	**20.3**	**25.1**	**28.1**	**41.7**	**65.1**	**69.6**	**82.7**	**108.4**

a As defined by the U.N. Statistical Office, but excluding Cyprus, Malta, Gibraltar, and the Faeroe Islands. Data taken from balance-of-payments sources were adjusted to cover those countries for which data were unavailable.

b Algeria, Ecuador, Gabon, Libya, Nigeria, Kuwait, Iran, Iraq, Indonesia, Saudi Arabia, Venezuela, Trinidad and Tobago.

c Preliminary.

d Excludes oil exports of the Netherlands Antilles.

e Covers all services, excluding investment income. Includes the petroleum sector's net income for the Netherlands Antilles.

f Gross bilateral grants and loans with maturities of over one year from OECD countries, gross flows from multilateral organizations other than IMF, and partial estimates for socialist countries.

g Includes reinvestment.

h Gross guaranteed private export credits of more than one year's duration, usually including their non-guaranteed portion and, in a few cases, other non-guaranteed credits.

i For 81 developing countries reporting to the IBRD.

j Payments on direct investments for those countries reporting balance-of-payments statistics to the IMF and payments on total investments in several sterling-area countries and in the United Kingdom's colonial territories.

k Recorded net short-term capital flows, net long-term capital movements by residents of developing countries, and errors and omissions.

l Plus sign signifies an increase.

m All payments on services, excluding investment income payments to foreigners and freight and merchandise insurance on imports.

SOURCE: Figures obtained from the Research Division, UNCTAD, Geneva.

D-2. Net Flow of Resources from DAC Countries to Developing Countries and Multilateral Institutions, 1965 and 1970-1973 ($ millions)

	1965[a]	1970[a]	1971[a]	1972	1973
Official	6,198.7	7,983.8	9,030.4	10,253.1	11,995.0
Official Development Assistance (ODA)	5,894.8	6,831.6	7,759.3	8,671.5	9,408.0
Bilateral	5,546.7	5,707.4	6,420.9	6,766.5	7,155.1
Grants and grant-like contributions[b]	3,713.7	3,323.1	3,634.2	4,369.7	4,481.3
Development lending and capital[c]	1,833.0	2,384.3	2,786.4	2,396.7	2,674.0
Contributions to multilateral institutions	348.1	1,124.2	1,338.6	1,905.0	2,252.7
Grants	180.7	553.3	707.4	991.9	1,045.3
Capital subscription payments	167.4	540.6	600.4	862.2	1,120.9
Concessional lending	—	31.5	30.6	50.8	86.4
Other official flows[d]	303.9	1,152.3	1,271.1	1,581.5	2,587.0
Private, at market terms	4,121.3	6,870.6	8,068.2	8,618.8	11,071.6
Private investment and lending[e]	3,370.1	4,728.9	5,237.0	7,189.6	9,873.0
Private export credits	751.2	2,141.7	2,831.3	1,429.2	1,198.6
Grants by voluntary agencies	n.a.[f]	858.3	912.8	1,035.9	1,362.2
Total	10,319.7	15,713.1	18,011.3	19,907.8	24,429.0

[a] Data for New Zealand, which joined DAC in 1973, are unavailable for years prior to 1972.

[b] Technical assistance, food aid, and other grants.

[c] New development lending, food aid loans, debt reorganization, and equities and other bilateral assets.

[d] Official export credits, debt relief, equities and other bilateral assets, and contributions to multilateral institutions.

[e] Direct investment, bilateral portfolio investment, and multilateral portfolio investment.

[f] Voluntary grants were not recorded by DAC before 1970.

NOTE: Official flows decreased from 60.1% of the total in 1965 to 49.1% of the total in 1973; total ODA fell from 57.1% to 38.5%; and bilateral ODA dropped from 53.8% to 29.3%. ODA contributions to multilateral institutions rose from 3.4% to 9.2%; other official flows increased from 2.9% to 10.6%; and private flows at market terms went from 39.9% to 45.3%.

SOURCE: Report by the Chairman of the Development Assistance Committee, *Development Co-operation, 1974 Review* (Paris: OECD, 1974), p. 233.

D-3. Net Flow of Resources from the United States to Developing Countries and Multilateral Institutions, 1965 and 1970-1973 ($ millions)

	1965	1970	1971	1972	1973
Official	**3,474.2**	**3,218.0**	**3,504.0**	**3,545.0**	**3,445.0**
Official Development Assistance (ODA)	3,417.7	3,050.0	3,324.0	3,349.0	2,968.0
Bilateral	3,348.8	2,657.0	2,893.0	2,724.0	2,337.0
Grants and grant-like contributions[a]	2,243.6	1,381.0	1,549.0	1,588.0	1,438.0
Development lending and capital[b]	1,105.2	1,276.0	1,344.0	1,136.0	899.0
Contributions to multilateral institutions	68.9	393.0	431.0	625.0	631.0
Grants	68.9	160.0	185.0	354.0	258.0
Capital subscription payments	–	233.0	246.0	271.0	373.0
Other official flows[c]	56.5	168.0	180.0	196.0	477.0
Private, at market terms	**1,859.0**	**2,394.7**	**2,785.0**	**3,360.0**	**3,996.0**
Private investment and lending[d]	1,846.4	2,312.0	2,595.0	3,025.7	3,721.4
Private export credits	12.6	82.7	190.0	334.3	274.6[e]
Grants by voluntary agencies	**n.a.[f]**	**598.0**	**599.0**	**669.0**	**905.0**
Total	**5,333.2**	**6,210.7**	**6,888.0**	**7,574.0**	**8,346.0**

[a]Technical assistance, food aid, and other grants.
[b]New development lending, food aid loans, and debt reorganization.
[c]Official export credits, debt relief, and equities and other bilateral assets.
[d]Direct investment, bilateral portfolio investment, and multilateral portfolio investment.
[e]Estimate.
[f]Voluntary grants were not recorded by DAC before 1970.

NOTE: Official flows decreased from 65.2% of the total in 1965 to 41.3% of the total in 1973; total ODA fell from 64.1% to 35.6%; and bilateral ODA dropped from 62.8% to 28.0%. ODA contributions to multilateral institutions rose from 1.3% to 7.6%; other official flows increased from 1.1% to 5.7%; and private flows at market terms went from 34.9% to 47.9%.

SOURCE: Report by the Chairman of the Development Assistance Committee, *Development Co-operation, 1974 Review* (Paris: OECD, 1974), p. 232.

D-4. Net Flow of Official Development Assistance from DAC Countries as a Percentage of Gross National Product, 1960, 1965, 1970-1975

	1960	1965	1970	1971	1972	1973	1974	1975
Australia	.38	.53	.59	.53	.59	.44	.53	.54
Austria	n.a.	.11	.07	.07	.08	.13	.13	.13
Belgium	.88	.60	.46	.50	.55	.51	.56	.62
Canada	.19	.19	.42	.42	.47	.43	.51	.51
Denmark	.09	.13	.38	.43	.45	.47	.49	.50
France	1.38	.76	.66	.66	.67	.58	.55	.51
Germany	.31	.40	.32	.34	.31	.32	.30	.28
Italy	.22	.10	.16	.18	.09	.14	.10	.08
Japan	.24	.27	.23	.23	.21	.25	.24	.24
Netherlands	.31	.36	.61	.58	.67	.54	.61	.65
New Zealand	n.a.[a]	n.a.[a]	n.a.[a]	n.a.[a]	.23	.27	.36	.47
Norway	.11	.16	.32	.33	.41	.45	.63	.65
Portugal	1.45	.59	.67	1.42	1.79	.71	.47	.42
Sweden	.05	.19	.38	.44	.48	.56	.69	.70
Switzerland	.04	.09	.15	.11	.21	.15	.15	.15
United Kingdom	.56	.47	.37	.41	.39	.35	.34	.32
United States[b]	.53	.49	.31	.32	.29	.23	.21	.20

DAC TOTAL

	1960	1965	1970	1971	1972	1973	1974	1975
ODA ($ millions)								
current prices	4,665	5,895	6,832	7,762	8,671	9,415	10,706	11,948
1973 prices	7,660	9,069	9,346	9,976	10,059	9,415	9,391	9,452
GNP ($ billions)								
current prices	898	1,340	2,010	2,218	2,550	3,100	3,530	4,100
ODA as % of GNP	.52	.44	.34	.35	.34	.30	.30	.29
ODA Deflator	60.9	65.0	73.1	77.8	86.2	100.0	114.0	126.4

[a]New Zealand became a member of DAC in 1973. ODA figures for New Zealand are not available for 1960-1971.

[b]In 1949, at the beginning of the Marshall Plan, U.S. Official Development Assistance amounted to 2.79% of GNP.

NOTE: Countries included are members of OECD Development Assistance Committee, accounting for more than 95% of total Official Development Assistance. Figures for 1973 and earlier years are actual data. The projections for 1974 and 1975 are based on World Bank estimates of growth of GNP, on information on budget appropriations for aid, and on aid policy statements made by governments. Because of the relatively long period of time required to translate legislative authorizations first into commitments and later into disbursements, it is possible to project today, with reasonable accuracy, ODA flows (which by definition represent disbursements) through 1975.

SOURCE: Robert S. McNamara, *Address to the Board of Governors of the World Bank Group*, Washington, D.C., September 30, 1974 (Washington, D.C.: World Bank, 1974).

D–5. Selected U.S. Personal Consumption Expenditures and Net ODA Disbursements, 1973 ($ billions)

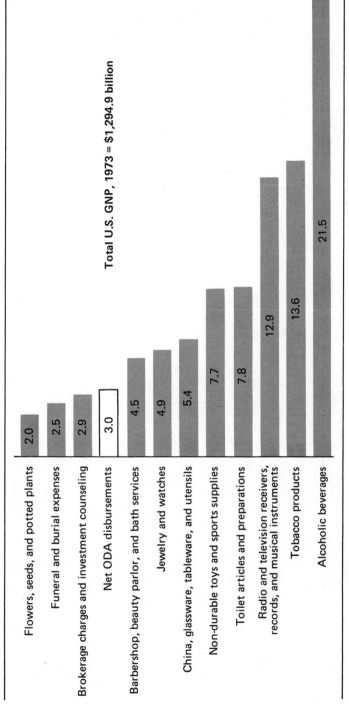

Total U.S. GNP, 1973 = $1,294.9 billion

Flowers, seeds, and potted plants	2.0
Funeral and burial expenses	2.5
Brokerage charges and investment counseling	2.9
Net ODA disbursements	3.0
Barbershop, beauty parlor, and bath services	4.5
Jewelry and watches	4.9
China, glassware, tableware, and utensils	5.4
Non-durable toys and sports supplies	7.7
Toilet articles and preparations	7.8
Radio and television receivers, records, and musical instruments	12.9
Tobacco products	13.6
Alcoholic beverages	21.5

SOURCE: U.S. Department of Commerce, *Survey of Current Business*, Vol. 54, No. 7, July 1974 , p. 24.

D-6. Ten Major Recipients of U.S. Official Development Assistance, Gross Commitments, FYs 1970-1974 ($ millions)

	FY 1970		FY 1971		FY 1972		FY 1973		FY 1974[a]	
	Rep. of Vietnam	477	Rep. of Vietnam	576	Rep. of Vietnam	455	Rep. of Vietnam	502	Rep. of Vietnam	654
	India	450	India	455	Bangladesh	286	Indonesia	241	Khmer Rep.	276
	Pakistan[b]	210	Indonesia	177	Rep. of Korea	252	Rep. of Korea	189	Pakistan	95
	Indonesia	203	Rep. of Korea	170	Indonesia	240	Pakistan	178	Indonesia	85
	Brazil	154	Brazil	118	Pakistan	165	Bangladesh	161	Bangladesh	78
	Rep. of Korea	141	Pakistan[b]	108	Colombia	116	Philippines	124	India	72
	Colombia	131	Colombia	98	India	114	Israel	110	Jordan	65
	Turkey	90	Turkey	83	Israel	104	Colombia	97	Philippines	61
	Laos	54	Khmer Rep.	77	Philippines	70	Khmer Rep.	93	Colombia	53
	Trust Territory of the Pacific Islands	53	Israel	56	Turkey	67	India	82	Israel	52
Total, 10 Recipients		1,962		1,906		1,868		1,776		1,491
Total, All Recipients		3,668		3,429		3,589		4,113		3,787
10 Major Recipients, as Percentage of Total		53.4%		55.5%		52.0%		43.1%		39.4%

[a]Preliminary.

[b]Includes Bangladesh.

SOURCE: Figures for FYs 1970-1973 are based on U.S. Agency for International Development, Office of Financial Management, Statistics and Reports Division, *U.S. Overseas Loans and Grants and Assistance from International Organizations: Obligations and Loan Authorizations, July 1, 1945-June 30, 1973;* those for FY 1974 are based on *U.S. Overseas Loans and Grants, Preliminary FY 1974 Data: Obligations and Loan Authorizations, July 1, 1973-June 30, 1974.*

D-7. Comparison of Per Capita GNP and Aid Commitments and Disbursements of Selected OPEC and Developed Countries, 1974

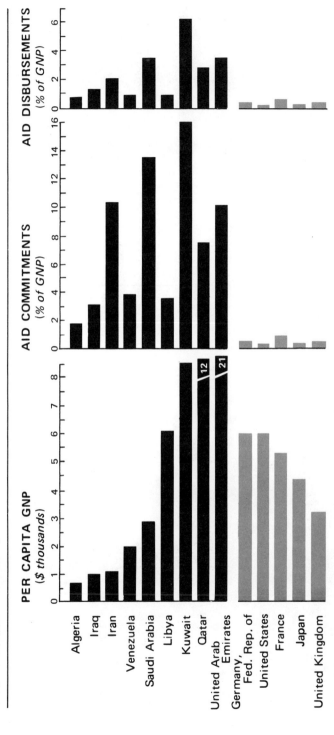

SOURCES: *The Economist*, February 15, 1975, p. 72, and Report by the Chairman of the Development Assistance Committee, *Development Co-operation, 1974 Review* (Paris: OECD, 1974), p. 44.

261

D-8. OPEC Aid Commitments and Disbursements, 1974 ($ millions and percentages)

| | Commitments | | | | | Disbursements[a] | | | | |
	Bilateral	Multi-lateral	Total	As Percentage of: Oil Revenues[a]	GNP[a]	Bilateral	Multi-lateral	Total	As Percentage of: Oil Revenues	GNP
	($ millions)					($ millions)				
Algeria	31	108	139	3.8	1.7	15	45	60	1.1	0.7
Iran	2,802	173	2,975	17.1	10.1	600	2	602	3.4	2.0
Iraq	222	58	280	4.1	2.9	80	35	115	1.7	1.2
Kuwait	957	384	1,341	19.1	15.8	460	70	530	7.6	6.2
Libya	178	241	419	5.5	3.4	45	60	105	1.4	0.9
Nigeria	1	16	17	0.2	0.2	1	15	16	0.2	0.1
Qatar	97	60	157	9.8	7.4	40	20	60	3.7	2.8
Saudi Arabia	2,568	453	3,021	15.1	13.4	650	115	765	3.8	3.4
United Arab Emirates	296	182	478	11.6	10.0	120	45	165	4.0	3.5
Venezuela	20	726	746	7.0	3.6	20	165	185	1.7	0.9
Total	7,172	2,401	9,573	12.1	8.2	2,031	572	2,603	3.3	2.2

[a]Estimate.

NOTE: Figures are subject to revision. Some of the disbursement estimates are highly tentative, as are all the comparisons of commitments and disbursements with oil revenues and GNP.

SOURCE: Organisation for Economic Co-operation and Development, Development Assistance Directorate, "Flow of Resources from OPEC Members to Developing Countries," Document No. DD-403, December 6, 1974, Table 2, p. 8.

D–9. Recipients of Bilateral Aid from OPEC Countries, 1974 ($ millions and percentages)

	Commitments		Disbursements[a]	
	($ millions)	(as percentage of total)	($ millions)	(as percentage of total)
Arab Countries				
Egypt	3,121[a]	43.5[a]	765	37.7
Syria	1,003[a]	14.0[a]	325	16.0
Jordan	185[a]	2.6[a]	140	6.9
Mauritania	153[a]	2.1[a]	25	1.2
Sudan	107	1.5	70	3.4
Somalia	82	1.1	25	1.2
Morocco	80	1.1	25	1.2
Tunisia	54	0.8	15	0.7
Bahrain	21	0.3	10	0.5
Yemen, Arab Rep.	19	0.3	15	0.7
Yemen, People's Dem. Rep.	12	0.2	10	0.5
Other	8	0.1	8	0.4
Africa				
Malagasy Republic	114[a]	1.6[a]	—	—
Guinea	16	0.2	5	0.2
Uganda	12	0.2	2	0.1
Senegal	11	0.1	5	0.2
Other	79	1.1	46	2.3
Asia				
Pakistan	957[a]	13.3[a]	355	17.5
India	945	13.2	75	3.7
Sri Lanka	86	1.2	35	1.7
Bangladesh	82	1.1	50	2.5
Latin America				
Guyana	15	0.2	15	0.7
Honduras	5	0.1	5	0.2
Europe				
Malta	5	0.1	5	0.2
Total	7,172[a]	100.0	2,031	100.0

[a]Estimate.

NOTE: Figures are subject to revision. Breakdown between Egypt, Syria, and Jordan is tentative. Commitment figures for Pakistan include $200 million by Saudi Arabia and Kuwait which were not made public but are believed to have been made.

SOURCE: Organisation for Economic Co-operation and Development, Development Assistance Directorate, "Flow of Resources from OPEC Members to Developing Countries," Document No. DD-403, December 6, 1974, Table 4, p. 10.

D-10. Economic Aid from U.S.S.R., Eastern Europe, and China to Developing Countries, Gross Commitments, 1969-1973 ($ millions)

	1969	1970	1971	1972	1973
Donors					
U.S.S.R.	474	194	865	581	622
Eastern Europe[a]	430	188	468	655	486
People's Republic of China	–	709	473	499	378
Total	904	1,091	1,806	1,735	1,486
Recipients					
Africa (excluding South Africa)	146	589	586	419	443[b]
East Asia (excluding Japan)	12	–	57	–	1
Europe (Malta, Spain, Portugal)	–	–	–	45[c]	–
Latin America (excluding Cuba)	31	107	259	331	5
Near East and South Asia	715	395	904	940	1,037[d]
Total	904	1,091	1,806	1,735	1,486

[a]Bulgaria, Czechoslovakia, German Democratic Republic, Hungary, Poland, and Romania.
[b]Of this, China committed $335 million, most of it for Zaire, Cameroon, Chad, Upper Volta, and Senegal. Note that China's total commitments to developing countries that year reached $378 million.
[c]All from China to Malta.
[d]India accounted for $455 million, Iran $291 million, Egypt $128 million, and Pakistan $71 million. The U.S.S.R. and Eastern Europe were the principal donors to this region. Over 85% of U.S.S.R. commitments went to India, which received $350 million (in the form of grain), and Iran, which received $188 million.

NOTE: Short-term commitments are excluded. Grants have, since 1954, made up only 5% of the total. Aid has concentrated on the public sector and is tied to the purchases of donor country goods. China probably accounted for most of the 1973 net transfers, i.e., gross disbursements less payments of principal and interest on earlier loans; this is in clear contrast with its position with respect to gross commitments. For 1973, the U.S.S.R.'s net transfer has been estimated at $50 million (its gross flow at $325 million) and Eastern Europe's as negative. Chinese credits are usually the softest: interest-free 10 to 30 year loans with a 10-year grace period. Eastern Europe's are generally 8 to 10 year loans at 3 to 3.5% interest; the U.S.S.R.'s are normally 12-year loans at 2.5 to 3% interest, with grace periods lasting until one year after the completion of the project or delivery of the goods.

SOURCE: U.S. Department of State, Bureau of Intelligence and Research, "Communist States and Developing Countries: Aid and Trade in 1973," Research Study INR RS-20, October 10, 1974.

D-11. Assistance from International Organizations to Developing Countries, Gross Commitments, FYs 1963 and 1967-1973 ($ millions)

	1963	1967	1968	1969	1970	1971	1972	1973	1946-1973[a]
International Bank for Reconstruction and Development	394.8	564.7	810.3	1,298.7	1,564.7	1,812.5	1,847.8	1,775.0	16,082.8
International Finance Corporation	20.9	45.6	45.3	83.5	100.4	100.8	106.2	155.1	787.6
International Development Association	256.4	348.8	105.4	369.3	569.4	559.0	671.0	1,706.5	5,595.5
Inter-American Development Bank	183.1	437.6	385.4	489.2	688.1	614.5	536.3	864.7	5,090.9
Asian Development Bank	—	—	5.0	65.6	91.5	223.2	265.9	360.6	1,001.7
African Development Bank	—	—	5.3	0.1	14.6	18.9	22.1	27.8	88.7
U.N. Development Programme	116.7	178.1	184.5	198.3	178.0	250.0	199.9	182.1	2,407.4
U.N. Children's Fund and U.N. Regular Programme of Technical Assistance and Specialized Agencies	67.0	42.6	56.5	51.5	53.0	84.4	62.9	76.5	854.2
European Community	123.0	182.3	189.9	141.1	98.5	173.3	188.9	251.9	2,203.8
Total	1,161.9	1,799.7	1,787.6	2,697.3	3,338.2	3,836.6	3,901.0	5,390.2	34,112.6

[a]Net commitments.

NOTE: Data for U.N. programs are calendar-year figures, shown in the fiscal year in which the calendar year ends. All other data are for U.S. fiscal years.

SOURCE: U.S. Agency for International Development, Office of Financial Management, Statistics and Reports Division, *U.S. Overseas Loans and Grants and Assistance from International Organizations: Obligations and Loan Authorizations, July 1, 1945-June 30, 1973*, p. 178.

D-12. Stock of Direct Private DAC Investments in Developing Countries, 1967, 1971, 1972 ($ billions and percentages)

	End 1967[a]		End 1971[a]		End 1972[a]	
	($ billions)	(percentages)	($ billions)	(percentages)	($ billions)	(percentages)
Europe	2.0	5.7	3.1	6.4	3.5	6.9
Africa	6.6	18.8	8.4	18.1	9.4	18.2
Central America[b]	6.3	18.0	9.5	20.4	10.3	20.0
South America	12.1	34.5	14.4	30.8	15.5	30.1
Middle East	3.1	8.8	3.5	7.5	3.9	7.6
Asia[c]	5.0	14.2	8.0	16.8	8.8	17.1
Total	35.1	100.0	46.9	100.0	51.6	100.0

[a]Estimates.
[b]Includes the Caribbean region.
[c]Includes Oceania.

SOURCE: Report by the Chairman of the Development Assistance Committee, *Development Co-operation, 1974 Review* (Paris: OECD, 1974), p. 144.

D-13. Publicized Euro-Currency Credits to Non-OPEC Developing Countries, 1973 and 1974 ($ millions)

	1973	1974		1973	1974
Third World Countries	4,819.4	6,188.8	Taiwan	—	183.0
Argentina	87.3	468.6	Thailand	—	9.7
Bahamas	30.0	—	Trinidad and Tobago	30.0	12.0
Bahrain	15.0	—	Turkey	20.3	—
Bolivia	6.0	52.0	Zaire	286.9	105.3
Brazil	718.1	1,437.5	Zambia	150.0	—
Colombia	170.0	8.0	**Fourth World Countries**	202.3	369.5
Costa Rica	11.0	10.0	Cameroon	—	10.0
Cuba	30.2	118.6	El Salvador	—	50.0
Dominican Republic	15.0	20.0	Guyana	12.5	15.0
Egypt	—	230.0	Haiti	10.0	—
Hong Kong	124.1	81.1	India	10.0	—
Jamaica	35.6	95.0	Ivory Coast	95.0	63.0
Korea, People's Dem. Rep.	65.3	—	Kenya	4.5	—
Korea, Republic of	142.0	221.8	Malawi	5.3	—
Lebanon	20.0	93.1	Senegal	65.0	—
Malaysia	—	140.0	Sudan	—	231.5
Mexico	1,572.5	1,517.2	**OPEC Countries**	3,012.6	740.6
Nicaragua	92.0	21.4	**Developed Countries**	13,160.1	19,379.9
Oman	35.0	—	**International Organizations**	50.0	144.0
Panama	251.0	101.0	**Unallocated by Country**	779.0	462.4
Peru	733.6	394.5	**WORLD TOTAL**	22,023.4	27,285.2
Philippines	178.5	869.0			

SOURCE: International Monetary Fund, *IMF Survey*, February 17, 1975, p. 50.

D–14. SDR Positions as of October 31, 1974 (million SDRs and percentages)

	Allocations (million SDRs)	Allocations as Percentage of Total	Net Acquisitions (+) and Use (−) (million SDRs)	Current Holdings (million SDRs)	Current Holdings as Percentage of Total
Developed Countries	6,959.1	74.7	263.1	7,222.2	77.5
United States	2,294.0	24.6	-364.1	1,929.3	20.7
United Kingdom	1,006.3	10.8	-326.1	680.2	7.3
Germany, Fed. Rep. of	542.4	5.8	904.9	1,447.3	15.5
France	485.0	5.2	-282.7	202.2	2.2
Japan	377.4	4.1	54.4	431.8	4.6
Canada	358.6	3.9	110.5	469.1	5.0
Italy	318.0	3.4	-128.8	189.2	2.0
Netherlands	236.5	2.5	242.9	479.4	5.2
Australia	225.6	2.4	-125.8	99.9	1.1
Belgium	209.3	2.3	373.8	583.1	6.3
Others	906.0	9.7	-195.3	710.7	7.6

Developing Countries					
India	326.2	3.5	-84.7	241.5	2.6
Argentina	152.5	1.6	-68.0	84.5	0.9
Brazil	152.5	1.6	10.3	162.8	1.8
Mexico	124.2	1.3	3.8	128.0	1.4
Venezuela	112.3	1.2	8.0	120.3	1.3
Indonesia	90.2	1.0	-34.5	55.7	0.6
Pakistan	81.6	0.9	-59.3	22.4	0.2
Egypt	65.2	0.7	-34.2	31.0	0.3
Iran	61.9	0.7	-17.4	44.5	0.5
Malaysia	60.6	0.7	–	60.6	0.7
Others	1,128.3	12.1	-463.6	664.3	7.1
Country Total	9,314.8	100.0	-477.0	8,837.8	94.9
Countries with Net Acquisition	–	–	1,768.6	–	–
Countries with Net Use	–	–	2,245.7	–	–
IMF Holdings	–	–	-477.0	477.0	5.1
Total	9,314.8	100.0	–	9,314.8	100.0

Developing Countries: 2,355.5 | 25.3 | -739.6 | 1,615.6 | 17.3

SOURCE: International Monetary Fund, *International Financial Statistics*, Vol. 27, No. 12, December 1974, p. 7.

D-15. Balance-of-Payments Projections for the Most Seriously Affected Countries, 1974 and 1975
($ millions)

	Projected Overall Deficit[a]		Current Account Deficit[a]		Net Inflow of Capital[b]		Projected Deficit as Percentage of Imports (c.i.f.)[a]	
	1974	1975	1974	1975	1974	1975	1974	1975
Bangladesh	375	407	612	657	237	250	28.3	30.0
Cameroon	25	42	43	67	18	25	5.6	8.2
Central African Republic	19	25	39	49	20	24	21.6	25.0
Chad	16	30	68	80	53	50	10.1	17.1
Dahomey	9	14	23	30	14	16	5.5	7.7
El Salvador	48	n.a.	78	n.a.	30	n.a.	10.0	n.a.
Ghana	23	82	-7	85	-30	3	3.6	10.9
Guinea	21	-10	92	70	71	80	13.9	-5.8
Guyana	16	16	74	48	58	32	5.9	5.2
Haiti	8	-8	50	67	42	75	7.4	n.a.
Honduras	33	44	84	104	51	60	8.9	10.2
India	820	880	1,919	2,270	1,099	1,390	16.8	15.7
Ivory Coast	57	77	153	203	96	126	5.7	6.7
Kenya	84	137	197	274	113	137	8.9	12.3
Lesotho	n.a.	n.a.	87[c]	95[c]	n.a.	n.a.	n.a.	n.a.
Malagasy Republic	32	25	88	82	56	57	10.3	7.6
Mali	42	32	53	46	11	14	30.9	24.6

Mauritania	17	16	26	28	9	12	9.6	8.3
Niger	30	22	31	23	1	1	21.1	19.6
Pakistan	155	78	485	513	330	435	8.6	3.8
Senegal	69	67	133	109	64	42	13.0	11.5
Sierra Leone	31	20	70	62	39	42	14.8	8.7
Somalia	27	29	56	59	29	30	18.6	18.7
Sri Lanka	69	100	152	185	83	85	9.7	13.0
Sudan	46	30	90	122	44	92	8.5	4.9
Tanzania	120	124	229	218	109	97	16.4	16.5
Upper Volta	10	17	82	73	72	56	7.4	12.6
Yemen, Arab Rep.	11	n.a.	54	n.a.	43	n.a.	5.0	n.a.
Yemen, People's Dem. Rep.	45	n.a.	70	n.a.	25	n.a.	12.2	n.a.
Total[d]	2,257	2,293	5,044	5,524	2,787	3,231		

[a]Minus sign indicates surplus.
[b]Minus sign indicates net outflow.
[c]Balance on trade account.
[d]Sum of listed amounts, excluding Lesotho.

NOTE: The countries listed, along with Ethiopia, Khmer Republic, and Laos, are the developing countries that, according to the United Nations, are most seriously affected by balance-of-payments difficulties in the current economic situation. Data were not available for Ethiopia, Khmer Republic, and Laos. Projections were made as of September 1, 1974.

SOURCE: "Completion of Tasks Assigned to the *Ad Hoc* Committee on Special U.N. Emergency Operation . . ." United Nations Doc. A/AC. 168/6/Add. 1, September 9, 1974.

D-16. Composition and Distribution of International Reserve Assets, Selected Months, 1973-1974
($ billions and percentages)

| | Distribution of Reserves, at End of Period | | | | Composition of Reserves |
	March 1973	September 1973	March 1974	September 1974	September 1974
	($ billions)				(percentages)
All countries[a]					
Gold stock	43.2	43.2	43.1	42.4	20
SDR	10.5	10.6	10.6	10.5	5
Reserve position in IMF	7.5	7.5	7.5	9.0	4
Foreign exchange	118.0	126.3	126.5	148.3	71
(U.S. liabilities)	(71.3)	(69.8)	(65.5)	(72.5)	(34)
Total	179.2	187.6	187.8	210.3	100
OPEC countries[b]					
Gold stock	1.4	1.4	1.4	1.4	4
SDR	0.4	0.4	0.4	0.4	1
Reserve position in IMF	0.3	0.4	0.4	1.0	3
Foreign exchange	9.8	11.0	16.8	35.6	93
Total	11.9	13.2	19.0	38.4	100

Industrial countries[c]

Gold stock	35.9	35.9	35.9	35.3	30
SDR	7.9	8.0	8.0	8.0	7
Reserve position in IMF	5.7	5.6	5.4	6.6	6
Foreign exchange	71.3	71.8	64.2	67.9	58
Total	120.8	121.2	113.5	117.9	100

Other countries[d]

Gold stock	5.8	5.8	5.7	5.7	11
SDR	2.2	2.3	2.3	2.1	4
Reserve position in IMF	1.5	1.6	1.7	1.4	3
Foreign exchange	36.9	43.4	45.6	44.8	83
Total	46.6	53.1	55.3	53.9	100

[a]Total of groups of countries listed in this table. Excludes communist countries except Yugoslavia.

[b]Algeria, Ecuador, Indonesia, Iran, Iraq, Kuwait, Libya, Nigeria, Saudi Arabia, and Venezuela. Qatar and the United Arab Emirates are not included because the IMF does not publish data for these countries.

[c]United States, Canada, Japan, Austria, Norway, Sweden, Switzerland, and all European Community countries except Ireland.

[d]Non-industrial countries other than OPEC countries; includes Yugoslavia.

SOURCE: *Economic Report of the President, Transmitted to the Congress February 1975* (Washington, D.C.: U.S. Government Printing Office, 1975), p. 206.

D-17. Debt and Debt Service for 80 Developing Countries, 1967-1972 ($ millions)

	External Public Debt Outstanding, Disbursed and Undisbursed					
	1967	1968	1969	1970	1971	1972
OPEC (8)[a]	7,326.1	8,448.5	10,010.1	12,083.7	14,989.7	17,666.6
Third World (39)[b]	23,446.2	26,318.2	29,424.2	33,835.7	39,039.9	46,579.8
Fourth World (33)[c]	14,687.9	16,644.7	18,052.0	19,795.9	22,129.4	24,101.6
TOTAL (80 Developing Countries)	45,460.2	51,441.4	57,486.3	65,715.3	76,159.0	88,348.0

	Debt Service Payments[d]					
	1967	1968	1969	1970	1971	1972
OPEC (8)[a]	301.1	399.4	521.9	712.9	1,020.6	1,510.8
Third World (39)[b]	2,347.2	2,786.0	3,130.7	3,644.5	3,836.2	4,393.8
Fourth World (33)[c]	771.2	835.2	957.3	985.1	1,204.6	1,239.4
TOTAL (80 Developing Countries)	3,419.5	4,020.6	4,609.9	5,342.5	6,061.4	7,644.0

[a]Algeria, Ecuador, Gabon, Indonesia, Iran, Iraq, Nigeria, Venezuela.

[b]Argentina, Bolivia, Brazil, Burma, Chile, Colombia, Costa Rica, Cyprus, Dominican Republic, Egypt, The Gambia, Guatemala, Jamaica, Jordan, Liberia, Malaysia, Mauritius, Mexico, Morocco, Nicaragua, Panama, Paraguay, People's Republic of the Congo, Peru, Philippines, Republic of Korea, Republic of Vietnam, Singapore, Swaziland, Syrian Arab Republic, Taiwan, Thailand, Togo, Trinidad and Tobago, Tunisia, Turkey, Uruguay, Zaire, Zambia.

[c]Afghanistan, Bangladesh, Botswana, Burundi, Cameroon, Central African Republic, Chad, Dahomey, El Salvador, Ethiopia, Ghana, Guyana, Honduras, India, Ivory Coast, Kenya, Lesotho, Malagasy Republic, Malawi, Mali, Mauritania, Niger, Pakistan, People's Democratic Republic of Yemen, Rwanda, Senegal, Sierra Leone, Somalia, Sri Lanka, Sudan, Tanzania, Uganda, Upper Volta.

[d]Amortization and interest payments.

SOURCE: Based on World Bank, *World Debt Tables: External Public Debt of LDCs*, World Bank Doc. EC-167/74, December 15, 1974, pp. 1-4.

About the Overseas Development Council
and the Authors

The Overseas Development Council is an independent, non-profit organization established in 1969 to increase American understanding of the economic and social problems confronting the developing countries, and of the importance of these countries to the United States in an increasingly interdependent world. The ODC seeks to promote consideration of development issues by the American public, policy makers, specialists, educators, and the media through its research, conferences, publications, and liaison with U. S. mass membership organizations interested in U. S. relations with the developing world. The ODC's program is funded by foundations, corporations, and private individuals; its policies are determined by its Board of Directors under the Chairmanship of Theodore M. Hesburgh, C.S.C. The Council's President is James P. Grant.

The authors of *The U. S. and World Development: Agenda for Action, 1975* are listed here in the sequence of the chapters they contributed.

James W. Howe, who directed the preparation of this study, is a Senior Fellow at the Council. Mr. Howe was previously a member of the Policy Planning Council of the Department of State and Director of the U. S. aid program to the East African Community. His recent articles have focused on monetary issues, new sources of development financing, and the international economic order.

Helen C. Low is a Research Associate at the Council. She previously worked in the international affairs division of the Atomic Energy Commission.

John W. Sewell is Vice President of the Overseas Development Council. Mr. Sewell was formerly with the Brookings Institution and with the Department of State. He is a board member of the American Freedom from Hunger Foundation.

James P. Grant has been President of the Overseas Development Council since its establishment in 1969. He was formerly Assistant Administrator of the U. S. Agency for International Development. Mr. Grant's recent analyses have centered on the world food situation, major structural changes taking place in the international order, and the effectiveness of various development strategies, with articles on the latter appearing in *Foreign Affairs* and *Foreign Policy*.

Robert H. Johnson is Charles Evans Hughes Professor of Government at Colgate University and a Visiting Senior Fellow at the ODC. He was formerly a member of the Policy Planning Council, Department of State. He has published articles on foreign affairs subjects in various journals.

Guy F. Erb, a Senior Fellow at the ODC, was formerly with the United Nations Secretariat and the U. S. Foreign Service, where he served in the Office of the Special Representative for Trade Negotiations. Sharon Hewitt and Stephen M. Taran assisted Mr. Erb in the preparation of Chapters IV and V, respectively.

Lester R. Brown, President of Worldwatch Institute, was formerly a Senior Fellow at the ODC and Administrator of the International Agricultural Development Service of the U. S. Department of Agriculture. He is the author of *Seeds of Change*, 1969; *World Without Borders*, 1972; *In the Human Interest*, 1974; and *By Bread Alone*, 1974.

Erik P. Eckholm is a Fellow at Worldwatch Institute and was formerly a Staff Associate at the ODC. He wrote, with Lester R. Brown, *By Bread Alone*, 1974.

Ali A. Mazrui, a noted Kenyan scholar, is currently a professor of political science at the University of Michigan. He was previously a professor at Makerere University, Kampala, Uganda, and a visiting professor at various universities worldwide. Most recently, he is the author of *World Culture and the Black Experience*, 1974; *Who Are the Afro-Saxons?*, 1975; *Soldiers and Kinsmen in Uganda*, 1975; and *A World Federation of Cultures: An African Perspective*, 1975.

Roger D. Hansen is a Senior Fellow at the Council and also is presently serving as a Senior Research Fellow at the Council on Foreign Relations while working on the Council's 1980s Project. He previously served as U. S. Deputy Assistant Special Trade Representative in the Office of the Special Representative for Trade Negotiations. Mr. Hansen is the author of *The Politics of Mexican Development*, 1971.

Mildred Weiss is Staff Associate at the Council and has prepared the statistical annexes of the *Agenda for Action* series since its inception in 1973.

Overseas Development Council
1717 Massachusetts Avenue, N. W.
Washington, D. C. 20036
(202-234-8701)

ODC Board of Directors

Chairman: Theodore M. Hesburgh

Robert O. Anderson
Roger E. Anderson
William Attwood
C. Fred Bergsten
Eugene R. Black
*Marvin Bordelon
*Robert R. Bowie
Harrison Brown
John F. Burlingame
John T. Caldwell
Anne Campbell
Wallace Campbell
Thomas P. Carney
Robert A. Charpie
Joel Chaseman
Mrs. William M. Christopherson
Frank M. Coffin
Owen Cooper
*Richard Cooper
Charles S. Dennison
John Diebold
*Thomas L. Farmer
Arthur S. Flemming
Luther H. Foster
William Franklin
J. Wayne Fredericks
*Orville L. Freeman
*William S. Gaud
Philip L. Geyelin
Stephen Girard
Arthur J. Goldberg
Kermit Gordon
*Lester E. Gordon
*Lincoln Gordon
*James P. Grant (*ex officio*)
*Edward K. Hamilton
J. George Harrar
Samuel P. Hayes
Ulric Haynes, Jr.
*Theodore M. Hesburgh
William R. Hewlett
Donald Hornig
Vernon E. Jordan
Nicholas de B. Katzenbach

*Tom Killefer
William C. Kokontis
Edward M. Korry
Peter F. Krogh
Anne O. Kruger
*Anthony Lake
*William J. Lawless
Walter J. Levy
*John P. Lewis
David E. Lilienthal
C. Payne Lucas
*Louis E. Martin
Edward S. Mason
C. Peter McColough
Francis McGuire
Lawrence C. McQuade
Malcolm Moos
Thomas A. Murphy
*Randolph Nugent
William S. Ogden
F. Taylor Ostrander
James A. Perkins
Hart Perry
Samuel D. Proctor
*Andrew E. Rice
James D. Robinson, III
David Rockefeller
Bruce W. Rohrbacher
John A. Schnittker
David H. Shepard
Joseph E. Slater
Edward B. Smith
*Davidson Sommers
Lauren K. Soth
*Stephen Stamas
John E. Swearingen
Charles B. Thornton
Raymond Vernon
*C. M. van Vlierden
Clifton R. Wharton, Jr.
J. Harvie Wilkinson, Jr.
Leonard Woodcock
Charles W. Yost
*Barry Zorthian

Member of Executive Committee

277

RELATED TITLES
Published by
Praeger Special studies

DEVELOPMENT IN RICH AND POOR COUNTRIES:
A General Theory with Statistical Analysis
Thorkil Kristensen

**EDUCATION AND DEVELOPMENT RECON-
SIDERED:** The Bellagio Conference
Ford Foundation/Rockefeller Foundation Report
edited by F. Champion Ward

NEW DIRECTIONS IN DEVELOPMENT: Latin
America, Export Credit, Population Growth, and U.S.
Attitudes
Colin I. Bradford, Jr.
Nathaniel McKitterick
B. Jenkins Middleton
William Rich
Paul A. Laudicina

U.S. AGRICULTURE IN A WORLD CONTEXT: Policies
and Approaches for the Next Decade
edited by D. Gale Johnson and
John A. Schnittker